HOW
TO BUY
FOREIGN
STOCKS
AND
BONDS

HOW TO BUY FOREIGN STOCKS AND BONDS

A Guide for the Individual Investor

GERALD WARFIELD

HARPER & ROW, PUBLISHERS, New York

Cambridge, Philadelphia, San Francisco, London

1817 Mexico City, São Paulo, Singapore, Sydney

HOW TO BUY FOREIGN STOCKS AND BONDS. Copyright © 1985 by Gerald Warfield. All rights reserved. Printed in the United States of America. No part of this book may be used or reproduced in any manner whatsoever without written permission except in the case of brief quotations embodied in critical articles and reviews. For information address Harper & Row, Publishers, Inc., 10 East 53rd Street, New York, N.Y. 10022. Published simultaneously in Canada by Fitzhenry & Whiteside Limited, Toronto.

FIRST EDITION

Designed by Ruth Bornschlegel

Library of Congress Cataloging in Publication Data
Warfield, Gerald (Gerald A.)
    How to buy foreign stocks and bonds.
    Includes index.
    1. Investments, Foreign—Handbooks, manuals, etc.
2. Stock-exchange—Handbooks, manuals, etc. I. Title.
HG4538.W325   1985   332.6'5   84-47625
ISBN 0-06-015327-X

85 86 87 88 89 10 9 8 7 6 5 4 3 2 1

This book is dedicated to
my great-aunt Fannie,
Mrs. Fannie Victoria Ramsey
of Olney, Texas

CONTENTS

APPENDIXES

ACKNOWLEDGMENTS

It is with gratitude that I acknowledge the many sources from which the information in this book has been compiled. Not only was material generously provided, but, in many cases, members of the stock exchange staffs read and corrected the chapters pertinent to their respective exchanges. In particular, I would like to thank individuals on, and departments of, the following exchanges. Their names are listed in the order that the relevant chapters appear in Part Two.

Division of Public Relations
Tokyo Stock Exchange

Mr. Peter Davis
Information & Press Department
The (London) Stock Exchange

Susan Walkington
External Communications
The Toronto Stock Exchange

The Public Relations Department
Frankfurt Stock Exchange

Josephine Coffey
Manager, Investor Services
The Sydney Stock Exchange Limited

Jacqueline H.Th. Granssen
Public Relations Department
Amsterdam Stock Exchange

Malcolm G. Duncan
Foreign Relations Department
Milan Stock Exchange

Ernest Backes
Luxembourg Stock Exchange

Gideon Uys
Public Relations Officer
The Johannesburg Stock Exchange

In addition, the following individuals and institutions provided assistance. Their names are listed in alphabetical order.

Fleuri Carpentier
Public Relations Officer
Brussels Stock Exchange

Dean Egly
Vice President, ADR Administration
Morgan Guaranty Trust

Fred Fischer
Financial Times (London)

Mark L. Hodge
J.B. Were & Son, Inc.

Robert H. James
Assistant Manager
Wood Gundy, Inc. (Florida)

Japan Securities Research Institute
Tokyo, Japan

Lipper Analytical Services, Inc.
Westfield, N.J.

Bernard H. Mass
Foreign Listing Consultant
American Stock Exchange

Thomas J. Niedermeyer
Nomura Securities

Raymond Reitzer
New York City

José Marie de C.H. Soares
The São Paulo Stock Exchange

Michael Steinberg
Nomura Securities

Robert Tepper
Algemene Bank Nederland

Dennis D.S. Tin
Conti Commodity

Harry M. Venedikian
Pace University
New York University

Among those personal friends who were of great help to me I would like to thank Paul Marcontell, Nina Hill, and David Loesch. Martin Gonzalez and Troy Stone helped greatly with early drafts of the manuscript.

I am grateful to the various sources from which I have quoted, in particular, Capital International Perspective, Geneva, Switzerland, which provided information for the six tables in Chapter 1.

Last, but certainly not least, I would like to thank Irving Levey of Barnes & Noble Books, who gave me the idea for this book.

HOW
TO BUY
FOREIGN
STOCKS
AND
BONDS

INTRODUCTION

GETTING STARTED

This book is for the individual investor: the person who takes, or wants to take, an active part in managing his or her assets. Little or no experience is assumed, and any terms or procedures that might be unfamiliar are explained as they arise in the text.

Further, this book is written for the individual who wants a greater investment return. The evidence seems to be irrefutable that internationally diversified portfolios will outperform portfolios made up only of domestic securities. Why, then, isn't international diversification already the norm? It is—but only for large portfolios. Today, one would be hard pressed to find a single major fund that doesn't commit a significant percentage of its assets to foreign securities (providing it is not restricted from doing so). United States retirement funds, for example, have invested massive amounts in foreign securities.

For the individual, however, it is a different story. Brokers (and here I am talking about the account managers with whom the individual investor usually deals) do not recommend foreign securities nearly as frequently as investment opportunities would seem to warrant.

There are generally two reasons for the neglect of foreign stocks and bonds: either lack of knowledge on the part of the broker, or lack of knowledge on the part of the investor. Brokers, after all, are salespersons, and when it is difficult to get an insular U.S. investor to buy utility stocks (much less something more imaginative), an account representative is usually reluctant to suggest anything else.

It is unfortunate that brokers themselves (i.e., the account managers) are not familiar with nondomestic instruments. Their training usually excludes all foreign securities except those which can be purchased in the United States as American Depositary Receipts (see Chapter 2). If brokers are not knowledgeable concerning foreign securities, then, obviously, foreign securities will not constitute part of their investment recommendations. For one thing, it would be too easy for a client to ask follow-up questions that the broker couldn't answer, and that is a good way for people to lose confidence in their broker—as well they should.

To begin acquiring foreign securities it may be that you have only to indicate your interest to your broker. Particularly if your account is with a large firm, the research and recommendations may already be available. If not, then you may be better off changing brokers. If you do end up shopping for a new broker, ask for a sample recommendation of foreign securities from their research department. By the time you have read this book you will be in a good position to evaluate the adequacy of such reports.

THE STOCK EXCHANGE PROFILES IN PART TWO

The first ten chapters in Part Two describe ten of the largest stock exchanges in the world, excluding those of the United States. It is not the intention of these chapters to present an exhaustive account of each market; obviously, exchange operations and the characteristics of their instruments may change from year to year. These chapters do, however, provide an overall picture of each exchange, its operations, and its instruments that will give the investor a meaningful perspective from which to view the market and interpret investment news and recommendations.

It is emphatically not the intention of these chapters to give specific investment recommendations. Investments, particularly international investments, should be made on the basis of the most current information available, both about general market conditions and about the specific security. Books take too long to publish to provide timely information in either of these areas.

The "Market at a Glance" charts can serve only as a rough guide. Data from individual exchanges is often not comparable and is certainly subject to different interpretations. For instance, it might make sense to discuss the volume of one exchange exclusive of its transactions in foreign securities when those transactions constitute only a small part of the volume. On an exchange where there are more foreign listings than domestic, such an exclusion could give a greatly reduced picture of the volume and be inappropriate for comparisons of volume on other exchanges. For this reason, the "Market at a Glance" charts vary somewhat from chapter to chapter; they attempt only to portray data relevant to and characteristic of each individual marketplace.

Although there is general conformity in the format of the exchange chapters, they are not entirely alike. Often, an aspect of a particular exchange or group of exchanges may be elaborated upon in some detail.

For example, there are special sections on roll-call trading on the Zurich exchange, newspaper quotations on London securities, rights on the Tokyo exchange, and the functioning of the Paris Stock Exchange under the new socialist government.

The discussions on tax are somewhat cursory. International tax laws are complex and change frequently. Circumstances under which you may obtain a reduced level of withholding vary from country to country. Often, the process is relatively automatic, but sometimes it will require special filings on your part. In all tax matters be guided by your broker and, if your investment is substantial, by an expert in international taxation.

In those sections where foreign investment terms are defined, the terms are usually given in English. It is assumed that the investor will be reading about the market or its securities in English. However, in a few chapters, particularly for those countries where investment information in English is not readily available, some or all of the terms are given in the original language as well.

In addition to those terms associated with foreign securities defined in the text, there are some applicable to domestic markets with which the reader may not be entirely familiar. A few are listed below:

amortization: The gradual repayment of an amount such as the principal amount of a bond, by a series of (usually) equal installments.

price-earnings ratio: Usually referred to as the PE ratio, it is the number of times the per-share price of a stock exceeds its per-share earnings. Thus, if a company earned two dollars per share, and its per-share market price were fifteen dollars, the PE ratio would be 7.5. The lower the PE ratio, the more valuable (presumably) the stock. Used as a rough guide, it is most meaningful when comparing similar securities within the same country. Different countries, and different industries within those countries, have different "norms" for their PE ratios.

secondary market: Transactions in securities after their initial sale. Thus, sales and purchases are between investors, and the issuer does not receive any of the sale revenues. One of the primary functions of a stock exchange is to provide a secondary marketplace.

straight bond: The usual type of bond with a coupon rate that remains fixed throughout the life of the bond. The term is usually used to distinguish a (straight) bond from a convertible bond.

Part One

UNDERSTANDING FOREIGN SECURITIES

1

WHY INTERNATIONALIZE?

OVERLOOKING THE OBVIOUS

There are many compelling reasons for U.S. investors to acquire foreign securities. However, before we consider those reasons, and certainly before we begin looking abroad for securities, it will be helpful to look at our own domestic market. Here, there are already a surprisingly large number of foreign stocks and bonds trading regularly.

As of yet, these securities are not highly visible because relatively few are listed on U.S. exchanges. The New York Stock Exchange (NYSE) trades only forty-one foreign stocks (of over 1,500 listings), and the American Stock Exchange (AMEX) trades fifty-four out of 950. Foreign bonds fare somewhat better, with over 150 listed on the NYSE, but only seven are listed on the AMEX. However, it is a different story with over-the-counter listings. About 250 foreign stocks are registered with the Securities and Exchange Commission (SEC), and all that are not exchange-listed are traded over the counter. Over 100 of the over-the-counter issues are Japanese, and that alone is as many as the exclusive domestic listings on the Pacific and the Midwest exchanges combined.

To overlook these securities is to ignore potential investments already at hand. One needn't trade abroad to acquire them, and investment information on the leading issues is becoming increasingly available. At this point, to restrict oneself to domestic securities is almost as arbitrary as restricting oneself to stocks and bonds from one side or the other of the Mississippi.

An important factor in the availability of foreign securities in the United States is the phenomenal growth of the over-the-counter (OTC) market. The National Association of Securities Dealers Automated Quotations (NASDAQ), in particular, provides an electronic system for quoting and trading securities which appeals increasingly to both U.S. investors and foreign companies who may want to list their securities here. In five years, from 1978 to 1983, trading on the NASDAQ system grew by 475%. This compares to only a 200% increase on the New York Stock Exchange. Also, brokers who make a market in OTC stocks (including foreign issues) realize a greater return on those securities than they do on exchange-listed stocks; thus, there is additional incentive to deal in these issues. The requirements for exchange listings (particularly those pertaining to financial reporting) have always been an impediment to foreign companies seeking a U.S. outlet for their shares, so NASDAQ, with its less stringent requirements and electronic support systems, represents a viable alternative.

At this point, a word should be said about the terms "NASDAQ" and "OTC"; they are not synonymous. Technically, any security not listed on an exchange is an over-the-counter security, but NASDAQ lists only about 4,500,[1] making their bid and asked prices available on quote terminals in brokers' offices throughout the country. Hundreds of shares, however, also trade over the counter, but they are not listed by NASDAQ (nor are they listed on an exchange). Their quotations, reported by the National Quotations Bureau, appear in the "pink sheets" distributed daily to U.S. brokerages. The term "over the counter" properly refers to both these markets although it is sometimes understood to refer only to NASDAQ securities. Over-the-counter stocks not listed by NASDAQ are referred to as securities that are "on the pink sheets."

WHY BUY FOREIGN SECURITIES?

The reason most people begin to look beyond the United States for investments is for profit opportunity. They want better performance from their investments than they have received in domestic markets. The briefest glance at the tables in this chapter demonstrates that better opportunities do exist.

Using data compiled by Capital International, S.A., in Geneva, Switzerland, Tables 1 through 6 compare the performance of nineteen stock markets around the world. Capital International (CI) is the major source of information concerning foreign markets, the data from which is entirely compatible. That is, the CI index of any country's equity market may be compared to the CI index for any other country's equity market.

When comparing the performance of various stock markets one immediately encounters the problem of compatibility of data. Indexes used by individual exchanges differ wildly. They usually originated in different years and were calculated from different numerical bases. The

[1]Counting warrants, units, different classes of common, etc.

weightings are different, and some are broadly based while others, such as the Dow-Jones Industrial Average (DJIA), are quite narrow. Some include different types of securities (for instance, both stocks and bonds); some include foreign issues, and others are made up only of domestic issues.

In order to form indexes which could be realistically compared to one another, Capital International created entirely new indexes for each country. All are calculated from a base of 100 as of January 1, 1970. The companies that constitute each index make up about 60% of the aggregate market value of the listed stocks in that country (irrespective of the exchange on which the security happens to be listed within that particular country). The indexes are thus both broadly based and directly comparable. However, they do not necessarily reflect the activity of a single exchange, since all of the constituent stocks will not necessarily be listed on the same exchange within that country. The indexes are more appropriately viewed as representing the performance of the equity market for an entire country rather than for a single exchange.

The chapters of this book which deal with individual exchanges contain the local indexes for those exchanges, since those are the ones most likely to be quoted in the media. It is the purpose of those indexes to document the performance of their respective markets. However, they are completely inadequate for comparing different exchanges. One must, instead, rely on information calculated consistently from data that is directly comparable.

One will find Capital International indexes quoted in financial periodicals such as *Barron's.* See, in particular, the excellent column, "International Trader." Capital International also calculates a world index made up of the average of all nineteen countries covered, so that one can easily determine whether a particular market outperformed or underperformed the average.

Table 1 shows the 1983 indexes for nineteen countries and the world average. The United States was sixteenth, behind Japan, with a 16.6% increase over its position a year earlier. The nation showing the greatest gain was Mexico, with a stunning 188.2% rise. Only Hong Kong, Austria, and Spain underperformed the United States.

However, such a table does not tell the whole story. The exchange rate between the respective local currencies and the U.S. dollar shifted during the year, and so Table 2, taking into account the U.S. dollar exchange rate, gives a more accurate picture for our purposes. In this table the U.S. position improves somewhat (beating Switzerland, Bel-

Table 1

PERFORMANCE OF WORLD STOCK MARKETS: 1983
CAPITAL INTERNATIONAL INDEXES*

COUNTRY†	% INCREASE FROM PREVIOUS YEAR	1982, END-OF-YEAR	1983, END-OF-YEAR	LOW-HIGH, 1983	% INCREASE OF HIGH TO LOW
1. Mexico	188.2	291.4	839.7	293.6–856.6	191.8
2. Denmark	95.4	252.1	492.7	255.4–501.3	96.3
3. Norway	91.5	160.7	307.8	158.9–314.0	97.6
4. Australia	63.1	88.8	144.8	88.8–146.7	65.2
5. Sweden	61.2	308.6	497.5	304.8–540.7	77.4
6. France	58.4	104.3	165.2	101.7–171.2	68.3
7. Netherlands	52.1	105.9	161.1	105.3–174.0	65.2
8. W. Germany	38.3	92.3	127.7	88.3–130.0	47.2
9. Belgium	36.1	103.0	140.1	100.5–141.7	41.0
10. Singapore	30.1	499.8	650.1	485.3–663.4	36.7
11. Canada	29.5	214.4	277.6	213.6–285.2	33.5
12. Switzerland	26.7	92.1	116.7	92.8–118.7	27.9
13. U.K.	24.5	26.3	281.8	226.3–286.5	26.6
14. Italy	22.3	114.2	139.7	111.1–154.0	38.6
The World	*21.6*	*149.6*	*181.8*	*148.2–185.2*	*25.0*
15. Japan	21.3	346.9	420.8	330.8–424.4	28.3
16. U.S.A.	16.6	134.2	156.4	132.0–163.9	24.2
17. Hong Kong	9.7	528.9	580.2	453.9–726.0	59.9
18. Austria	9.5	100.9	110.5	97.0–115.5	19.1
19. Spain	4.1	56.1	58.4	53.7–65.7	22.3

*Calculated from a base of 100, Jan. 1, 1970.
†An average of 60% of each country's stock capitalization is represented irrespective of which exchange within that country lists a particular stock.
Source: Capital International Perspective, Geneva, Switzerland.

gium, the United Kingdom, and Italy), coming in twelfth, just under the world average. The gains for Mexico, still number one, were trimmed by a weak peso to a merely spectacular 164.3%.

While it is traditional to compare markets by the position of their year-end indexes (as in Tables 1 and 2), it is also distorting. A market could have risen to impressive heights (and, presumably, one could have taken profits) at midyear and have fallen back to its original position or lower by the end of the year. It would therefore rank relatively low on tables such as 1 and 2. To account for this possibility, the next-to-last column of Table 1 shows the yearly high and low for each market. The percentage of the yearly high to the low is shown in the last column. The year's winner, Mexico, shows little change in this category. The biggest surprise is Hong Kong, probably the most volatile of all foreign markets, which registered only a 9.7% increase for the year but whose yearly high showed a 59.9% gain over the year's low.

One year, of course, never tells the whole story. Let us now go back a year and compare the same indexes in 1982. That was the year the

Table 2

PERFORMANCE OF WORLD STOCK MARKETS: 1983
ADJUSTED FOR CURRENCY EXCHANGE WITH U.S. DOLLAR

COUNTRY	% INCREASE FROM PREVIOUS YEAR	CAPITAL INTERNATIONAL INDEXES	
		1982, END-OF-YEAR	1983, END-OF-YEAR
1. Mexico	164.3	23.5	62.1
2. Norway	75.1	162.8	285.1
3. Denmark	65.8	225.8	374.4
4. Australia	49.6	77.7	116.2
5. Sweden	47.0	218.7	321.4
6. Netherlands	30.9	145.7	190.7
7. Singapore	29.2	730.1	943.0
8. Canada	29.1	188.0	242.8
9. France	28.2	85.7	109.8
10. Japan	23.1	532.6	655.4
11. W. Germany	20.9	141.8	171.5
The World	*18.6*	*155.2*	*184.0*
12. U.S.A.	**16.6**	**134.2**	**156.4**
13. Switzerland	16.0	198.4	230.0
14. Belgium	15.6	107.1	123.8
15. U.K.	11.8	152.3	170.3
16. Italy	1.0	52.1	52.7
17. Austria	−4.9	157.1	149.4
18. Hong Kong	−8.6	453.3	414.2
19. Spain	−16.5	31.3	26.1

Source: Capital International Perspective, Geneva, Switzerland.

Table 3

PERFORMANCE OF WORLD STOCK MARKETS: 1982

CAPITAL INTERNATIONAL INDEXES*

COUNTRY†	% INCREASE FROM PREVIOUS YEAR	1981, END-OF-YEAR	1982, END-OF-YEAR	LOW-HIGH, 1982	% INCREASE OF HIGH TO LOW
1. Sweden	57.2	196.3	308.6	179.2–308.6	72.2
2. U.K.	21.3	186.6	226.3	182.1–235.1	29.1
3. Netherlands	15.2	91.9	105.9	85.3–110.0	29.0
4. U.S.A.	15.1	116.5	134.2	98.1–138.4	41.1
5. Belgium	14.0	90.4	103.0	89.0–106.9	20.1
6. Denmark	13.3	222.5	252.1	212.3–259.0	22.0
7. W. Germany	12.6	82.0	92.3	78.7–93.9	19.3
The World	*11.6*	*134.0*	*149.6*	*116.1–153.3*	*32.0*
8. Switzerland	11.1	82.9	92.1	75.4–95.7	26.9
9. France	6.6	97.9	104.3	95.3–117.7	23.5
10. Japan	4.4	332.3	346.9	289.1–349.0	20.7
11. Canada	1.1	212.1	214.4	147.9–225.0	52.1
12. Austria	−7.9	109.6	100.9	93.8–109.6	16.8
13. Italy	−9.4	126.0	114.2	100.9–139.0	37.8
14. Australia	−15.4	105.0	88.8	78.0–105.0	34.6
15. Singapore	−16.0	595.3	499.8	392.0–615.6	57.0
16. Norway	−17.6	195.0	160.7	153.1–198.8	29.8
17. Spain	−20.3	70.4	56.1	53.5–72.1	34.8
18. Mexico	−33.3	436.9	291.4	218.4–469.1	114.8
19. Hong Kong	−40.0	881.9	528.9	454.7–914.5	101.1

*Calculated from a base of 100, Jan. 1, 1970.

†An average of 60% of each country's stock capitalization is represented irrespective of which exchange within that country lists a stock.

Source: Capital International Perspective, Geneva, Switzerland.

great bull market began in August, a very different year from 1983. Table 3 shows that the United States fared much better, ranking fourth behind Sweden, the United Kingdom, and The Netherlands. After accounting for the enormous strength of the dollar during that year, the United States dislodged both the United Kingdom and The Netherlands to rank second in the world (see Table 4). The 1983 star, Mexico, was next to last in 1982 and, after accounting for foreign exchange, came in dead last. Sweden's first place was for a healthy 19.1% increase over the previous year—after accounting for the exchange rate between the krona and the dollar (see Table 4).

In terms of volatility, Mexico was first with a 114.8% difference between the yearly high and low. Unfortunately, this did not present many opportunities for investors since the high appeared early in the year and the direction of the market was down for the remainder of the period. The same could be said for Hong Kong, which showed a difference between the yearly high and low of just over 100%, and for Singapore, which showed a difference of 57%.

Table 4

PERFORMANCE OF WORLD STOCK MARKETS: 1982
ADJUSTED FOR CURRENCY EXCHANGE WITH U.S. DOLLAR

| | | | CAPITAL INTERNATIONAL INDEXES | |
COUNTRY	% INCREASE FROM PREVIOUS YEAR		1981, END-OF-YEAR	1982, END-OF-YEAR
1. Sweden	19.1		183.7	218.7
2. U.S.A.	15.1		116.5	134.2
3. Netherlands	8.3		134.6	145.7
4. Germany	6.2		133.6	141.8
The World	5.8		146.6	155.2
5. U.K.	3.1		147.7	152.3
6. Switzerland	0.2		198.0	198.4
7. Belgium	0.1		106.9	107.1
8. Denmark	−0.9		227.8	225.8
9. Japan	−2.3		545.1	532.6
10. Canada	−2.6		193.0	188.0
11. France	−9.7		94.9	85.7
12. Austria	−13.0		180.6	157.1
13. Singapore	−18.6		897.2	730.1
14. Italy	−20.6		65.6	52.1
15. Australia	−26.5		105.8	77.7
16. Norway	−32.1		239.8	162.8
17. Spain	−38.5		50.9	31.3
18. Hong Kong	−47.5		863.7	453.3
19. Mexico	−88.7		208.2	23.5

Source: Capital International Perspective, Geneva, Switzerland.

Table 5

PERFORMANCE OF WORLD STOCK MARKETS: 1981
CAPITAL INTERNATIONAL INDEXES*

COUNTRY†	% INCREASE FROM PREVIOUS YEAR	1980, END-OF-YEAR	1981, END-OF-YEAR	LOW-HIGH, 1981	% INCREASE OF HIGH TO LOW
1. Sweden	66.2	118.1	193.3	112.4–201.0	78.8
2. Denmark	45.2	153.2	222.5	153.2–228.9	49.4
3. Spain	23.6	57.0	70.4	55.8–80.7	44.6
4. Japan	23.0	270.3	332.3	270.3–359.3	32.9
5. Italy	14.2	110.4	126.0	107.3–182.4	70.0
6. Singapore	13.7	523.6	595.3	472.6–734.1	55.3
7. U.K.	5.7	176.4	186.6	157.8–200.3	26.9
8. Belgium	1.4	89.1	90.4	71.8–92.0	28.1
9. W. Germany	−1.3	83.1	82.0	80.5–90.3	12.2
The World	*−2.3*	*137.2*	*134.0*	*125.0–145.7*	*16.6*
10. Netherlands	−7.5	99.3	91.9	79.6–103.6	30.2
11. U.S.A.	**−9.3**	**128.5**	**116.5**	**107.7–131.2**	**21.8**
12. Hong Kong	−9.8	977.3	881.9	700.6–1194.4	70.5
13. Norway	−10.7	218.3	195.0	160.7–221.5	37.8
14. Switzerland	−11.1	93.2	82.9	77.6–94.7	22.0
15. Austria	−13.3	126.4	109.6	102.7–126.4	23.1
16. Canada	−14.3	247.5	212.1	199.1–264.1	32.6
17. France	−17.3	118.4	97.9	81.1–120.7	48.8
18. Australia	−23.6	137.5	105.0	96.0–140.3	46.1
19. Mexico	−35.6	678.2	436.0	371.9–717.4	92.9

*Calculated from a base of 100, Jan. 1, 1970.
†An average of 60% of each country's stock capitalization is represented irrespective of which exchange within that country lists a stock.
Source: Capital International Perspective, Geneva, Switzerland.

Moving to a year earlier (see Table 5), the U.S. equity market in 1981 was down to eleventh, outperformed by ten other countries and even by the world average. After accounting for foreign exchange its position improved to sixth, beaten by Sweden, Denmark, Singapore, Japan, Spain, and the world average (Table 6).

From our brief survey of world equity markets we can see that in two of the last three years the United States ranked below the world average. Before 1981 (in the years for which CI has data) the ratio is about the same. Thus an internationally diversified portfolio had a better than even chance, if considering market averages, of outperforming a domestic portfolio.

At the time of this writing, the six-month figures for 1984 have just come in. According to Capital International Perspective, fourteen foreign stock markets, as measured in their own currencies, outperformed the United States. Adjusting for foreign-exchange fluctuations, the number was lowered only to thirteen. The overall picture, in fact, resembles 1983, when eleven foreign markets outperformed the

Table 6

**PERFORMANCE OF WORLD STOCK MARKETS: 1981
ADJUSTED FOR CURRENCY EXCHANGE WITH U.S. DOLLAR**

| | | % INCREASE | CAPITAL INTERNATIONAL INDEXES | |
| | | FROM PREVIOUS | 1980, | 1981, |
COUNTRY		YEAR	END-OF-YEAR	END-OF-YEAR
1.	Sweden	31.7	139.5	183.7
2.	Denmark	19.4	190.9	227.8
3.	Singapore	16.2	772.3	897.2
4.	Japan	13.8	478.8	545.1
5.	Spain	1.2	50.4	50.9
	The World	*−7.9*	*159.2*	*146.6*
6.	**U.S.A.**	**−9.3**	**128.5**	**116.5**
7.	Italy	−11.4	74.1	65.6
8.	Switzerland	−12.5	226.2	198.0
9.	Germany	−13.5	154.4	133.6
10.	Canada	−14.4	225.4	193.0
11.	U.K.	−15.9	175.7	147.7
12.	Hong Kong	−18.6	1061.1	863.7
13.	Netherlands	−20.0	168.3	134.6
14.	Norway	−20.4	301.2	239.8
15.	Austria	−23.5	236.1	180.6
16.	Belgium	−23.9	140.6	106.9
17.	Australia	−27.1	145.0	105.8
18.	France	−34.4	144.7	94.9
19.	Mexico	−42.9	364.5	208.2

Source: Capital International Perspective, Geneva, Switzerland.

United States. The countries, in order of their performance, are listed
in Table 7. Note that the United States (−8.1%) was again beaten by
the world average (−4.9%).

Table 7

**PERFORMANCE OF WORLD STOCK MARKETS: FIRST HALF OF 1984
ADJUSTED FOR CURRENCY EXCHANGE WITH U.S. DOLLAR**

COUNTRY	% INCREASE FROM BEGINNING OF YEAR
1. Spain	26.0
2. France	7.4
3. Italy	7.3
4. Japan	5.6
5. Hong Kong	4.3
6. Belgium	3.8
7. Norway	3.8
8. Netherlands	3.6
9. Mexico	−.8
10. U.K.	−1.5
11. Sweden	−4.6
The World	*−4.9*
12. W. Germany	−4.9
13. Austria	−5.6
14. U.S.A.	−8.1
15. Switzerland	−10.5
16. Singapore	−17.3
17. Canada	−17.7
18. Australia	−19.3
19. Denmark	−22.1

Source: Capital International Perspective, Geneva, Switzerland.

ARE U.S. MARKETS OVERANALYZED?

It has been suggested that one of the problems of the U.S. securities
market is that it is overanalyzed. While it is the exceptions (i.e., the
surprises) that one hears about in the news, the majority of securities
in this country find their price equilibrium as a result of the vast amount
of information that is available on each. Furthermore, prices tend to
stay at their same general levels until there is either a major market
move or until new information becomes available that is pertinent to
the securities.

It is true that the securities industry in this country is larger and
more developed than in any other country. The same data is sifted
through again and again by brokers, analysts, investment letter writers,

columnists, financial planners, and portfolio managers of every type imaginable. There is even a growing number of amateur analysts who make use of increasingly sophisticated tools such as advanced charting techniques and computer screening.

However, the analyses themselves do not constitute the "problem." It is the *dissemination* of the analyses, or, at least, of the results of the analyses. When a major brokerage or financial analyst reaches a conclusion regarding a security, customers and readers across the country receive the recommendation, and the security's price usually responds, positively or negatively, both to the analyst's predictions and to the increased attention.

Security analysis in other countries is often on a par with our own. However, there is undoubtedly less of it, and less dissemination of the results. Consequently, there is a greater chance of coming across a relatively unappreciated security. It is likely that an incipient IBM would remain undiscovered far longer in a foreign country than in the United States.

In an "efficient" market, all things are known about all securities, and the prices of those securities reflect what is known and what is projected. Prices of securities change as a result of broad market movements or when developments within a company or in the marketplace (this includes, of course, business cycles, interest rates, etc.) change either the facts or one's expectations. No country has an entirely efficient market, but the U.S. equities market has probably come closer than the markets of most other countries because of the sheer volume of dissemination of high-quality analysis. This has not made for a market of complete predictability—there are certainly surprises—but there is somewhat less risk (certainly less risk than in more volatile markets), and for that lessened degree of risk there is a correspondingly lower degree of potential return.

If the movement of stock prices in the United States were averaged over the ten years from 1970 to 1980, the resulting cumulative returns (dividends and capital gains) for all U.S. stocks would be a disappointing 16%. Thus, the country with the majority of market capitalization, with the largest number of financial instruments, and with the most sophisticated analytical techniques, offers only a mediocre return to its investors. Do not think, however, that the case for foreign diversity rests on the fact that it is wilder or woollier out there in foreign markets. The recommendation for internationalization is based on the fact that greater oppportunities often exist in foreign markets than in domestic markets. Finding the right investment or uncovering the overlooked company takes time and diligence. A broker with a good international department is a major component of successful internationalization, as is care, curiosity, and watchfulness on the part of the investor.

WHAT MAKES FOREIGN SECURITY PRICES MOVE?

How different are foreign securities with respect to the way their market prices fluctuate? What forces are brought to bear on securities in Japan, in the United States, or The Netherlands, that cause their prices to rise or fall?

The basic mechanism of any marketplace is the same no matter where the market: it is supply and demand that moves prices. Specific differences between countries are those imposed by regulation or custom. For instance, a limitation on the daily price movement, such as the 5% limit imposed by the Frankfurt Stock Exchange, protects a security from extreme fluctuations within a single trading day. While this can inhibit price movements in the face of extraordinary news, it also offers a certain degree of price stability. United States stock exchanges, by comparison, do not impose such restrictions, but limitations on daily price movement are standard on the more volatile U.S. commodity exchanges.

Another example would be the fact that high PE ratios,[1] typical of Japanese stocks, do not have the negative effect on security prices in Tokyo that they have in New York. It is simply customary for the Japanese to buy stocks at higher PE ratios than we do in the United States.

The bottom line, under all these circumstances, is supply and demand, and these two forces function within whatever guidelines are imposed by regulation or custom of the marketplace. If supply or demand change, the prices of securities will move, so long as they are permitted to do so.

In the following chapters the specifics of each stock exchange are explained, as are certain conditions external to the exchange. Also given are the salient features of each investment instrument. With these facts, you will have at least a limited perspective with which to interpret foreign financial news, evaluate security recommendations, and, simply, to talk to your broker more intelligently.

Figure 1 illustrates the fact that general market forces are everywhere the same. The original version, by Nomura Securities, was in-

[1]See "price-earnings ratio" on p. 3.

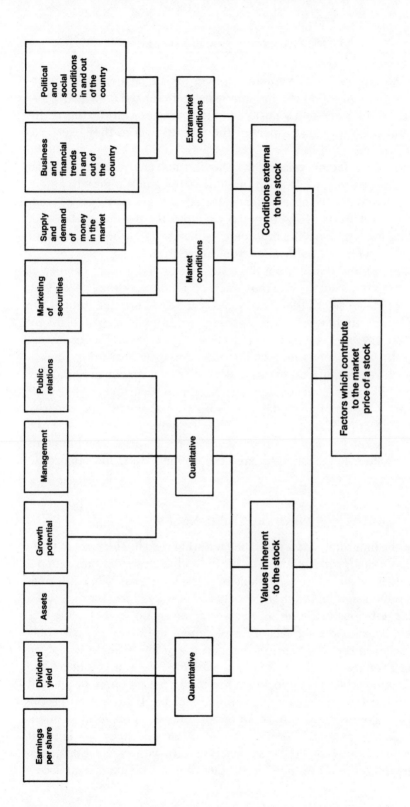

Figure 1. Factors which contribute to the market price of a stock.

tended to explain the movement of prices on the Japanese stock market. In its present expanded and somewhat generalized form, all factors relevant to the price of a security (anywhere in the world) are categorized and related to that aspect of the security where they exert the most influence.

Some of the factors relating to a stock's value are quantitative, such as earnings or assets, while others are qualitative, such as growth potential or management. Those factors external to the security come from either general market conditions (for example, the recommendation of a leading analyst or a shift in foreign exchange rates) or extra-market conditions (such as a political crisis or a rise in imports).

Keep in mind that it is not the status quo or the present balance of these forces that causes price movement. It is *change*—real, perceived, or expected—in any of the above areas that causes prices to move. For example, one might read of a new government regulation in a relatively small country (say, The Netherlands) that would channel more money from retirement funds and unions into domestic securities. Such a change in regulations, an extra-market condition, might precipitate a rise in stock prices that would affect all Dutch securities.

Almost any bit of news, data, or information that can affect security prices is accommodated in Figure 1. By knowing only the basics of a foreign market you can begin to interpret its financial developments and more knowledgeably evaluate your options, risks, and opportunities.

WHAT ARE THE DANGERS?

One of the first rules of international investing is *do not attempt to trade quickly on small price moves.* For the individual investor, international investing is usually more reasonable over the long term. While information is now disseminated more widely than ever before, there is still a time lag. Obviously, the rest of the world does not operate during U.S. business hours, and a significant development in Europe or Japan may likely occur in the wee hours of the morning or late at night when you are not keeping an eye on the economic news. Even if you heard the news immediately, your broker's office might not be open, or when it is open, the foreign stock exchange may not be. It may often be the following day before you have an opportunity to react to investment news. (See Appendix 1 for time zones of various stock markets.) It therefore behooves one to be especially careful with speculation, keeping such investments in the United States where one has instant access

to the news and the market. There will, of course, be foreign speculative situations that will be very attractive, but try to limit them to a few.
For the most part, one is better off adjusting one's expectations of
foreign investments to a longer time frame.

Another danger to watch for is thin markets or a security with a thin
float (i.e., a relatively small number of shares available for trading). If
you have purchased a thinly traded stock it may be subject to erratic
price movement on an imbalance of buy or sell orders. Liquidity
becomes crucial at the most important moment for your investment: at
the time you want to sell. Difficulty in finding a buyer will certainly
bring the price down.

Currency exchange is, of course, an ever-present risk with foreign
investment. However, one can also think of this risk as extra leverage
which will either augment or diminish the price of the security once it
is translated into dollars. Chapter 3 is devoted to this subject, so we will
not go into detail now except to say that it is a manageable risk; it is also
a risk foreign investors must be willing to accept if they are to invest
abroad.

SAFETY OF INTERNATIONAL DIVERSIFICATION

An important reason to buy foreign securities is diversification. Anyone
knows that risks are higher when all one's eggs are in one basket.
Diversity is the classic protection against the poor performance of a few
stocks, and foreign securities are, in fact, the ultimate in diversification.
Yet, the portfolios of typical U.S. investors are seldom diversified, either
with respect to markets or currencies.

When you confine your investments to one market (typically, the
New York Stock Exchange) you are, no matter how careful your stock
selection, subject to the overall performance of that particular market,
not to speak of the movement of the currency. Recalling the relative
performance of the major foreign markets shown in Tables 1 through
6, it is easy to see that your chance of selecting securities in markets that
will outperform the U.S. markets is excellent.

Do not, however, be lulled into thinking that the mere fact of
diversification is going to guarantee good performance for your portfolio. A shotgun approach will not usually be of much benefit. It goes
without saying that care in selecting both securities and currencies is
essential.

It is expected that when some markets are down, others will be up.
However, in comparing the performance of various markets, it should

be cautioned that markets do not move with complete independence (although neither do they move in tandem). The strong bull market that began on the New York Stock Exchange in August 1982 soon affected most foreign markets as well. The interesting observation for the international investor is that while foreign markets frequently respond to strong movement on the NYSE, that response can lag, sometimes by days and sometimes by months. Thus, when you feel that a strong market in New York is running out of steam you should be able to locate investments in other countries where the market still has strength. Getting a feel for this kind of market switching takes some experience, but investments based on strong market moves can provide excellent returns for the international investor.

A DIMINISHING PERCENTAGE OF WORLD CAPITALIZATION

For many years the United States has enjoyed the lion's share of world capitalization. It has been estimated that, with 5% of the world's population, U.S. markets represent almost 55% of the world's capitalization. Japan is second with just over 17%, and the United Kingdom third with 7%.

This seems like an enormous percentage until one compares it with the figure ten years ago. In 1974, U.S. securities represented almost 75%(!) of the world's capitalization. Although the United States still has a strong lead, there can be no doubt that foreign centers of capital are increasing in importance. It is arguable whether a more equitable distribution of capital will benefit world economics; likely it will. At any rate, as larger amounts of capital become centered in other countries, increased investment opportunities soon follow.

KEEPING INFORMED

Perhaps the most serious impediment to investment abroad is the difficulty in obtaining information. The timely receipt of annual and interim reports can still be a problem. However, space-age communications are making price quotations and limited data increasingly available on an international basis. It will only be a matter of time before foreign quotations will be accessible, at least on a limited basis, on most quote terminals in the United States.

In the chapters in Part 2 on individual stock exchanges the major sources (in English) of investment information are given. Addresses included are those of the stock exchange, major brokers, periodicals, regulatory agencies, banks, etc. In the chapter on the London stock exchange, price quotations from the *Financial Times* are explained for stocks, bonds, and mutual funds.

It may seem like a big step for U.S. investors to look abroad for investments, but foreign diversification has been standard practice in Europe for hundreds of years. It is probably because we enjoy such a large and diverse market in the United States that investors have tended to keep their money in domestic securities. However, times are changing. The investing public is gradually awakening to the degree to which we are already involved in foreign securities as news of foreign companies is increasingly reported in major newspapers and financial periodicals. Not only are investors beginning to purchase more foreign securities at home, but they are shopping abroad in increasing strength. In the last quarter of 1982, records of the Commerce Department show that U.S. investors, led by large pension funds, were heavy net buyers of foreign securities: purchases outnumbered sales by $1.3 billion. In 1983 the trend increased, with $2.8 billion more purchases than sales in the first two quarters alone.

Figures like these, of course, will not march in the same direction forever. There will doubtless be quarters when U.S. investors will be net sellers of foreign securities. Nevertheless, the overall pattern seems to be established. Foreign securities are becoming a standard part of U.S. investment portfolios and, with the help of modern communications and trading facilities, they are likely to remain so.

2

AMERICAN DEPOSITARY RECEIPTS

A DOMESTIC INSTRUMENT FOR FOREIGN SECURITIES

American Depositary Receipts, usually referred to simply as ADRs, are negotiable certificates created by U.S. banks to facilitate the trading of foreign securities in the United States. ADRs serve as surrogate certificates for foreign shares,[1] and, from the point of view of the investor, they may be traded in the United States exactly as if they were domestic shares.

ADRs are created in the following way: a U.S. bank, which we will call the "depositary" bank, decides that it will create an ADR issue (for reasons we will consider later). It contacts a bank in the country of the issue and appoints that bank the "custodian bank." The custodian bank may be a branch of the depositary bank, a branch of some other U.S. bank, or it may be a foreign bank. A depositary bank may even have more than one custodian bank in a country. At any rate, the shares of a specific company—let us call it "company F"—are acquired on the foreign stock market (or from a foreign broker or foreign bank) and placed with the custodian bank. The depositary bank then prints and issues the certificates (ADRs) that represent those shares in the United States.

Sometimes one receipt is issued for each foreign share, and sometimes, particularly with Japanese stocks, one receipt may represent two, five, ten, or even twenty shares of the underlying stock.

The share certificates of the original shares never leave the country in which they were issued—they remain in the keeping of the custodian bank. The ADR certificates, issued in the United States, are sold in the United States through stockbrokers. (Banks in the United States, of course, may not sell shares directly to investors.) If the original shares are in registered form, then a nominee for the custodian bank (usually a partnership set up for this purpose) becomes the holder of record on the books of company F, and the investor who has purchased the ADR

---

[1] A few ADRs are created for bonds, in particular, long-term issues of foreign governments.

certificates becomes the beneficial holder of the shares in the United States. Either the investor or the broker will become the registered holder, depending on whether the ADR is held in street name or not. The depositary bank, although the creator of the ADRs, has served only as an intermediary in this process.

However, the depositary bank continues to be involved with the ADR issue in a number of ways, such as effecting transfer of ownership. The depositary is the conduit through which dividends are distributed in this country. More important, the depositary continually adjusts the number of ADRs (and therefore the number of shares held by the custodian) depending on market demand. For example, if U.S. investors become net sellers of a specific ADR, the market makers in the United States (brokers with a private inventory of the security from which they stand ready to buy or sell in at least limited quantities over the counter) will sell the security abroad, in order to reduce their inventories. They then return the ADRs to the depositary bank to obtain release of shares for delivery in the country of issue.

WHY ARE ADRs NECESSARY?

Before going into more detail concerning the structure of ADRs, it might be helpful to discuss them from a functional point of view. Why are they necessary, and what role do they play in U.S. securities markets?

Among the most obvious reasons why share certificates from most other countries do not trade in the United States is the fact that the shares are often different types of instruments than they are in the United States. For instance, some foreign shares are in bearer form rather than the registered form to which we are accustomed. Bearer shares are different in many ways. There is no name (i.e., of the owner) on the certificate, and the company does not keep records—it doesn't know who owns its shares. Each certificate has a page of numbered dividend coupons[2] attached to it, and the distribution is to whoever presents them.

However, one cannot blame the problem of foreign share transfer entirely on bearer-form stock certificates. Many countries issue only registered shares, and those that issue both types are showing a definite

---

[2]The coupons are numbered, not dated. This is so the issuer can use an extra coupon, if necessary, for a special distribution. Thus more coupons may be needed in one year (and at different times) than in another.

preference for the registered form. There are other problems, such as getting shares and records through international mail in a reasonable amount of time, certificates that are in other languages, and rules of ownership transfer which vary from country to country.

It is important to realize that ADRs are *not* always necessary. The share certificates of many foreign companies, particularly Canadian, are traded in this country every day because those companies have appointed transfer agents (usually banks) here to effect transfer of ownership. In fact, the single greatest impediment to trading foreign share certificates in this country has to do with transfer of ownership. The procedures are complex and involve the coordination of brokerages, the relevant stock exchange, transfer agents, company records facilities, and, often, the Depository Trust Company.[3] The efficiency with which huge volumes of shares have been processed in recent years would be greatly impeded if a bearer-form instrument were introduced. Any changes in the future are likely to be in the direction of "paperless" transfers (such as those made possible because of the Depository Trust Company) rather than the opposite, which is what the accommodation of bearer shares would mean.

From the investor's point of view, ADRs are a convenience. One of the most important of those conveniences is that the dividends are received in U.S. dollars. While there may be a small charge for this service (anywhere from $.0025 to $.02 per share), at least the currency exchange has been taken care of and dividends can be deposited without further bother. It should be mentioned with respect to foreign dividends that quarterly payments are not the norm. Most foreign companies pay semiannually, and some even pay annually. In the chapters on specific exchanges the normal dividend schedule will be given for listed securities, but you should always verify the specific dividend payment dates with your broker for any security you purchase.

Another advantage of ADRs is that the number of underlying stocks represented by each ADR can be adjusted so that the price per ADR is within a range considered respectable by U.S. investors. For example, the price of Japanese stocks often falls within a bracket that might cause the U.S. investor to think of them as "penny stocks." A ratio of one ADR to five, ten, or even twenty underlying shares places the price of the ADR within a more comfortable range.

[3]The Depository Trust Company (DTC) is a depositary used by U.S. brokers for U.S. shares whose ownership registration can be transferred (as is the case for all U.S. shares). It serves as a collateral base by which brokers can effect ownership transfer among themselves through debits or credits to their accounts with the DTC.

At their most basic level, ADRs are instruments of arbitrage. They create a market whereby banks buy securities in a foreign country and sell them in the United States, and brokers, in addition to buying and selling for their customers in the United States, buy ADRs here and sell the shares abroad. (In the latter case, the ADR certificates are returned to the depositary bank for delivery of the shares wherever they are sold.)

All the above problems in trading foreign shares apply also to foreign countries where U.S. shares are traded. In Amsterdam, for instance, where shares are normally in bearer form, fifty-five American stocks are traded. The Dutch have accommodated American shares by creating a "paperless" instrument called the American Shares Amsterdam System (ASAS). The U.S. shares are held by an Amsterdam depositary, and trading is effected by electronic transfer of ownership. So efficient is this system that the price of the ASAS shares seldom varies from the underlying U.S. security by more than a quarter of a point. Any change in the U.S. ADR system in the future may very well be along these lines.

SPONSORED AND UNSPONSORED ADRs

Few people realize that there are two different kinds of ADRs: those created through a sponsored account and those created through an unsponsored account. The difference can be important in terms of dividend yield and the reliability with which one may or may not receive financial reports.

The banks themselves do not usually initiate creation of an ADR. In one case, a foreign company approaches the bank to request that ADRs be issued for the company's stock. The result is usually a "sponsored" deposit agreement in which all costs of creating and administering the ADRs are paid for by the company. Subsequent listing of the ADR on NASDAQ or an exchange, as well as SEC reporting, are also at the initiation and expense of the company.

Unsponsored accounts are not usually initiated by the company. In this case, U.S. brokers who feel that they have determined a sufficient market for the securities of a specific foreign company approach a bank with a branch or an affiliate in the country of issue. The bank then contacts the company for a "no objection" letter. It is possible such an expression of interest could lead to a sponsored account, but, more likely, the account will be unsponsored, which means it will be created and administered at no cost to the company.

HOW ADRs ARE ADMINISTERED

For a sponsored account, the company reimburses the bank for the cost of distributing the dividends, and for distributing annual or semiannual reports to ADR holders. Annual reports, proxies, and other materials are sent in advance of the annual meeting, and dividends are sent afterwards. In cases where the ADRs are in street name then the brokers are also reimbursed for distribution of this material. The brokers pass the expense on to the bank, which, in turn, passes it on to the company.

Costs of administering an unsponsored account are not covered by the company. To pay for these continual expenses the depositary bank deducts a 1 to 2 cents per-share fee for each dividend distribution. Sometimes, for an unsponsored account, a company will pay for distribution of an annual report. Unless this happens, however, annual reports are sent only on direct request of the shareholder, and even then on an as-available basis.

Subscription rights for new issues are only forwarded to ADR holders if the new issues are registered with the SEC. Otherwise, rights are sold in the country of issue, and the proceeds, in U.S. currency, forwarded to the ADR beneficial holder. For unsponsored accounts, there is a charge for this service.

There are also cases where ADRs trade so infrequently in the United States that new ADRs must be created for every purchase. When this happens, there may be a small charge (around 5 cents per ADR).

A BIRD'S-EYE VIEW OF ADRs

Figures 1 and 2 illustrate the ADR operational structure. The only difference between the two at this level is that for sponsored accounts financial reports are sent directly to the depositary and not to the custodian bank. In either type of account, whenever ADRs are held by the investors (i.e., not in street name) dividends and financial reports are sent directly to them from the depositary.

EXCHANGE LISTING

All ADRs on the NYSE and AMEX must be of the sponsored type. An investor can thus be assured of receiving timely information about the company and of having no deductions from his or her dividends if ADRs are purchased on one of these two exchanges. The regulation that exchange-listed ADRs be sponsored addresses a major deterrent to the acquisition of foreign stocks by U.S. citizens: the difficulty of getting information about a company. Exchange regulations also prohibit the

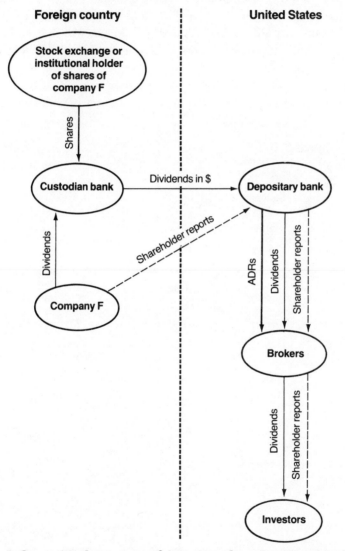

Figure 1. Operational structure of American depository receipts (sponsored account). NOTE: This assumes the ADR is held in street name. If it is registered in the name of the investor, the "broker" step is skipped once the initial transaction has been made.

security, if it is common stock, from being nonvoting. However, there are ways around this regulation, as you will see in Chapter 6, on Japan.

Because of differences among foreign business practices and corporate structures, the exchanges and NASDAQ cannot apply the same listing and reporting requirements that they do for domestic companies. Attempts to accommodate these differences include allowances made for minimum numbers of shareholders, and allowances for the market value of publicly held shares. For instance, the calculation of these figures is allowed on shares held worldwide, not just within the country of issue.

An ADR issue carries all the risk of a domestic stock. It may carry more if the reporting requirements in the country of issue are substan-

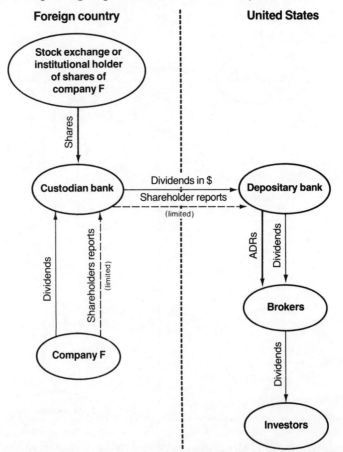

Figure 2. Operational structure of American depositary receipts (unsponsored account). NOTE: Shareholder reports will have to be requested especially from the depositary bank.

tially lower than in the United States. There is also the added risk of currency exchange (discussed elsewhere). However, many of the problems are solved by the ADR mechanism. ADRs, it is safe to say, constitute a positive step toward the creation of a world market in equity securities.

3

THE EFFECT OF CURRENCY EXCHANGE

THE EXTRA STEP

Currency exchange is the "extra step" in foreign security transactions, having the power both to increase or decrease either your profits or your losses. There is even the potential to change profits *into* losses, and vice versa.

Although it is complicated in its detail, currency exchange need not be a mysterious "black box." In principle, its effect is simple. If, for example, the British pound appreciates against the dollar, and you happen to own a security denominated in pounds, the value of your security (with respect to U.S. dollars) appreciates accordingly. If the pound falls against the dollar then your security decreases (in dollar value) accordingly.

It is the interaction of the exchange rate with the market price of a security that determines what you will pay for a security, and what you will get for it when you sell. To determine the dollar value you simply multiply the two together. You can think of it in musical terms: over a period of time the generally slower-moving wave (the exchange rate) will modulate the more widely fluctuating market price. The resulting "wave" plots the dollar price of the security. Although the movements in price or exchange rate would never be as regular as those shown in Figure 1, this example nevertheless shows the effect of the one on the other.

If the exchange rate had remained unchanged at £ = $1.50 for the two weeks then the fluctuation of the security price in dollars would have been between $1.50 and $1.575, a difference of 7½ cents. With the change in the exchange rate, the lowest value of the security in the course of the two weeks is $1.50 and the highest $1.68, a difference of 18 cents.

BUYING MONEY

Foreign exchange is the price of money in a different currency. It is, in fact, not exchange at all. You may think of it as the *conversion* of one currency into another, but it is closer to the truth to think in terms of "buying" money.

When one inquires at a bank about foreign exchange, two prices are usually quoted: a higher one if you are buying currency, and a lower one if you are selling currency. The higher price at which you may buy is called the "asked" price, and the lower one at which you may sell is the "bid" price.[1] The difference between those two prices is the quotation "spread," and that is where the bank is compensated for its foreign

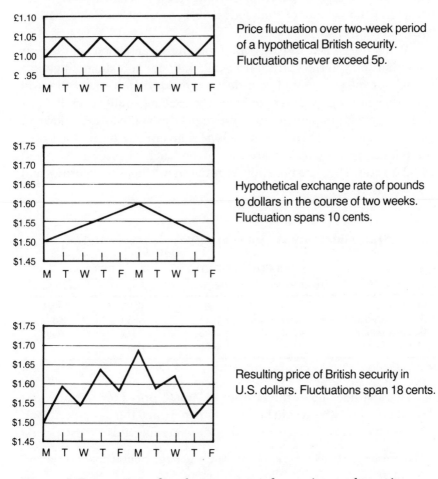

Price fluctuation over two-week period of a hypothetical British security. Fluctuations never exceed 5p.

Hypothetical exchange rate of pounds to dollars in the course of two weeks. Fluctuation spans 10 cents.

Resulting price of British security in U.S. dollars. Fluctuations span 18 cents.

Figure 1. **Interaction of exchange rate and security market price.**

[1]It is sometimes easy to confuse the "asked" and "bid" prices (as to which one is the higher), but remember that the quotations are the bank's, not yours. Therefore, the higher price will be what the bank is *asking,* the lower one what the bank is *bidding.*

exchange transactions. Foreign exchange in this light is not a service for which one pays a fee but simply purchases and sales. The bank, for its part, is following the most tried-and-true of all trading principles: buying low and selling high.

WHAT PRICE MONEY?

The exchange rate your broker charges will depend on the rate at which he or she is able to obtain the currency. A large international broker may be able to purchase currency at fractionally lower prices because of the volume of transactions or because of special affiliations with banks or money brokers.

At any rate, when you are contemplating a transaction your broker can either tell you the current exchange rate or approximate it closely enough for the purposes of your decision-making. However, there will be times when you will want to know the exchange rate yourself. Most of the large daily papers publish exchange rates in the format shown in Table 1. The *current spot* or *cash rate* is given only on the first line. Sometimes, *forward rates*[2] are also given, such as the 30-, 60-, and 180-day rates. These do not apply to retail transactions of securities and can be ignored.

Table 1

STANDARD FORMAT FOR PUBLISHING EXCHANGE RATES

	U.S. $ EQUIVALENT		CURRENCY PER U.S.$	
	THURSDAY	WEDNESDAY	THURSDAY	WEDNESDAY
* Britain (pound)	1.4588	1.4605	.6855	.6847
30-day forward	1.4594	1.4611	.6852	.6844
60-day forward	1.4613	1.4629	.5843	.6835
180-day forward	1.4636	1.4652	.6832	.6825

Current spot rate.

The first line shows the current or "spot" prices for the previous day, "Thursday" (this would be Friday's paper), and the day before that, "Wednesday." There are three things to remember about these prices:

1. They are interbank rates applicable only to large transactions ($1 million or more).

[2]Forward rates are prices for large quantities of currencies traded between banks and large multinational corporations for settlement and delivery at the future time specified. Minimum amounts are usually over 100,000 units of currency.

2. They are yesterday's (and the previous day's) prices.
3. They are asked prices; bid prices are fractionally lower.

Checking the spot price in the first column, we see that yesterday the British pound was $1.4588. It is usual in quotations such as this to take the quote out to hundredths of a cent. Although the price today will be fractionally different, it is easiest to go ahead and work with yesterday's price. You can see that Thursday's price varies from Wednesday's price by only .17 of a cent (i.e., $.0017).

The $1.4588 is the interbank spot asked price. As a rule of thumb, you will receive a conversion rate for securities transactions of about 2% more (which allows for fractionally higher prices for lower quantities and for the services from the broker), which is called the "retail" rate. Two percent of the current spot rate is $.0291 (rounded off), making for an estimated retail exchange rate of $1.4879.

If you are considering buying 100 shares of British XYZ quoted at £13.74 per share, you would calculate the charge simply by multiplying.

> £1374 price of 100 shares of British XYZ
> × $1.4879 retail exchange rate
> $2044.37 price (rounded off) in U.S.$

If you are considering selling shares then you needn't tack on the extra 2% for the rough estimate since the bid price is slightly lower anyway.

When you do make a purchase, you should keep a record of the exchange rate. Sometimes it doesn't show on your brokerage receipt. If you are not sure what it is, write down the interbank rate for that day (it will be quoted in the following day's paper). That way it will be easier to keep track of currency exchange rate fluctuations.

WHERE DOES FOREIGN EXCHANGE ENTER THE TRANSACTION?

Most people at one time or another have had to buy foreign currency to send abroad, perhaps for a purchase. In that case, an international money order or cashier's check is usually purchased at a bank, in the applicable currency (i.e., the conversion takes place at this point), and then mailed to the foreign payee. When the money order is received at its destination, it is already denominated in the appropriate currency and can be deposited without further currency exchange.

When purchasing foreign securities you will probably be paying for them in the United States, with U.S. dollars.[3] There are a variety of ways transactions can be handled and a variety of places where foreign exchange can enter the picture. Of course, if you are buying ADRs or the actual shares in this country you will not be concerned with foreign exchange. Foreign exchange is only necessary when you must, in some sense, actually "go" to the foreign market for your transaction.

Figure 2 shows the most common method by which foreign securities are purchased. You place an order with your broker for a Japanese security and send him or her payment in U.S. dollars. The broker sends your order on to a Japanese broker who, as a member of the Tokyo Stock Exchange, will obtain the security on the Tokyo trading floor. At the same time your broker obtains a currency exchange with a U.S. bank in order to get the necessary yen. (Those yen were probably obtained, in turn, from a Japanese bank.) After obtaining the yen, the U.S. broker then sends payment, in yen, on to the Japanese broker. Many other steps, of course, also take place, but these are the ones relevant to the foreign exchange part of the transaction, as shown in Figure 2.

Even if your broker in the United States is a branch of a foreign brokerage firm, the currency exchange will probably take place in the United States, as shown in Figure 2. This is, in fact, what happens when you buy Japanese securities through a U.S. branch of a Japanese broker. One of the standard deviations from this pattern is that the U.S. broker might deal directly with a Japanese bank for the foreign exchange and skip a U.S. intermediary, but this would probably be done only for large transactions.

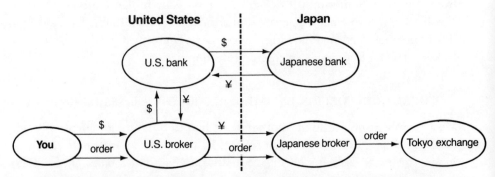

Figure 2. Purchase of foreign securities through a U.S. broker (or U.S. branch of a foreign broker).

[3]If you use a broker in another country it is possible you could send a foreign money order but it is unlikely you could obtain a significantly better exchange rate, counting the charge for the money order.

In the next case, shown in Figure 3, you would have to have an account in a foreign country with a foreign broker. You would still pay directly in U.S. dollars and the currency exchange would be handled entirely within that country. This would be the case, for instance, in the United Kingdom because U.S. branches of U.K. brokers do not usually handle retail accounts in the United States.

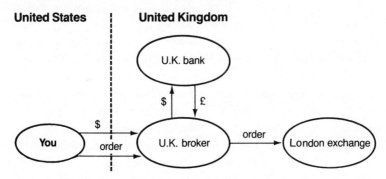

Figure 3. Purchase of foreign securities through a foreign broker in a foreign country.

In many foreign countries, such as Germany, banks also serve as brokers. In fact, they conduct all types of "investment banking" such as underwriting, portfolio management, and safekeeping, etc., in addition to regular banking services such as foreign exchange. If you had an account with a German bank, it would effect the foreign exchange in-house, as shown in Figure 4.

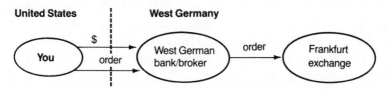

Figure 4. Purchase of foreign securities through a bank in a foreign country.

WHICH WAY WILL EXCHANGE RATES GO?

Predicting exchange rates is a bit like predicting interest rates: at best, it's half science and, at worst, a mixture of alchemy and fortune-telling. Obviously, the financial condition of a country affects exchange rates, but that effect is not always predictable. For instance, if a country runs a large budget deficit, it can have a *positive* effect on its currency's exchange rate because interest rates will probably rise, making the currency more attractive to foreign traders.

Politics and the perception of safety, as in the case of the dollar, play an important role. News, too, has a strong effect, although sometimes it may only move currency rates for the short term. When considering the effect of news it becomes immediately apparent that exchange rates can never be predicted with precision because news, by definition, cannot be predicted.

How, then, is an investor to view exchange rates? First of all, do not be alarmed by short-term volatility. This is often the result of speculation in the currency markets and cannot usually alter a currency's fundamental strength or weakness. For long-term exchange rate movements there are two important fundamentals to watch: higher or lower inflation rates (in relation to U.S. rates), and higher or lower real interest rates (in relation to U.S. rates). Movement in either of these areas may be the result of a shift in the balance of payments, a shift in the balance of trade, or an increase or decrease in the money supply.

Also important are activities of major financial institutions. However, these institutions will usually react after the fact or attempt to maintain the status quo rather than precipitate change on their own. Specifically, we are referring to the activity of international agencies such as the International Monetary Fund (IMF) or the European Economic Community (EEC), or activity of a central bank, particularly a change in the support level of the country's currency. And, of course there is always the wild card: adverse or supportive political developments.

Information or data from any of the above areas must be interpreted in relation to other data. In isolation, facts are often not very helpful. For instance, it is not necessarily informative to know that inflation in country X is 5% unless you know that that is higher or lower than inflation in the U.S.

As far as foreign exchange is concerned, it is *change* to which rates are the most sensitive. Presumably, current rates will already reflect current circumstances. It is when the relationship between comparable factors *changes,* or is *expected* to change, that currency rates begin to move.

EFFECTIVE EXCHANGE RATE

By means of an exchange rate the value of one currency is established with respect to another. However, in a system where the value of all currencies more or less floats freely, a view of the relationship of only two currencies can be ambiguous and even misleading. For example, let us say that the yen is increasing in value against the French franc. From the perspective of the U.S. resident we still need to know more about those currencies, since any one of the following situations could be true:

- The yen is appreciating faster than the French franc is appreciating.
- The yen is appreciating while the French franc is holding steady.
- The yen is holding steady while the French franc is falling.
- The French franc is falling faster than the yen is falling.

By evaluating a single currency against a *group* of currencies (called a "basket" of currencies in foreign exchange jargon), one gains a more accurate view that is closer to what most would call an objective evaluation of a currency. Figure 5 plots the exchange rate of the U.S. dollar against a basket of seventeen major currencies. When the line ascends, the dollar is gaining in value over the combined value of those currencies, and when it drops, it is losing ground with respect to their combined value. You can see that the U.S. dollar dropped in relation to those currencies from 1977 through 1978 and then experienced an extraordinary rise in 1981 and 1982. The index representing the seventeen-

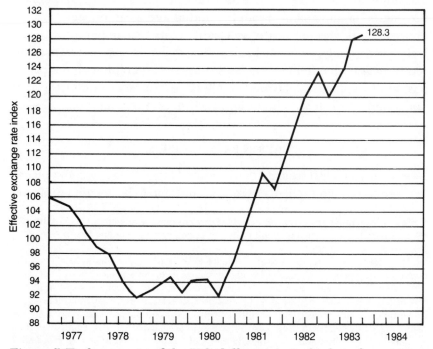

Figure 5. Exchange rate of the U.S. dollar against a basket of seventeen major currencies.   Source: *Federal Reserve Bank of St. Louis*

currency basket is the effective exchange rate index.

The index numbers on the left- and right-hand side of Figure 5 are arbitrary and only used to show comparison of values. They do not represent any unit of currency.

Graphs of the kind shown in Figure 5 are prepared using various numbers of currencies and employing various weightings of those currencies within the index.[4] The effective exchange rate used in this book is calculated from the exchange rate of the currency in question and those of seventeen other major currencies, with weights derived from the International Monetary Fund's "Multilateral Exchange Rate Model."[5]

Each chapter in Part Two on a major stock exchange contains a chart such as the one shown in Figure 6 for the deutschemark. On the left of the graph the increments are labeled in U.S. dollars. The solid line, representing the deutschemark, shows a dramatic appreciation from 1977 through 1979, and an even more dramatic fall from 1980 to 1981.

The dotted line shows the effective exchange rate of the deutschemark. The increments on the right, which apply to the effective exchange rate, are labeled with arbitrary numerical values to establish the degree of movement. From the dotted line it can be seen that the deutschemark was not nearly so volatile as its exchange rate with the U.S. dollar would lead one to believe. The dollar, in fact, moved precipitously against all other currencies. Compare this graph with the previous one in Figure 5 showing the effective exchange rate of the U.S. dollar and you will see almost an exact inverse relationship.

FOREIGN EXCHANGE RISK

As soon as you buy a security denominated in another currency you are exposed to foreign exchange risk. You continue to be exposed until you

---

[4]Different weightings of currencies in an index means that the movement of one currency affects the index more than movement by the same proportion of another (presumably, less important) currency.

[5]Each weight represents the model's estimate of the effect on the trade balance of the country in question of a change of 1% in the domestic currency price of one of the other currencies. The weights, therefore, take account of the size of trade flows as well as of the relevant price elasticities and the feedback effects of exchange rate changes on domestic costs and prices. The measure is expressed as an index based on average exchange rates during 1975. For more information see Jacques R. Artus and Rudolf R. Rhomberg, "A Multilateral Exchange Rate Model," *International Monetary Fund Staff Papers* (November 1973), pp. 591–611.

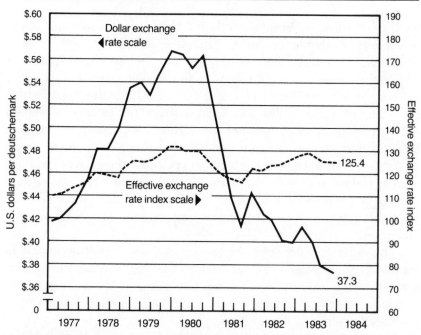

Figure 6. Exchange rate of the deutschemark with the U.S. dollar and the effective exchange rate with other major currencies.
Source: *Federal Reserve Bank of St. Louis*

sell the instrument or close your position (or, with an option, until it expires). On that day, the foreign exchange rate, in relation to the exchange rate when you initiated your position, will be crucial in determining the extent of your profit or loss.

Studies have shown that exchange rates do not usually constitute a significant risk to large institutional portfolios as long as the currency exposure is "hedged." (Hedging, in this context, means taking on a risk which will counterbalance another risk.) The standard method of hedging currency is to buy or sell currency forward contracts or currency futures. For example, one might protect a large exposure in French francs (say, bonds) by selling French francs forward. If the value of the franc fell against the dollar then the value of your forward contract would increase. If the franc rose against the dollar then the dollar value of the bonds would increase but you would have lost on your forward contract.

The point of hedging is not to *make* money, it is to *keep* money. You hedge when you want to avoid risk, and the result of a successful hedge is that you end up essentially where you began. Also, what is protected in a currency hedge is the value of the currency, not the value of the security. If you hold French bonds and the value of the bonds themselves declines then a forward contract in French francs will not help.

Forward contracts and futures contracts, which we will examine here only cursorily, are similar in a number of ways. Both require delivery at a future date and at a set price. (This is the aspect which offers the protection.) With a forward contract, for instance, you could sell deutschemarks nine months in the future at a specific price and thus be protected against a drop in the value of the deutschemark in the meantime. If such a drop were to occur you could close the contract for a profit and regain most of what your other instruments, denominated in foreign currency, lost when the exchange rates fell. You could also sell deutschemarks when the contract matures at the higher rate specified.

The difference between the two is that futures contracts come in standard contracts, amounts, and dates. Forward contracts are tailor-made for each transaction. They are not as negotiable, because of the variations which exist in the contract, but they are more adaptable to the specific needs of the investor.

Unfortunately, individual investors seldom have foreign holdings substantial enough to successfully hedge with respect to currency. The typical hedging instrument has definite time limits so that periodic transactions would be required to maintain the hedge. The repeated cost of these transactions would constitute a significant percentage of the yield that should be expected from foreign investments. As a result, the individual investor is better off accepting foreign currency risk without the benefit of hedging. So long as one diversifies among several currencies, foreign exchange risk is manageable.

If you *were* to hedge, then you would not only be protected against a drop in the value of the currency but you would also be protected against a *rise* in that currency(!). Thus, if the currency were to appreciate against the dollar it would be of no benefit to your holdings. This is not usually the position desired by the individual investor.

Again, currency hedging is not usually for the individual. Before purchasing any foreign security, check with your broker concerning the outlook for exchange rates. If the prospects do not look good then it may be best to find a security in another currency. For the international investor there is never a lack of investment opportunities.

4

INTERNATIONAL MUTUAL FUNDS

WHEN IS AN INTERNATIONAL FUND APPROPRIATE?

One of the dangers of international investing is insufficient diversification. The number of securities or currencies which constitutes adequate diversity is debatable; but the less diversity, the heavier the responsibility will rest on each individual component for the performance of the portfolio.

Currently, conservative brokers suggest that only 5% to 10% of a portfolio should be in foreign securities. It is the author's feeling that three times this amount is appropriate. But whatever the percentage, if you have only a few thousand dollars to invest abroad, you may want to think of an international mutual fund instead. You will receive the benefits of diversification and professional management, along with the quarterly reports which, in themselves, are often sources of information on foreign markets and specific foreign securities. Of course, you would not want to use a mutual fund report as a shopping list, since the statement of holdings will be several months out of date and, even more dangerous, some mutual funds do not indicate whether a security on their list is one which they hold or one which they have shorted.

Predictions of market conditions found in mutual fund reports can be particularly helpful. Such forecasts are made, for example, to explain the shift of fund emphasis from one country to another. If the expected market rise or currency appreciation has not already taken place by the time you read the report, you may want to check with your broker to determine whether those predictions remain viable. The same goes for specific companies. Check with your broker on the price history of the security you are considering. As always, be guided by the most current information you or your broker can obtain. If the price of a security has already appreciated, your mutual fund may have already taken a profit by the time you read the report, and your subsequent purchase could be timed very badly. If the security hasn't appreciated since the date of the mutual fund report you may consider it a cautious recommendation. However, the fact that a stock has not significantly appreciated in three months cannot necessarily be interpreted as a positive sign.

TYPES OF MUTUAL FUNDS

International mutual funds are generally divided into three categories: global funds, international funds, and regional funds. Although the names used are sometimes different, the fund types remain the same. In this chapter, "international" is used to describe all three of these types as well as referring specifically to the middle type only. The context should make the meaning clear.

Global funds in themselves represent maximum diversification in that they divide their capital among many countries, including the United States. There are often stated limits for holdings in any one country. If you already own U.S. securities or U.S. mutual funds, you may not achieve the international diversification you desire with a global fund since a good percentage of such a fund will usually be invested in the United States.

International funds are much the same as global funds except that they do not invest in the United States. Thus, an international fund is the most efficient way of controlling your desired percentage of international diversification, since you are assured of having the entire sum invested in foreign securities.

If you have an interest in a particular geographic location or country, you may want to consider a *regional fund*. Such funds have the advantage of focus when there is strong share-price movement in a particular country. However, there is also more risk because of the lack of diversification. One of the most disheartening examples was the recent Mexico Fund (although this is specifically a closed-end fund, not a mutual fund). Almost immediately after the fund was launched, international oil prices fell; the peso was devalued, and the economy became so weakened that the Mexican government nationalized banks (some of the shares of which were held by the fund). From an initial $10 a share the price tumbled to a mere $2. On the other side of the coin, however, some regional funds have been among the year's best performers (see Table 3).

In each of the chapters that cover individual stock exchanges, a few mutual funds or mutual fund management groups are mentioned. There is, however, a special problem with obtaining information from and sometimes with purchasing shares of foreign mutual funds (that is, mutual funds that are *based* outside the United States). None are registered with the SEC which means, among other things, that their shares may not be publicly offered here. The manner in which individual funds interpret this restriction affects the accessibility of of the funds to U.S. investors. In some cases you may obtain a prospectus and purchase shares of a specific fund by simply calling or writing a U.S. branch of a foreign bank (assuming the home office of that bank is either the manager of the fund or that the bank owns the management group that is). In other cases you will have to write to the home office of the management group and even then you will sometimes be refused a prospectus on the grounds that it might constitute solicitation in the United States. In the chapters that follow, addresses for all funds mentioned are given in the sections entitled "Useful Addresses" so that you may write directly to the funds if you choose to do so.

Countries with a particularly strong history of well-managed funds are The Netherlands (Chapter 14), Switzerland (Chapter 10), Germany (Chapter 9), and the United Kingdom (Chapter 7). The funds of these countries offer diversification through many different combinations of domestic and international securities. Many will have a large percentage of their holdings in the United States, however, and you may want to take this into consideration if you are seeking purely international diversification.

A SELECTION OF U.S. FUNDS

Tables 1, 2, and 3 are by no means comprehensive. They contain only major funds based in the United States. Most have toll-free numbers, and a prospectus can be obtained with the ease of a phone call. You should request several prospectuses and compare them before you

Table 1

U.S. GLOBAL FUNDS

FUND	% GAIN, 1983	% GAIN, 1978–83	% YIELD, 1983
First Investors International (800) 221-3847	30.07	—	.7
Keystone International (617) 338-3200	13.52	89.81	1.0
Putnam International Equities (800) 225-1581	27.89	109.73	1.4
Templeton Foreign (800) 237-0738	36.51	—	1.4
United International Growth (800) 821-3664	28.28	75.91	3.2

make up your mind. A few of the funds are no-load, meaning that there is no sales charge deducted from your investment. Those that do charge a load do not usually charge more than 8.5%.

International mutual funds do not always outperform domestic funds, but in 1983 international funds (meaning any of the three categories mentioned earlier) performed better than any other type of fund. According to the Lipper Analytical Service, which monitors all U.S. mutual funds, international funds turned in an impressive 32.1% average gain for the year, while the average domestic share fund performed at 20.2%. This strong return was all the more amazing since it was in the face of a strengthening U.S. dollar, which reduced the value of the funds' holdings when translated into dollars.

For each fund listed, the one-year and five-year percentage gain is calculated, assuming all dividends were reinvested. The yield is made up of the entire last year's income divided by the closing net asset value.

The Scudder International Fund is the oldest of the international funds, founded in 1953. Until 1975, the fund only grew to $12 million in assets, but in the last eight years it has mushroomed to a healthy $112 million. The Transatlantic Fund is the second oldest; it is also one of the

Table 2

U.S. INTERNATIONAL FUNDS

FUND	% GAIN, 1983	% GAIN, 1978–83	% YIELD, 1983
Kemper International Fund (800) 621-1048	28.04	—	1.3
T. Rowe Price International Fund (no-load) (800) 638-5660	28.61	—	1.5
Scudder International (no-load) (800) 225-2470	29.72	92.26	1.4
Transatlantic Fund (no-load) (212) 747-0440	32.98	64.62	1.2

Table 3

U.S. REGIONAL FUNDS

FUND	% GAIN, 1983	% GAIN, 1978–83	% YIELD, 1983
Canadian Fund (800) 221-5757	25.45	111.1	3.1
G.T. Pacific Fund (no-load) (800) 824-1580	37.37	43.55	2.0
Merrill Lynch Pacific (212) 692-8162	37.93	91.21	1.8

most expensive, with an initial deposit requirement of $5,000 and additional deposits of a minimum of $1,000. T. Rowe Price International Fund, the youngest, is also the largest, with net assets of nearly $130 million.

There are also specialized international mutual funds, such as gold-share funds or technology funds. An example of the latter is Sci/Tech Holdings, Inc., a new fund jointly managed by Merrill Lynch in the United States, Nomura Capital Management in Japan, and Lombard Odier International in Europe. It specializes in holdings in science and technology with present emphasis in Japan and the United States, and, to a lesser extent, in Europe. Shares can be obtained through Merrill Lynch.

An example of an excellent gold fund is United Services Gold Shares, which specializes in gold shares throughout the world. It is a no-load fund with an initial minimum investment of only $500. It has an excellent record, topping the Lipper Investment Service five-year performance chart with a total return of 544.54% at the end of 1983. It is headquartered in San Antonio, Texas (800-531-5777).

Another gold fund, International Investors, topped the Lipper Investment Service fifteen-year list with a total return of 1,316%. It is a load fund (8.5%) headquartered in New York (212-687-5200).

5

HOW DIFFERENT ARE FOREIGN SECURITIES?

MEANINGFUL DIFFERENCES ARE FEW

There are surprisingly few differences between foreign and domestic securities other than those of mere terminology. Meaningful differences are becoming fewer and fewer as stock exchanges modify their operations to increase their compatibility with other exchanges. Most are members of the Fédération Internationale des Bourses de Valeurs (FIBV), an international organization of stock exchanges that seeks to promote closer relationship and cooperation among world exchanges.

In this chapter we will consider briefly only differences between U.S. and foreign securities, or between U.S. and foreign markets, likely to affect the individual investor. There are, in fact, a wide variety of operational changes being adopted by world stock exchanges that have to do with transfer of ownership. One of the results of these changes will be to make international transfer of security ownership easier and more efficient. Since these are, however, "back office" procedures, we will not consider them here.

BEARER-FORM SHARES

In the United States, all stocks are issued in registered form. That means two things. First of all, the owner's name is inscribed on each certificate. That is, every certificate is issued to a specific person. Secondly, it means that the owner's name is also inscribed on the books of the corporate issuer so that the company knows who its stockholders are and can be in touch with them. When ownership of the stock changes, a new certificate is usually issued with the new owner's name on it, and the company adds the new owner's name to its books and deletes the name of the former owner.

Many foreign shares are also issued in registered form, but there is still a significant proportion in bearer form. (The tendency now, except for a few countries, is to issue registered shares.) The only experience U.S. investors are likely to have had with bearer-form securities is with

U.S. municipal bonds issued before 1983. No name was inscribed on the certificate so that the owner was assumed to be the bearer of the certificate, and the municipality did not know who its bondholders were. Dated coupons were attached to each certificate, and the appropriate one was clipped and sent in to claim an interest payment.

Bearer-share certificates are the same, with one important difference. The coupons attached to the stock certificate are usually numbered instead of dated. This allows the company to use an extra coupon when needed, for claiming an extra distribution. Thus, if the company normally pays dividends twice a year, only two coupons would be needed, but if there were additional dividends, the investor might need three or even four coupons. When the coupons run out (i.e., the last number is used) the company sends out a new sheet.

DIVIDENDS

Dividend payments are not always quarterly, as we expect in this country. Sometimes they are semiannual, and sometimes they are even annual. In the chapters on the individual markets the schedule for dividend payments is given so that you will know the norm in each country. However, for any security you purchase you should verify with your broker when and how many times the dividend is distributed.

In many countries it is customary to declare the dividend as a percent of par value (like preferred shares here). If you see stock quotations in foreign newspapers or periodicals you may still see dividends reported in percent of par value, although now it is customary to use units of local currency. At any rate, the par value of common stock takes on a greater significance for foreign shares than in the United States, and often you will see the name of the stock followed by its par value. See, for example, the quotation examples from *The London Times* in Chapter 7.

INTEREST

Bonds frequently pay interest only once a year rather than semiannually as in the United States. In the chapters on individual exchanges the payment schedules are usually given for the major bond types. However, schedules may vary even within the same category, so you should verify the interest-payment schedule with your broker for any bonds you are considering for purchase.

Foreign bonds may also amortize their principal (face value) over the life of the bond or over its last five or ten years. The principal will show up as extra amounts on your dividend receipts. If you do not desire this gradual return of the principal you should watch for it among bonds you are considering for purchase as it is quite common, particularly among European bonds. Also, amortization will affect the price at which you may buy or sell a bond, if you do so after the amortization has begun. Although interest from foreign government and municipal bonds is often paid without foreign withholding tax, there are no tax-exempt foreign municipal bonds as far as your own tax returns are concerned. The tax exemption of municipal bonds in the United States is a creation of the individual states, and regulations vary (as to which state's bonds are tax-exempt) from state to state.

PRICES AND TRADING LOTS

Prices of stocks in other countries are often lower, on the average, than in the United States. Thus, a blue-chip stock on a foreign exchange will sometimes seem like a penny stock to a U.S. investor. This is particularly true on the Tokyo Stock Exchange, the second largest equity market in the world. More detail is given in Chapter 6 on Tokyo, but suffice it to say here that it is traditional on a number of foreign markets to keep the unit price of equities low by the frequent issuance of additional shares. The price does not indicate a greater degree of speculation or risk but merely that the number of shares outstanding is higher than is customary here.

Because the per-share price is low does not mean that small-sized transactions (in terms of dollars) either are invited or are practical. Usually, the size of the trading lots for low-priced issues is set at a number substantially higher than 100 shares. The cost of the average transaction is thereby increased accordingly.

In each of the following chapters the standard trading lot sizes are given. Usually, they are on a sliding scale based on the per-share price of the security. In Tokyo and Sydney, for instance, many issues are traded in 10,000-share lots. Odd lots may or may not be difficult for the nonresident to obtain.

NEW INSTRUMENTS

There are no entirely new investment instruments on any of the major stock exchanges; however, there are some which combine features of several instruments in ways that do not appear on domestic U.S. markets. For instance, nonvoting shares in the United States are generally preferred shares. On some foreign stock exchanges nonvoting common shares appear as a matter of course. These issues have been created to keep voting control of the corporation within the country of the issue. The voting shares will sometimes be available only to residents while nonvoting shares (often designated as class B shares) are restricted to investors outside the country.

Some countries, such as Switzerland and Japan, have adopted strict regulations to keep domestic corporate voting entirely within their own borders. In the case of Japan, all nonresident shareholders must appoint a Japanese proxy for the purpose of corporate voting. In itself, this is not a great cause for concern; the process is fairly automatic, and one usually appoints a Japanese broker as proxy. Unfortunately, there is a hefty charge for this "service"—about $70 (see Chapter 6 on the Tokyo Stock Exchange).

Other relatively unique investments are shares in mutual funds, in that they are traded on the floors of many foreign stock exchanges. Both open-end and closed-end funds are usually listed. However, many of the so-called closed-end funds, or trusts, more closely resemble open-end funds (in the United States) because there are so few restrictions—in some cases, none—on the issuance of new shares. In most cases the prices of these shares (or certificates) stay relatively close to their net asset value.

One of the relatively unique types of instruments, at least from the point of view of the issuer, are the "savings shares" available on a few exchanges, most notably on the Milan Stock Exchange. They resemble preferred shares in that they are nonvoting and the dividends (which are higher than the dividends of common stock) are cumulative and have preference over the dividends of other shares. Their innovation lies in the fact that the dividends are tax-deductible *for the company,* thus providing considerable incentive to issue these high-yielding shares. (See Chapter 15 on the Milan Stock Exchange.)

ROLL-CALL TRADING

Many foreign stock exchanges practice a roll-call form of trading instead of the continuous trading to which we are accustomed in this country. In roll-call trading, the names of all listed securities are called out one at a time by an exchange clerk. Most of the traders are situated around a central circle or pit, and after each name is called, transactions in that specific security take place.

The specific mode of exchange trading does not usually directly affect the investor but there are cases where it is helpful to know that this kind of trading is the norm. For instance, an order may not be executed on the same day it is received if the last round of trading in that particular security has already taken place. There are also a few types of orders used on some exchanges (see the specific exchange chapters) which wouldn't make sense unless you knew the trading was by roll call.

Dates for settlement tend to be different on every exchange. In general, payment may be required by anywhere from one day to three weeks. If you have your account with a broker in a foreign country (specifically *in* another country, not with a branch of a foreign brokerage in the United States), then the settlement schedule of that country will apply. In the case of next-day settlement, as is the case in The Netherlands, it may be necessary to have the funds in your account in advance of your order. If you are purchasing foreign securities through a U.S. broker, then you will be required to pay according to the U.S. settlement schedule—within five business days.

Part Two

STOCK EXCHANGE PROFILES

6

THE TOKYO STOCK EXCHANGE

Courtesy of the Tokyo Stock Exchange

THE LARGEST STOCK EXCHANGE OUTSIDE THE UNITED STATES

As you might gather from the picture above, the Tokyo Stock Exchange is not small. Second only to the New York Stock Exchange in terms of market capitalization, Japan's share of the total world equity market was 17.4% in fiscal 1983, more than the world market shares of Germany, France, and the United Kingdom combined. (The U.S. share was 55.5%.) Average daily volume in 1983 was approximately 200 billion yen. Over the last two years, market capitalization increased at an annual rate of 17%. During the same period, U.S. market capitalization increased at an annual rate of 5.1%.

There are eight stock exchanges in Japan, with Tokyo conducting about 80% of all trading. The other exchanges are located in Fukuoka,

Hiroshima, Kyoto, Nagoya, Niigata, Osaka, and Sapporo.

Nonresidents may sell Japanese securities freely, but there are a few restrictions on purchases. In case you're a big spender, nonresidents may not acquire more than 10% of a corporation without permission of the Minister of Finance. There is also a group of eleven stocks for which total foreign ownership limitations have variously been set, usually between 25% and 50%. There are indications that the Japanese government may lift this restriction, although for now it still stands. Most are oil companies, and none, except Hitachi Ltd., are available as ADRs. (Hitachi is listed on the New York Stock Exchange.)

The size alone of the Tokyo exchange makes it an important market. While individual investors seem to have discovered Japan only recently, institutional investors, particularly pension funds, have for years invested in Japan on a massive scale. No large international portfolio has been without major Japanese holdings for long.

The Japanese government, however, has not always encouraged foreign investment. While most of the restrictions that existed before 1980 have been relaxed or lifted altogether, nonresidents still may not sell short (except under extremely limited circumstances), and they are required to appoint a Japanese proxy for all Japanese stock owned.

The proxy requirement (see "When Your Broker Trades in Tokyo")

THE TOKYO STOCK MARKET AT A GLANCE

Capitalization:
Market value of shares (only) in U.S.$* . . . . $547.5 billion
Percent of total share capitalization represented by ten largest
    companies. 14.8%
Volume:
Average daily volume of shares . . . . 365 million†
Percent of total volume represented by ten most active shares. 15.8%
Listings:
Domestic equities. 1,441
Domestic fixed-income securities 594
Foreign equities 11
Dividend (average yield) 1.54%
PE ratio (average) 26.5
Rank in the world:
Capitalization 2nd
Turnover/shares 1st

*Exchange rate as of Dec. 31, 1983: $1 = ¥232.35.
†Down from 377 million shares in 1981.
Source: Tokyo Stock Exchange, 1984 Fact Book.

is understandable given both the homogeneity of Japanese culture and the paternalistic attitude of Japanese businesses. However, such a requirement is an anomaly in a leading international marketplace, and it is hoped that it will be rescinded or significantly modified in the near future.

Any decision to invest abroad should take into consideration the general economic and political condition of the country in question. In this case, Japan is a stable democracy and a staunch political ally. It is both a major trading partner of the United States and a formidable competitor. The disagreements over quotas, barriers, and international market shares (which at times almost resemble corporate rivalry) are addressed politically with various mixtures of self-interest and concern for the common good.

Japan is particularly safe in terms of market size (thereby guaranteeing liquidity), and its currency is strong. Japanese management's ability, both on the corporate and national level, is almost legendary. Japan's area of greatest weakness is dependency on foreign energy sources. In fact, 99.8% of its crude oil and 75% of its coal must be purchased abroad. Offsetting this weakness is one of Japan's greatest assets, the unity with which its people can address problems of national import. For example, from 1973 to 1980, as a result of the oil crises, the Japanese, through extraordinary conservation measures, reduced their imports of crude oil by 10% while at the same time more than doubling their nominal[1] gross national product! That took determination and cooperation on a massive scale.

A BIT OF HISTORY

The Tokyo Stock Exchange has the astonishing distinction of having emerged almost directly from the demise of feudalism. One of the primary functions of the exchange, founded in 1878, was to provide a marketplace for bonds that had been issued to commute the feudal stipends of the samurai. Thus, one of the tools with which feudalism was dismantled became an instrument of a far more progressive institution: the Tokyo Stock Exchange.

Although Japan may have started late, it did some fast catching up. By 1881 there were 137 stock exchanges throughout the country. This proliferation was due in part to the organization of the exchanges as profit-making entities. They derived their revenues from a hefty cut of

---

[1]Without adjusting for inflation.

the commissions, usually over 50%, and even issued their own stock. (Shares of the Tokyo exchange were actively traded until the beginning of World War II.) Gradually, however, the government reduced the number of exchanges so that by 1914 there were only ten.

Despite what some people think, war is not always good for capitalism. With the beginning of the China War in 1937, the government began regulating monetary flow. Prices of securities were artificially maintained, and by 1943 all Japanese stock exchanges were merged into a government agency where they eventually ceased to function as marketplaces. On August 9, 1945, three weeks before the surrender, all stock exchanges were closed. A small amount of over-the-counter trading began after the war but the Allied occupying authority forbade the reopening of the exchanges, despite the fact that they were badly needed. It was not until May 16, 1949, that trading resumed on the Tokyo, Osaka, and Nagoya exchanges. These and the other exchanges were organized under a securities exchange law modeled after the U.S. Securities Exchange Act of 1934.

Since World War II, the rise of the Japanese securities market has been far from smooth. Japan has been adversely affected by a number of events in the Far East as well as by events farther from home, such as the U.S. Interest Equalization Tax, the U.S. 10% import surcharge of 1971 (referred to as the "Nixon shock"), and the two oil crises of 1973 and 1979. Despite these setbacks, the performance of the Tokyo exchange has been impressive. The graph in Figure 1 compares the Tokyo Stock Exchange price index (a more broadly based index than the Nikkei-Dow) with the broadly based indexes of four other major markets. (For the sake of comparison, all indexes are calculated from a base of 100 in 1975.) One's enthusiasm for this performance might be somewhat dampened by the low dividend yield of these stocks (discussed later), but with respect to capital gains, the Tokyo exchange has outperformed the exchanges of the United States, the United Kingdom, and West Germany for most of the last seven years.

Even more impressive than the appreciation of stock prices in Japan is the rise of its gross national product. In Figure 2 Japan's real GNP (i.e., adjusted for inflation) is compared to the real GNP of its major competitors: the United States, the United Kingdom, and West Germany. (All are calculated from a base of 100 in 1973.)

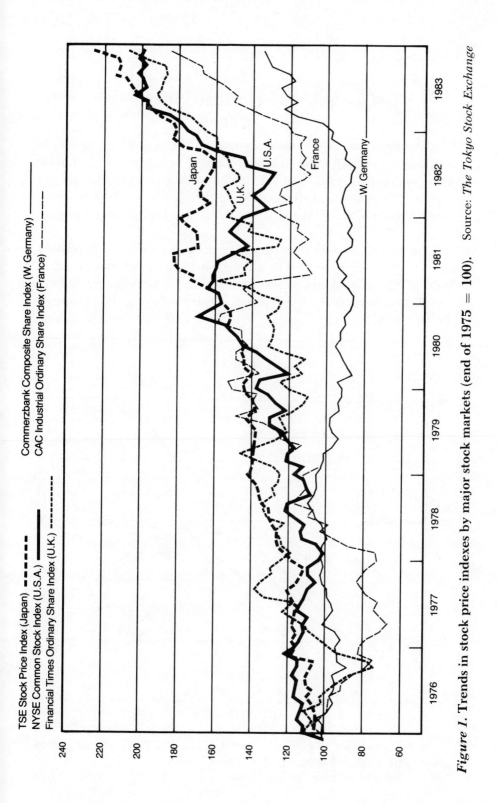

Figure 1. Trends in stock price indexes by major stock markets (end of 1975 = 100).   Source: *The Tokyo Stock Exchange*

JAPANESE CURRENCY AND EXCHANGE RATE WITH
THE U.S. DOLLAR

The standard unit of Japanese currency is the yen, whose symbol is ¥. It may appear in print as ¥10 (ten yen) or ¥1 million (one million yen). Coins are minted in values of 1, 5, 10, 50, and 100 yen while bank notes are printed in denominations of 500, 1,000, 5,000, and 10,000 yen—worth a bit over $2, $4, $21, and $42, respectively, at current exchange rates.

The yen floats freely with respect to all other currencies. The Minister of Finance is empowered to intervene in the exchange market when there are (1) unusual movements in the exchange rates, (2) problems in the domestic economy, and (3) extraordinary swings in the balance of payments.

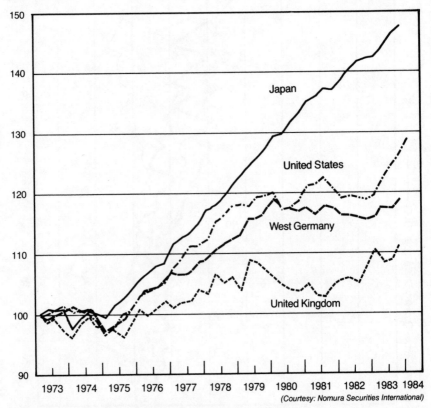

(Courtesy: Nomura Securities International)

Figure 2. **Japan's real GNP compared to the real GNP of the United States, the United Kingdom, and West Germany.**
Source: *Nomura Securities International*

The solid line on the graph in Figure 3 shows the interbank exchange rate (the rate quoted in the press). Room is left for you to continue the graph if you like. Regular charting is not necessary, but a dot here and there as you observe the exchange rates may be useful to you later.

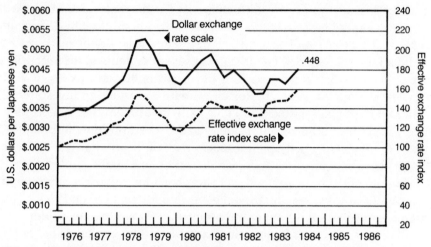

Figure 3. **Exchange rate of the Japanese yen with the U.S. dollar and the effective exchange rate with other major currencies.**
Source: *Federal Reserve Bank of St. Louis*

The effective exchange rate (see p. 40), indicated by the broken line, reveals a trend not seen in any other major currency. Since 1976, the yen consistently has been valued above the average of other currencies (as represented by the average of the seventeen currencies making up the effective exchange rate).

HOW DIFFERENT ARE JAPANESE STOCKS?

One of the first differences that a U.S. investor notices is that the per-share price of many of the most important companies is very low; they literally appear to be "penny stocks" (averaging from $.50 to $4). This should not put off the U.S. investor; it is simply customary (even among the bluest of blue-chip companies) to have a large number of shares outstanding. Whenever a company's earnings rise, causing its stock's price also to rise, the usual practice is for Japanese companies to declare stock dividends rather than to increase their monetary dividend. This tends to keep share prices low because of dilution. It does not necessarily reflect on the stability or instability of a company or indicate a high or low degree of speculation, although it is typically the case that a Japanese corporation is highly leveraged.

In the past, only about 20% of a Japanese company's capitalization was normally represented by equity stock; the rest was in the form of direct loans from banks. Although there is currently a shift toward greater equity capitalization, the percentage is still low by U.S. standards. This can result in a degree of greater volatility of share prices should there be sudden changes in the supply or demand for a security. But even though stock prices in Japan are quite sensitive to market news, U.S. investors are better off (as with most foreign investments) thinking of Japanese stocks as a long-term investment. For the present, anyway, time and distance make rapid short-term trading impractical.

Another aspect of Japanese stocks that a U.S. investor will notice is that dividends are usually lower than they are in the United States. Thus, it must be understood from the beginning that the investor in Japanese stocks is seeking capital gains rather than dividend yield. The Japanese government apparently encourages this attitude on the part of Japanese investors by granting exemption from capital gains tax for the first forty-nine trades(!), or the first 200,000 shares, during each calendar year. (This is an advantage not shared, unfortunately, by U.S. investors.) As a result, the annual turnover of stocks in Japan averages about twice that of the United States.

Dividends are calculated from par value and, as explained earlier, often have no relation to earnings. The average return in 1959 was 4% to 5%, and those same dividends, because of an increase in the price of the stock, have today become yields of only 1% to 2%. The compensation for the investor who has held Japanese stocks for a long time is that he or she will have acquired a relatively large number of shares by virtue of stock dividends (which are more common in Japan than in the United States) so that the *total* dividend return will have increased as a result of the additional number of shares acquired.

It may be the low dividend yield which has brought about a change in the demographics of stock ownership in Japan. Over the last thirty years the percentage of individual ownership (as opposed to institutional ownership) has decreased dramatically. In 1950, 61% of all Japanese stocks were owned by individual investors. Now the proportion is less than 30%.

Dividends are usually calculated around the three-week registration period beginning September 30. During this time an investor cannot conveniently sell shares, and in fact it would not be advantageous to do so under ordinary circumstances since the dividend would thereby be missed.

If you have ever looked into the fundamentals of a Japanese stock you may have been surprised by the high price-earnings (PE) ratio. For the last six years the average PE has been about 26. This was partly the result of accounting differences (such as the heretofore reporting of earnings on an unconsolidated basis). Hitachi, for example, sold at a PE of 31.4 in 1983: if the earnings had been consolidated on the annual report, the multiple would have been about half that figure. A new law, which took effect in March 1984, will now require companies to report earnings of all subsidiaries (i.e., on a consolidated basis). This will probably reduce Japanese PE ratios by about 20%. Other accounting differences to watch for in Japanese corporate reports are accelerated depreciation and hidden assets. Some properties, for example, are still reported on balance sheets at their post-World War II costs. A study by Nomura Securities International has shown that the current PE of Japanese stocks is only about 1% higher than the average PE of U.S. stocks once differences between the two countries' accounting systems and reporting systems are taken into consideration.

SECURITIES TRADED ON THE TOKYO EXCHANGE

common stocks: As mentioned earlier, prices often seem low; however, on the Tokyo exchange many stocks can conveniently be bought only in lots of 1,000 shares, which quickly brings their price up to a "respectable" level. (Trading in amounts less than normal-sized round lots is somewhat complex. See "Trading Lots," later in this chapter.) Dividends are usually paid semiannually on March 31 and September 30, but some are paid annually. There is only one preferred stock in Japan, issued in 1976 by the Hitachi Shipbuilding and Engineering Company.

rights: These instruments are more common in Japan than in the United States. They expire in (and therefore trade only for) about two months. As always, any rights assigned to stocks you presently own must be registered with the SEC to be distributed. This means you may receive a cash equivalent (see "A Word about Rights" later in this chapter).

bonds: The bond market is dominated by government securities, including local issues. Most corporate bonds are electric utilities or very large corporations, and most are traded over the counter. Interest is normally paid semiannually. Bonds of less than five years' maturity are issued at discount, and do not pay interest until maturity.

investment trusts: There are many types. Low-risk funds specialize in fixed-income securities. Higher-risk funds usually aim for capital growth through stocks.

Nonresidents are required by law to have an individual or institution in Japan serve as their proxy for all corporate voting. If you purchase Japanese stocks through ADRs, this will be done for you by the custodian bank holding the original certificates. If you purchase shares directly from the Tokyo exchange, there will be an annual fee charged by your broker for this service (see "When Your Broker Trades in Tokyo").

The market in stocks is quite active, with a great deal of turnover. The largest and most widely held stocks make up what are called the "first section" stocks on the Tokyo exchange. Admission to first section listing requires that a company have substantial capital (in excess of ¥1 billion), a large number of shareholders (more than 3,000), and that it have granted a 5-yen dividend per share for each of the previous three fiscal years.

There is a small over-the-counter market in stocks which is analogous to NASDAQ listings in the United States. What formerly constituted the over-the-counter market was absorbed by the Tokyo exchange as second section stocks. They are not traded on the floor but are accommodated by a completely computerized division of the exchange. Bonds make up the bulk of over-the-counter trading except for convertibles, which by regulation must be traded on an exchange. There are over 300 convertible bonds listed.

There are over 1,000 issues designated first section, about 400 second section, and 110 over the counter. Recent changes in regulations, however, may revive the over-the-counter market. Until 1983, brokers weren't permitted even to recommend these stocks.

It is unfortunate that there are so few foreign stocks listed on the Tokyo exchange. At present, there are only ten; nine American, and one Dutch. These stocks are traded on the floor during two thirty-minute periods each day: one at 10:30 A.M., and one at 2:30 P.M. A depository system is used to settle transactions; actual shares are not traded.

As far as nonresident trading in Japan goes, it has grown steadily for the last three years. In 1983, according to statistics from the Tokyo Stock Exchange, nonresident trading accounted for 10% of the total turnover on the Tokyo, Osaka, and Nagoya exchanges. Three years earlier, that figure was only 5%. Another change is the increase in U.S.

holdings in Japan. Traditionally, European and Middle Eastern investors dominated foreign purchases. Today, the United States accounts for at least half of all foreign holdings in Japan. Among restrictions for nonresidents are that they may not sell short (except under extremely limited—and complicated—circumstances). Most other types of orders are permitted except stop-loss and when-issued.

THE NIKKEI DOW-JONES AVERAGE

The stock index you will see quoted most often is the Nikkei Dow-Jones average. This average, originally designed by Dow-Jones & Company, is an unweighted arithmetic average based on 225 issues. Like the Dow-Jones Industrial Average (DJIA), it does not reflect total market activity (although a base of 225 issues is better than the thirty issues of the DJIA). It is also too susceptible to the activity of high-priced, thinly traded shares. Nevertheless, by popular demand it is the average that most often represents the Tokyo exchange. Shown in Figure 4 is a fourteen-year comparison of the Nikkei Dow-Jones and the DJIA of the New York Stock Exchange.

A more broadly based index, the Tokyo Stock Exchange Index (TSE Index), was established in 1968. Based on the nearly 1,000 issues on the first section of the exchange, it is subject to less distortion than the Nikkei-Dow because, among other things, it takes into consideration the number of shares outstanding, something the older index does not. (The TSE Index was the index used in Figure 1 in this chapter, which compares Tokyo exchange prices to those of four other countries.)

TRADING JAPANESE SECURITIES IN THE UNITED STATES

The first Japanese ADR was a Sony issue of two million shares in 1960. Today, there are more ADRs available in the United States for Japanese stocks than for the securities of any other country. That makes them, with the exception of Canadian stocks, the most accessible foreign securities here. Most are available over the counter; so if you have an account with a broker who makes a market in these stocks you may get a better price. At least you will save on commissions, since brokers who make a market in a specific over-the-counter security cannot charge a commission for transactions in that security. The broker's profit is the difference between the bid and ask price.

Quotations for ADRs on exchanges or over the counter are per ADR; per-share prices can be determined by dividing the number of

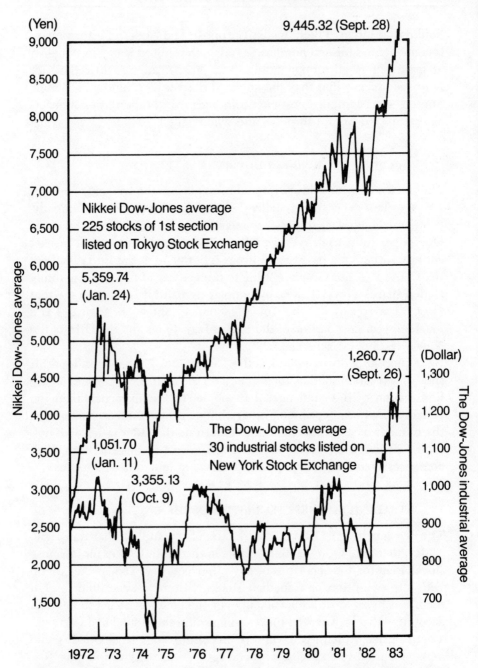

Figure 4. Stock price indexes (Dow-Jones Average) of the Tokyo and the New York stock exchanges. Yearly highs and lows in old TSE stock price average.

Source: Securities Market in Japan, *Japan Securities Research Institute*

shares per ADR into the ADR price. In the following lists the ratio of foreign shares to ADRs is given in parentheses.

AVAILABLE ON THE NEW YORK STOCK EXCHANGE
All are ADRs except the Japan Fund.

Hitachi, Ltd. (10:1)—largest producer of general electronics in Japan; computers, TVs, videotape recorders, appliances, semiconductors, and power plant equipment; plants in sixteen countries.

Honda Motor Co., Ltd. (10:1)—largest motorcycle manufacturer in the world; makes cars and trucks; plants also in the United States and Belgium.

Japan Fund (common shares)—leading closed-end investment company specializing in Japanese stocks.

Kubota, Ltd. (20:1)—largest manufacturer of agricultural machinery in Japan; industrial and building materials: nineteen plants in Japan.

Kyocera Corp. (2:1)—this is the former Kyoto Ceramic Co.; 60% of world market in ceramic casings for semiconductors; also ceramic parts for machinery, medical instruments, and electronics; nine plants in Japan, six in the United States.

Matsushita Electric Industrial Co. (10:1)—largest producer of consumer electronics in the world; Panasonic and Quasar; all lines of home appliances, communication equipment, and lighting; plants in twenty-five countries.

Pioneer Electric Corp. (2:1)—second largest producer of high-fidelity equipment in world; videodiscs and telephones; twelve plants in Japan, one in United States, one in Belgium.

Sony Corp. (1:1)—consumer electronic products such as TVs, videotape recorders, digital recorders, radios; eight plants in Japan, two in the United States, one in the United Kingdom.

TDK Corp. (2:1)—largest manufacturer of audio and video recording tape in the world; automation and memory devices, ceramic components for semiconductors; sixteen plants in Japan, three in the United States, one each in Brazil, South Korea, Mexico, and Taiwan.

AVAILABLE OVER THE COUNTER

There are almost 100 Japanese stocks available as ADRs in the United States. However, the mere fact that the ADRs are traded does not mean they are readily available. For example, if you wish to buy shares of Kawasaki Steel Corp., an ADR would be created (10:1) specially for your purchase at an extra charge of 5 cents per ADR above the commission. When you sell, the ADR will probably be dissolved and the shares will revert to the Tokyo exchange for trading. The advantage of buying ADRs (and thus paying for the ADR conversion) is that the proxy requirement is taken care of without charge by the depositary bank.

The following is a list of major Japanese ADRs available in this country on the NASDAQ system. The ratio of shares to ADRs is also given.

Canon, Inc. (5:1)—cameras and business machines
The Daiei, Inc. (2:1)—retailing
Fuji Photo Film Co., Ltd. (10:1)—chemicals and film
Ito Yokado (4:1)—retailing
Japan Air Lines Co. (10:1)
Kirin Brewery Co., Ltd. (10:1)
Marubeni (10:1)—retailing
Mitsui & Co., Ltd. (20:1)—retailing
NEC, formerly Nippon Electric Co., Ltd. (25:1)—electronics
Nissan Motor Co., Ltd. (10:1)
Shiseido Co., Ltd. (10:1)—chemicals
The Tokyo Marine & Fire Insurance Co., Ltd. (50:1)
Toyota Motor Co., Ltd. (2:1)
Trio Kenwood Corp. (10:1)—electronics
Wacoal Corp. (1:1)—textiles

The following bonds are available on the American Stock Exchange. (These are not ADRs; the certificates are in English.)

Ito-Yokado Co., Ltd. (6% debentures due in 1992)
Ito-Yokado Co., Ltd. (5¾% debentures due in 1993)
Komatsu Ltd. (7¼% debentures due in 1990)
Kubota, Ltd. (6¾% debentures due in 1991)

WHEN YOUR BROKER TRADES IN TOKYO

When a Japanese stock is not available as an ADR in the United States, the original shares must be purchased on a foreign market, presumably the Tokyo Stock Exchange. Discount brokers do not usually make purchases or sales outside the country (with the exception of Canada), so these transactions must be conducted through a U.S. full-service broker with U.S. offices.

Currently, only Japanese brokers are members of the Tokyo exchange. That means any U.S. broker who takes a purchase order from you for a non-ADR Japanese stock will, in turn, have to go through a Japanese broker to effect the transaction on the Tokyo trading floor. While Japanese commissions are low, and the interbank broker commission (what your broker has to pay the Japanese broker) is only about 80% of that already low rate, your U.S. broker must add his or her own charges so that the eventual rate, a double commission, will be higher than the Tokyo rates, although still not terribly out of line with typical U.S. broker fees.

In choosing a U.S. broker, select one who offers research in Japanese stocks (as well as the stocks of other countries in which you are interested). United States brokers licensed to trade in Japan are Merrill Lynch, Prudential-Bache, Goldman Sachs, Smith Barney, and Salomon Brothers. A British broker offering excellent research in Japanese stocks is Vickers da Costa. With Vickers, however, individuals will have to have their account in London unless it is a sizable amount.

Major brokers of foreign countries often have branches in the United States, but those branches are usually set up only to handle institutional accounts. Japanese brokers are an exception. Most have U.S. offices that accept accounts from individuals. In fact, with the excellent Japanese brokerage services in this country, there is no reason whatever to have your account in Japan. Communication, including the fourteen- to seventeen-hour time lag (depending on where in the United States you are), makes an account in Japan very awkward.

The four largest Japanese brokers with offices in this country are Nomura International (a major investment institution with a net worth exceeding that of Merrill Lynch), The Nikko Securities Co., Daiwa Securities American, Inc., and Yamaichi International America, Inc. (See "Useful Addresses" at the end of this chapter.) All offer research and comprehensive investment guidance for stocks and fixed-income instruments in Japan and other major market areas in the Pacific basin. It is often worth your while to use a Japanese broker, not only for the extensive research they can provide, but for their low commissions, the lowest of any major market (see below). However, Japanese brokers in the United States tend to prefer clients with large accounts, while some U.S. brokers, such as Prudential-Bache, are willing to handle foreign investments of any size.

COMMISSIONS, SETTLEMENT, AND THE PROXY FEE

Following are the commissions set by the Tokyo Stock Exchange. The minimum, ¥2,500, is only about $10.50 at current exchange rates. These rates will be slightly higher for over-the-counter stocks.

PURCHASE AMOUNT	COMMISSION
Less than ¥200,000	¥2,500
¥200,000–1 million	1.25%
¥1 million–3 million	1.05% + ¥2,000
¥3 million–5 million	.95% + ¥5,000

For bonds the commission rates are:

Government bonds	.4%–¥5 million, .35%–¥10 million
Government-guaranteed bonds, mostly local government bonds	.6%–¥5 million, .5% –¥10 million
Corporate bonds	.8%–¥5 million, .65%–¥10 million

Settlement is required three business days after the transaction. Although the exchange is open a half day on Saturday (except for the second Saturday of each month, when it is closed), Saturdays do not count as delivery days, so that purchases on Wednesday settle the following Monday (except on the second Wednesday of each month, in which case settlement is the following Tuesday). In the United States, because of the time difference, you may be given an additional day for settlement.

Another fee you must pay to a broker is a proxy fee. Japanese law requires that foreign shareholders appoint someone (usually your broker) in Japan to function as proxy for the purpose of corporate voting. The fee for this service is ¥2,000 per holding plus ¥.2 per share. The minimum is ¥20,000 (about $85 at current exchange rates) and the maximum is ¥400,000. Banks (which may also hold securities for you) charge a slightly higher fee. The minimum will apply to most individuals since it would take a holding in excess of 90,000 shares to exceed the ¥20,000 minimum. The fee, which does *not* apply to debt instruments, is levied annually on September 30. Obviously, purchases immediately after, or liquidations immediately before this date would be particularly timely. However, this means you would have held the security for less than a year, and capital gains would be taxed in this country at short-term rates. Also, as mentioned before, you would miss the dividend.

The proxy fee makes it necessary for any long-term investment in Japanese stocks to be substantial. Otherwise this yearly charge will take too large a bite from your total investment (unless, of course, the capital gains are extraordinary).

Another small fee that will be charged only on sales is the transfer tax. For stocks it is .55% of the total sale amount. For government bonds it is .03%, and for other bonds it is .045%.

TRADING LOTS

The size of trading lots varies on the Tokyo exchange depending on the par value of the stock. Most stocks are issued at a par value of ¥50 (sometimes ¥20), and the trading lot is 1,000 shares. This often comes as a surprise to the first-time investor in Japanese securities. If the par value of the stock is ¥500, the normal trading lot is 100 shares. Stocks with an exceptionally high market price can, if designated by the exchange, trade in 100-share lots, as can some second section stocks. Exceptions to the above round lot specifications are Sony, Fanuc, TDK, Kyocera, and NTV, which may be purchased in lots of 100 shares.

Since 1982, certificates have not been issued for odd lots. Therefore, investors receiving odd lots as share dividends have their ownership recorded only on the books of the company. When such dividends accumulate to a round lot the stockholder receives a certificate.

Odd lots without a certificate (i.e., those issued after 1982) cannot be sold on the exchange. Instead, the investor must demand purchase of all certificateless odd lots from the company. Thus, when you sell your holdings of a Japanese security your broker will likely sell the round lot portion on the exchange and the odd lot back to the company (at the market price).

Certificates for odd lots (which must have been issued before 1982) can still trade on the exchange. However, they are gradually disappearing, and one cannot buy odd lots without finding such a certificate since regulations now prohibit a company from registering the certificateless transfer of less than the standard unit of shares.

Because the U.S. owner of Japanese shares must pay a yearly proxy fee (explained earlier) it is generally impractical to acquire less than a round lot as an initial purchase because the proxy fee will constitute such a large percentage of your purchase price. Your broker will handle all aspects of the selling of odd lots, but it is good to know something of the procedure since Japanese stock dividends are constantly creating new odd lots.

A WORD ABOUT RIGHTS

Rights are a means of distributing a secondary offering to present stock-holders. Investors receive one right for every share currently held. At a set date the share offering will be made and investors may purchase the new shares at a price substantially lower than the current market price. Sometimes one right will allow the purchase of one share, but it more likely will take many rights, depending on the size of the new offering in relation to the number of shares outstanding. The point of the rights mechanism is to enable shareholders to maintain the same *proportion* of ownership in a company by purchasing the same propor-tion of a new issue. If a shareholder does not purchase the new shares, his or her holding in the company will be proportionally reduced in value through dilution.

Shares usually trade ex-rights three days before the final date of registration for rights offerings. At that time the shares generally drop from the former price to one which is the average of the old and new prices. For example, if a stock were priced at ¥1,000 and rights offerings were made enabling one to buy an equal number of shares (a ratio of 1:1) at par value (probably ¥500), then after the issuance of the new shares the price of all shares would be ¥750; that is ¥1,000 (the price of the old shares) + ¥500 (the price of the new shares) = ¥1,500 (the total value of one old share and one new share) divided by 2. In practice, however, there will be a slight difference in price between the old and new shares until the first dividend is passed (see below).

It has been common in recent years for rights to enable one to purchase new shares at a modest discount from the current market price (rather than at par value) so that the drop in share price may not be so precipitous. An issuance of rights does not cause investors to lose money. The rights can be sold at a fair market price, thus compensating investors in cash for the dilution in value of the shares already held.

Your broker will notify you of a rights issue and send you a form on which you will indicate your instructions regarding the rights. Usually, your choice is to exercise them or to sell them. Since rights can be a bit complicated, you should always consult your broker on the best strategy given the particular security and your financial circumstances.

There is one condition under which you cannot exercise rights. If the issue is not registered with the SEC it may not be distributed in the United States. Your rights will then be sold, and you will receive the cash.

The distinction between "old" shares and "new" shares (i.e., new shares being those recently issued through a rights offering) is maintained until the next registration period (when dividends are declared —usually September 30) because the dividend of the new shares will be in an amount proportional to the time that they were in existence during the year. For instance, if the new shares were out only three months by the time of registration their dividend would be half that of the old shares, assuming biannual dividends. After a dividend has been declared the distinction between old and new shares is no longer maintained since the shares are then considered equivalent.

TOKYO TRADING OPERATIONS

Membership in the Tokyo exchange is limited to licensed securities firms. There are two major categories: regular members, who buy and sell for their own accounts and the accounts of their clients; and Saitori members, who serve as intermediaries for regular members. Saitori members process transactions only in securities to which they have been assigned and try to match buy and sell orders insofar as possible. They are not like specialists on the NYSE in that they cannot buy or sell for their own accounts, and thus do not make a market in any of "their" securities. Regular members also have the option of trading among themselves without using the Saitori, except that all trades between regular members must still be reported to the Saitori, whose job it is to record the transactions. Since the Saitori do not make markets in securities, they receive a monthly commission from the regular members, based on the number of shares traded in their issues, regardless of whether they were participants in the trades or not.

The mechanism of trading is basically the same on the Tokyo floor as it is on most exchanges, including the United States: buyers compete with other buyers, and sellers compete with other sellers to get the best prices for their clients. Prices of securities move with the balance of orders. More sellers drive the price down, and more buyers drive the price up.

At present, the number of regular members on the exchange is limited to eighty-three firms, and the number of Saitori members is limited to twelve. This seems surprisingly small when compared to New York Stock Exchange membership of 1,360. However, unlike the NYSE, membership is corporate, not individual, and each member may be represented by as many as ten floor traders. There are also over 2,000 clerks and support personnel who assist in trading and reporting operations. Recently, the exchange's ban on foreign membership was lifted, but to date no foreign firms are members.

In the illustration at the beginning of this chapter you can see the raised seats along the sides of the trading floor where the telephone clerks of the regular members sit; traders and other clerks (also of regular members) are conducting transactions on the floor. Inside the fourteen large horseshoe-shaped booths are the traders and clerks of the Saitori members along with the TSE staff. Surrounding the exchange, on all four walls, are the huge quote boards.

The exchange building, constructed over fifty years ago, will soon be replaced by a new fifteen-story complex scheduled for completion in late 1984 (and ready for trading in 1985). Daily trading is made up of two sessions: 9:00 A.M. to 11:00 A.M., and 1:00 P.M. to 3:00 P.M.

A little-known aspect of the Tokyo exchange is its limits on daily price fluctuations. This aspect somewhat resembles the limits imposed by commodity exchanges in this country. The amount of permitted variation depends on the price of the issue and, generally, those that are lower-priced have a greater margin for movement than higher-priced issues. Table 1 gives the daily allowable price fluctuations:

Table 1

PER-SHARE PRICE, IN YEN	TOTAL DAILY FLUCTUATION ALLOWED, IN YEN
Up to 100	± 30
100–200	50
200–500	80
500–1,000	100
1,000–1,500	200
1,500–2,000	300
2,000–3,000	400
3,000–5,000	500
5,000–10,000	1,000

The types of orders available include limit orders and market orders (the same as in this country), and discretion orders, which give your broker authority to transact your order at what he or she considers the best time and price. Stop-loss orders are not available. Short selling is permitted only under extremely limited circumstances (i.e., one can sell short against the box during the registration period—usually beginning September 30—when converting convertible bonds into stock). Margin trading is permitted with 50% margin (soon to be raised to 60%), and settlement must be within six months.

All exchanges in Japan are closed during national holidays, the longest of which is New Year's (sometimes four or five working days). Other holidays include the Spring Equinox, the Fall Equinox, and Respect for the Aged Day (September 15). The Emperor's Birthday, also a holiday, is April 29.

In this chapter, as in many of the following chapters, lists are given of companies whose shares have the greatest total market value and companies whose shares enjoy the greatest market turnover. Inclusion of a security on such lists should not be interpreted as a recommendation to buy. However, the extent of capitalization, in particular, can sometimes be an indication of the stability of a company.

Table 2

THE TWENTY LARGEST STOCK ISSUES ON THE TOKYO STOCK EXCHANGE

COMPANY	MARKET VALUE IN BILLIONS OF YEN
1. Toyota Motor	3,627
2. Matsushita Electric Industrial	3,147
3. Hitachi	2,315
4. N.E.C.	1,741
5. Tokyo Electric Power	1,547
6. Fujitsu	1,471
7. Nissan Motor	1,435
8. Nomura Securities	1,192
9. Dai-ichi Kangyo Bank	1,162
10. Nippon Steel	1,153
11. Nippondenso	1,131
12. Mitsubishi Bank	1,114
13. Fuji Bank	1,114
14. Sumitomo Bank	1,114
15. Sanwa Bank	1,114
16. Toshiba	1,108
17. Sharp	985
18. Honda Motor	969
19. Nippon Oil	920
20. Kansai Electric Power	913

Source: Tokyo Stock Exchange, *1984 Fact Book.*

INVESTMENT COMPANIES

Either closed-end investment companies or mutual funds should be seriously considered by all international investors. Such funds guarantee two of the most important safety factors: diversity and professional guidance. The major closed-end investment company specializing in Japanese securities is The Japan Fund, whose shares are listed on the New York Stock Exchange. The quarterly reports of this and other funds will list the portfolio holdings, making these reports an additional source of investment suggestions.

A recent mutual fund with a large stake in Japan is Sci/Tech Holdings, Inc. Currently, 35% of its portfolio is in Far East securities. The goal of the fund is long-term capital appreciation through investment in science and technology issues. The sales charge is 8.5% of the offering price (which constitutes 9.29% of the net amount invested). Over 50% of its capital is invested in North America and a bit over 10% in Europe.

The G.T. Pacific Fund is a no-load mutual fund that invests in the common stock of Far Eastern companies. Long-term capital gains are the objective, and current income is not considered in stock selection. Merrill Lynch also has a mutual fund, Merrill Lynch Pacific, that invests heavily in Japan.

Table 3

**THE TEN MOST ACTIVE STOCKS ON THE
TOKYO STOCK EXCHANGE**

COMPANY	VOLUME IN MILLIONS OF SHARES
1. Nippon Steel	2,956
2. Nippon Express	2,009
3. Japan Line	1,824
4. Mitsubishi Metal	1,736
5. Keisei Electric Railway	1,712
6. Mitsui Mining & Smelting	1,704
7. Hitachi	1,645
8. Sanko Steamship	1,566
9. Mitsubishi Heavy Industries	1,300
10. Nippon Light Metal	1,300

Source: Tokyo Stock Exchange, *1984 Fact Book.*

ABOUT BONDS: GOVERNMENT AND CORPORATE

Like the stock market, the Japanese bond market is second in size only to that of the United States. As is the case in many countries, it is dominated by issues of the government, both national and local. Most bond transactions are over the counter but Tokyo does list over 600 separate issues, including those of the government. In Japan, yields are calculated such that returns, by U.S. standards, are understated by about .75%.

Short-term government bonds are issued for maturities as brief as two months. Longer-term government bonds are for various maturities from one to ten years. Any bond with a maturity of less than five years may be sold at a discount, and therefore will not pay interest until redeemed at maturity. Yields are about .5% below good-quality corporate bonds of similar maturities.

Government bonds are issued monthly, and the minimum denomination is usually ¥1,000,000. Interest is paid semiannually and most are coupon-bearing.

Corporate bonds (also called industrial bonds) make up only about 5% of the total bond market, and the majority of those (about 80%) are issued by nine electric power companies, JAL, and the Nippon Telegram and Telephone Company. Over thirty corporations (such as Nippon Telegram) may issue bonds backed by the government. You may want to ask your broker about these particular issues if your primary goal is safety of principal.

Most corporate bonds are straight but a few are convertible. They are issued in maturities of from one to twelve years, and pay interest semiannually. Minimum denominations are usually ¥100,000 and their yields are only slightly greater than government bonds (about .5%). As with government bonds, maturities of less than five years may be issued at discount. Corporate bonds are graded according to a scale of AA, A, BB, and B. These ratings reflect the degree of safety of the issue and result in about a quarter-point difference in yield.

The term "bond" is properly used in Japan only when the instrument is secured by *specific* assets of a company. Bonds secured by general assets are called "financial debentures."

Samurai bonds are bonds denominated in yen and issued in Japan by a foreign country or corporation. The first nongovernment to issue a Samurai bond was the Sears Roebuck Co. in 1979. Samurai bonds are in bearer or registered form, pay semiannually, and are free of withholding tax. They have maturities of ten to fifteen years. They are denominated at ¥1,000,000, and about half of each issue is usually purchased by nonresidents.

There is an active market in treasury bills, which are issued in the same way as short-term government bonds. They are in discount form with sixty-day maturities, and in denominations of ¥1,000,000. They may be subscribed through one of the four major security dealers or they may be obtained through banks on the secondary market. Relatively low yields, however, do not make them popular with nonresident investors.

BANKS

Nonresidents may open savings or checking accounts with any of the "city banks" in Japan in yen or other currencies. Securities may be bought, sold, or held in special accounts. The largest of these banks are the Dai-ichi Kangyo Bank, the Fuji Bank, the Sumitomo Bank, and the Mitsubishi Bank. Balances may be transferred outside the country without restriction.

The Bank of Japan, wholly owned by the government, implements the economic policy of the government. It establishes the discount rate, and all other interest rates fall in line. Banks are usually in an overloaned position, so any change in the discount rate has a swift effect.

WITHHOLDING TAX

Withholding tax on interest is 10%, and on dividends it is 15%. Withholding for nonresidents is not charged on bills or bonds issued at discount (i.e., government bonds with less than 5 years maturity), Samurai bonds, or Euroyen bonds. All withholding may be claimed as tax credits on U.S. tax returns.

Stock dividends are common in Japan. However, there are two kinds: one is termed a "stock dividend" and the other is called a "free issue." They affect the capital structure of a corporation differently, but to an investor they are the same (i.e., a free distribution) except for taxes. Stock dividends are considered the same as ordinary dividends and are thus taxed, while free issues are not. It is important that you know which kind of shares you have received.

JAPANESE INVESTMENT JARGON

bond: This term is only used for debt instruments backed by *specific* assets of a corporation, as opposed to financial debentures (see below).

discount bond: Both government and corporate issues of less than five years' maturity are often issued at discount, meaning that the purchaser pays less than face value and no interest is paid until maturity, at which time the bond is redeemed at face value. They are taxed at issue so that discount bonds purchased on the secondary market are entirely free of withholding tax.

financial debenture: Bond backed by *general* assets of a company, issued usually by banks. See "bond."

first section: Consists of all stocks regularly listed on the Tokyo Stock Exchange, as opposed to second section stocks.

free issue: Same as gratis issue.

gratis issue or *offering:* Similar to a stock dividend except it is not taxable as income, whereas a stock dividend is.

Saitori member: A member firm of the Tokyo Stock Exchange that serves as a go-between for the trades of regular broker members. A Saitori member is assigned specific securities, and may not buy or sell for its own accounts or for the accounts of retail clients. A Saitori member is strictly a broker's broker.

Samurai bond: A bond denominated in yen and issued in Japan by foreign governments or corporations.

second section: A category of stocks traded on the Tokyo Stock Exchange made up of the securities of smaller companies. These transactions are handled by computer in a separate room of the exchange, not on the trading floor.

unit of shares: A round lot.

SOURCES OF INFORMATION

The Asian Wall Street Journal and *The Asian Wall Street Journal Weekly,* published by the Dow-Jones Company, are major sources of information. Obviously, Japan is one of the countries thoroughly covered. There are excellent articles on specific companies and detailed earnings reports. There are even lists of recommendations and reports from Japanese (and other) brokers on Asian securities. The weekly contains closing prices for over 300 Japanese stocks, and is a must for the serious investor in Japan. Other countries covered include Hong Kong, Singapore, Australia, Malaysia, Thailand, and the Philippines. The single-copy price for the weekly is $2, and a year's subscription is $125.

An obvious source of information is your broker. Both Japanese and U.S. brokers (those with international departments) issue reports on companies, sometimes in newsletter format. Those of Nomura Securities and Vickers da Costa (of the foreign brokers) are the most extensive.

Two other English sources to consider are weeklies—the *Japan Economic Journal,* and *The Japan Stock Journal.* They are, however, of a technical nature and may not interest the average investor.

Annual reports are important sources of information, and many of the larger companies print editions in English. (But see Chapter 2 on ADRs concerning sponsored and unsponsored accounts.) Those companies that report to the SEC use one of two forms: 20-F for annual reports, and 6-K for all others. These reports are available to the public from the Washington office of the SEC for the price of copying. (Branch offices of the SEC do not usually have 6-K forms on file.)

USEFUL ADDRESSES

TOKYO STOCK EXCHANGE

6, Nihombashi-Kabuto-cho
I-chome, Chuo-kes
Tokyo, Japan

MUTUAL FUNDS

Nomura Capital Fund of Japan
(see address for Nomura below)

SCI/TECH Holdings, Inc.
633 Third Avenue
New York, NY 10017

G.T. Pacific Fund
G.T. Capital Management, Inc.
601 Montgomery St., Suite 1400
San Francisco, CA 94111

LEADING JAPANESE BROKERS
Addresses given are of U.S. offices that usually accept retail accounts.

Nomura Securities International, Inc.
180 Maiden Lane
New York, NY 10005

The Nikko Securities Co.
140 Broadway
New York, NY 10005

Daiwa Securities America, Inc.
333 S. Grand Ave., Suite 3636
Los Angeles, CA 90071

Yamaichi International America, Inc.
333 S. Hope Street
Los Angeles, CA 90071

THE LONDON STOCK EXCHANGE

Courtesy of The Stock Exchange

A BRIEF LOOK INSIDE

The London Stock Exchange is not its real name; in a style characteristically British, it is simply The Stock Exchange. It is the third largest exchange in the world (in terms of market capitalization), New York being first and Tokyo second.

Interestingly enough, The Stock Exchange is not much older than the New York Stock Exchange. It was founded in 1773, and the NYSE was founded after the Revolution in 1792. (The NYSE was also predated two years by the founding of the Philadelphia Stock Exchange.) Another historical similarity is that early operations of both exchanges were conducted in coffee houses. In fact, employees who carry messages on the floor of the London exchange are still referred to as "waiters." The Stock Exchange is the product of the amalgamation of the London stock exchange with the thirteen provincial exchanges, all of which used to make up the Associated Stock Exchange of the United Kingdom and Ireland.

The Stock Exchange has always welcomed foreign investment, and many of its 7,000 listings (more than any other exchange) are foreign companies. The foreign country with the most listings is the United States (166 securities) and second is South Africa (ninety-seven securities).

The international perspective of The Stock Exchange is visible even on the trading floor of the exchange. The far wall of the room supports a huge map of the world beneath which clocks (the small squares in the photograph) give the time for major financial centers of the world: San Francisco, Toronto, New York, Zurich, etc.

More important than maps and clocks, however, are new systems (some still under development) to facilitate the trading of securities abroad. Transfer of ownership, which must take place every time a security changes hands, is complicated enough when it is between parties and brokers within the same country, but it is more complicated when the transfers must cross international borders and involve two different currencies.

Most exchanges use electronic transfers and bookkeeping as long as the transactions are entirely within their own or affiliated regional ex-

---

THE LONDON STOCK MARKET AT A GLANCE

Capitalization:
Total market value of all securities in U.S.$* . . . . $1,197,390.4 million
Market value of shares (only) in U.S.$* . . . . $247,556.6 million
Percent of total share capitalization represented by ten largest
companies. 27.6%
Volume:
Average daily volume of shares (estimate) . . . . over 100 million
Listings:
Total of all securities 7,055
Public sector 783
Eurobonds 1,041
Company securities 5,231
Rank in the world:
Capitalization 3rd

*Exchange rate as of March 30, 1984: $1 = £1.4390.
Source: The Stock Exchange Fact Book, March 1984, and the Report and Account, 1983.

changes. But London is developing systems that operate beyond usual exchange procedures. First of all, the Irish exchanges are accommodated within The Stock Exchange even though a different currency is involved—the Irish punt. Secondly, an operational branch of The Stock Exchange has established an office in Johannesburg that is linked by computer directly to London to facilitate transfer of London-listed South African securities. Thirdly, The Stock Exchange has entered into an agreement with France to become the London and South African settlement agent (implementing ownership transfers) for French securities. And lastly, the London exchange has begun negotiations for the establishment of depositaries in foreign financial centers of the world such as Australia, Canada, and the United States.

A depositary serves as a collateral base for the electronic transfer of securities. Such a system greatly enhances the facility and *safety* with which ownership of securities can be transferred internationally. Note that the American ADR system also makes use of a depositary, but in our case it is stock-by-stock, each ADR created anew to accommodate a specific security. The London system is more general and created to accommodate all London-based issues. It remains to be seen which approach will serve as a model for international depositaries and computer transfer systems of the future.

BRITISH CURRENCY AND EXCHANGE RATE WITH THE U.S. DOLLAR

The standard unit of British currency is the pound, also known as "pound sterling," which contains 100 pence. In print, it appears as £9 (nine pounds), £10.95 (ten pounds, ninety-five pence), and 9p (nine pence, pronounced "pee"). Prices of securities on the London exchange are quoted in pence until they reach £10, so that 523p is, in fact, 5 pounds, 23 pence. However, to be idiomatically correct one would say five hundred and twenty-three pence. The more exotic British currencies, such as the shilling and the sovereign, are no longer in use. The term "quid," incidentally, is slang for "pound."

Many of the financial institutions and practices of the United Kingdom have evolved over long periods of time, and the monetary system is no exception. Pound sterling, for example, dates back to 1066 when, for obvious reasons, Norman coins became part of English currency. It turned out that exactly 240 Norman coins of a specific alloy (92.5% silver, 7.5% copper) made up a troy pound. Because those coins had a starling on them, this measure became known as a "pound starling," later corrupted to "pound sterling."

In Figure 1 the solid line indicates the interbank exchange rate (as is quoted in the newspaper). As you can see, the pound has lost about a third of its value against the U.S. dollar since 1980. From the effective exchange rate, however (see p. 40), it is clear that the pound has held its own against other currencies.

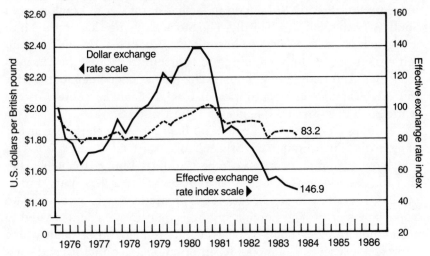

Figure 1. Exchange rate of the British pound with the U.S. dollar and the effective exchange rate with other major currencies.
Source: *Federal Reserve Bank of St. Louis*

Room is left for you to continue the graph, if you like. Regular charting is not necessary, but a dot here and there as you observe currency shifts may be helpful if you hold or plan to acquire British securities.

There are no restrictions on the flow of capital or currencies in or out of the United Kingdom (controls were lifted in 1979). The value of the pound floats freely on the exchange markets although the government sometimes intervenes when foreign exchange fluctuations become excessive. Nonresidents may open the same types of bank or brokerage accounts as residents, and revenues may be repatriated at will.

SECURITIES TRADED ON THE LONDON STOCK EXCHANGE

Before listing the investment instruments it should be pointed out that the words "stock" and "share" are used more loosely in the United

Kingdom than they are here. In the United States we use both only for equity instruments, and we reserve the word "bond" for debt instruments. Do not be misled by references in the foreign press to "loan shares" or "government stock"—both are bonds.

The instruments available on the London exchange are:

stocks: More commonly called "shares" or "equities." They are all in registered form, and both common and preferred (called "preference shares") are available although there is relatively little trading in the latter. Dividends are usually paid semiannually (not quarterly), and some are paid annually.

rights and *warrants:* Issues of rights (granting additional shares) from stock you already own must be registered with the SEC in the United States for you to receive them, and they most likely will be, if the company is listed on a U.S. exchange. Otherwise, you will receive a cash equivalent. Warrants are relatively rare.

options: There are two kinds available, those that cannot be traded once you have bought them (only exercised or allowed to expire), and those that can (see the section entitled "Options").

bonds: Both corporate and government. Government bonds are called "gilts," a leftover from the nineteenth century when the bond certificate was, literally, gilt-edged. Both corporate bonds (sometimes called "loan stock") and gilts are discussed under the section "About Bonds: Corporate and Government."

investment companies: Just as in this country, shares of closed-end investment companies are traded on stock exchanges. In the United Kingdom they are called "investment trusts." Do not confuse them with unit trusts, which more closely resemble mutual funds.

In general, stocks (equities) are more popular with investors and the issuing institutions than are corporate bonds. Part of the reason for this may be the high rate of inflation that eats away at the yield of fixed-income securities in the United Kingdom. Gilts, on the other hand, are extremely popular because the interest (sometimes called the "dividend") is paid gross if held for at least 366 days.

New issues of shares may be underwritten by either brokers or banks. One aspect of new issues in the United Kingdom that favors the small investor is that all subscriptions of 500 shares or less will probably be filled even if the issue is oversubscribed (that is, even if there are more requests for the issue than shares to go around). Institutional purchases will be cut back, if necessary, to ensure that members of the investing public receive the shares they request.

Among new issues to appear in the United Kingdom have been shares of companies formerly owned by the government. The Conservative Party, in its efforts to dismantle socialism in the United Kingdom, has been returning state-owned industries to the private sector. Since 1981, part or all of companies such as British Aerospace, Cable & Wireless, Amersham International, and Britoil have been sold through shares. The biggest offering is yet to come with the planned sale of 51% of the United Kingdom telephone company, British Telecommunications. The offering, which constitutes the largest sale of stock in history, is valued at about $6 billion (U.S.). To date the largest equity offering has been the 1983 $1.17 billion sale of AT&T stock.

Receiving information about your shares, as mentioned elsewhere, can be a problem. Reporting by corporations is required only twice a year in the United Kingdom (not quarterly), and only the annual report requires an outside audit. However, if the stock you purchased is listed on the NYSE or AMEX you will automatically receive semiannual reports, and, if you do not receive quarterly reports, the quarterly earnings will at least be released to the press so that you will be able to find them in *The Wall Street Journal* or other financial publications.

MAJOR STOCK INDEXES

The Financial Times Industrial Ordinary Share Index, the "FT Index," is the most often quoted of all London indexes, and consists of thirty industrial stocks,[1] much like the Dow-Jones Industrial Average (DJIA). It was begun in 1935 by the *Financial Times* of London. It calculates an unweighted geometric mean based on the ratio of each security's current price to its value in the base data, adjusted for capital gains.

In Figure 2 you can compare the performance of the FT Index and the DJIA. For the sake of comparison, the DJIA is recalculated to start at 410, where the FT Index stood at the beginning of 1976.

There are other financial indexes including an FT 500 Share Index and an FT All Share Index. The latter is the broadest and is made up of the securities of 750 companies.

---

[1]These companies are the English equivalent of those that make up the DJIA. They are Allied-Lyons, Associated Dairies, Beecham Group, BICC, Blue Circle Industries, Boots, Bowater Corporation, BOC Group, British Petroleum, BTR, Cadbury Schweppes, Courtaulds, Distillers, General Electric, Glaxo Holdings, Grand Metropolitan, GKN, Hanson Trust, Hawker Siddeley, ICI, Imperial Group, Lucas Industries, Marks & Spencer, P&O, Plessey, Tate & Lyle, Thorn EMI, TI Group, Trusthouse Forte, and Vickers.

In 1984 a new index, the SE-100 (Stock Exchange 100), was begun by the London exchange. It is a capitalization-weighted index with a January 30, 1983 base of 1,000. It represents about 70% of the market value of all U.K. shares.

The London exchange has no ticker, and it is interesting to observe how its absence affects implementation of an index. Clerks must be sent directly to the jobbers (brokers assigned to trading in specific stocks) on the floor to obtain the latest prices for those stocks in the index. After the information is gathered it is fed into a computer.

It remains to be seen whether this particular index will catch on. Several indexes were launched a number of years ago but were eventu-

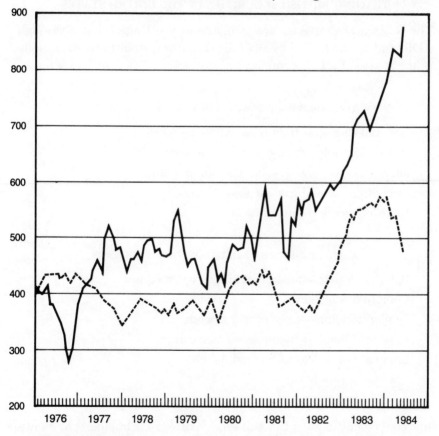

Figure 2. Financial Times Ordinary Share Index, or FT Index (solid line), and the **Dow-Jones Industrial Average** (dashed line), recalculated, for comparison, to 410 from 1976.
Source: *The Stock Exchange,* 1983 Fact Book, *and the Dow-Jones Co., Inc.*

ally abandoned. One of the reasons for starting another now is that the London International Financial Futures Exchange wants to establish a new futures contract based on a London stock index. The FT Index is only updated hourly, and that's not frequently enough for a so-called "real time" index. The SE-100 is updated every *minute,* which keeps the clerks literally running in circles. If the SE-100 does catch on, obviously, the next step is to automate the information-gathering process. An exchange the size of London should have a ticker, anyway, to reflect the flow of prices and volume.

TRADING BRITISH SECURITIES IN THE UNITED STATES

The following companies are available in the United States through ADRs and can be traded by any full-service or discount broker as easily as the shares of a U.S. company.

AVAILABLE ON THE NEW YORK STOCK EXCHANGE

Imperial Chemical Industries (ICI)—chemicals

Plessey Co.—electronic equipment systems

Shell Transport and Trading Co.—petroleum

Tricentral—oil and gas; car dealership

Unilever—food, commodities

AVAILABLE ON THE AMERICAN STOCK EXCHANGE

B.A.T. Industries—tobacco, retailing, commodities

Courtaulds—textiles

Dunlop Holdings—tires, sporting goods

Imperial Chemical Industries—chemicals

Imperial Group—tobacco, food, hotels

WHEN YOUR BROKER TRADES IN LONDON

It is convenient to use a U.S. full-service broker for buying U.K. securities, particularly one with an active foreign securities department, or at least one that provides some foreign security analysis. If your broker conducts a large volume of foreign transactions he or she may be able to obtain a fractionally better exchange rate for you. Also, the interbroker commission rate is a negotiated one, and your broker will be in a position to bargain for the best possible commission on the British end of the transaction.

Incidentally, if you ask a U.S. broker about a foreign security that has come to your attention, be certain you have the full name of the company, and, if possible, the spelling. There are no ticker symbols for many foreign stocks, and the individual with whom you speak may not be as familiar with foreign shares as with domestic. There are many chances for confusion. "Harties," for example, a gold-mining stock on the London exchange frequently listed in U.S. papers, is apparently not available in the U.S. except that, in fact, it is Hartebeestfontein, a South African gold-mining company available in the U.S. as an ADR.

When you ask your broker for a quotation for a security available only on the London exchange the price will probably already include the commission for the U.K. broker who must conduct the trade on the London floor. There are two ways to avoid a double commission. One way is for your broker to find a foreign broker that makes a market in that particular security and to buy it directly from that broker's inventory. In such a case your broker would only have to pay the ask price for the security. The other way is to have an account with, and make your purchase directly through, a U.K. brokerage firm.

While on the subject of U.K. brokers, we should note that banks in the United Kingdom also perform brokerage services. They accept discretionary accounts (they will trade for you within guidelines that you stipulate), and they offer types of savings accounts not available in the United States (for instance, accounts denominated in foreign currencies). However, as in the case of brokerages, branches of U.K. banks in this country either do not accept individual accounts, or they are completely "Americanized" and offer only the same services as domestic banks.

When dealing with U.K. firms, should you ever have a problem with any securities transaction for which the responsibility lies in the United Kingdom, you may lodge a complaint with the Secretary of the Council of The Stock Exchange (see "Useful Addresses" at the end of the chapter). One of the council's services, for instance, is the Compensation Fund which was set up by the exchange to reimburse investors for losses as a result of broker default.

The ten companies in Table 1 constitute over 27% of the capitalization represented on the London exchange. All but Shell T&T, B.A.T., and Racal Electronics are among the thirty-share FT Times Index.

LONDON TRADING OPERATIONS

The most common orders on the London exchange are the same as in this country:

at the market: The broker is to take the best offer available; referred to as "best offer."

limit order: A purchase or sale price is not to be above or below a stated price limit.

However, here are some differences:

selling short: Covering purchase must usually be within a specific time period (see below), and may be permitted only for a few days (i.e., for arbitrage) by your U.S. broker.

margin purchases: Not usually permitted; some "loan account" business is done by a few brokers.

discretionary orders: Although accepted on the London floor, they are not usually permitted by U.S. brokers.

odd lots: Orders for odd lots are not necessary since shares can be purchased in any quantities.

The hours of the London exchange are 9:30 A.M. to 3:30 P.M. weekdays except for bank holidays. There are almost 4,000 brokers and almost 500 jobbers. The jobbers take on the same role, roughly, of specialists in this country. However, every security has at least two jobbers (usually more) so that they compete with one another, increas-

Table 1

THE TEN LARGEST STOCK ISSUES ON
THE LONDON STOCK EXCHANGE

COMPANY	% OF TOTAL MARKET CAPITALIZATION
1. General Electric	5.1
2. British Petroleum	4.8
3. Shell T&T	4.1
4. Marks & Spencer	2.6
5. B.A.T. Industries	2.0
6. Beecham Group	2.0
7. Imperial Chemical	1.9
8. Glaxo Holding	1.9
9. Grand Metropolitan	1.8
10. Racal Electronics	1.4
Total	27.6

Source: Capital International Perspective, Geneva, Switzerland.

ing liquidity and the chances for favorable prices. Each jobber has a position (called a pitch) by one of the trading posts (the hexagonal structures in the photograph) where they may be found. Brokers will always go to several jobbers to get quotes, and take the offer most favorable. Brokers may not trade among themselves.

There is a small over-the-counter market made up of about 150 equities. Prices are quoted in the *Financial Times,* but these shares are not recommended, as they are less regulated with respect to disclosures than securities listed on The Stock Exchange. By the way, becoming listed on The Stock Exchange is called "obtaining a quote."

SETTLEMENT AND FEES

Fixed commissions in the United Kingdom are in the midst of being phased out, a process to be completed by 1986. For that reason the rates are not given here.

Should you open an account with a British broker, the following settlement schedule will apply. Government bonds require settlement the next day, and all stocks and corporate bonds purchased within each two-week account period are to be paid for, in one lump sum, on the settlement day one week following that account period.

The settlement day is usually a Monday, so that, as you can see in Figure 3, if you make a purchase the last day of the account period (usually a Friday) you have one week in which to make payment (actually, six business days, counting the last Monday). If you make a purchase the first day of an account period, usually a Monday, you will have three weeks in which to make payment. If your transaction is a sale, then the above applies to the period of time in which payment must be sent. It may be that this built-in period of credit is one of the reasons purchases on margin are not permitted. To complicate things a bit further, there are also two three-week settlement periods set at the beginning of the year to accommodate bank holidays.

Payments for all transactions during the same account period are due in one lump sum, although if you purchase and sell a security all within the same account period you pay a commission only for the

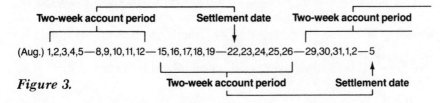

Figure 3.

purchase or only for the sale, whichever is greater. (You are also exempt from the stamp duty for those transactions.) When selling short you must make a covering purchase within the same account period unless you get an extension (called a "contango") into the next account period.

All purchases are subject to stamp duty except gilts, foreign government bonds, corporate bonds (except convertible bonds), mutual funds (unit trusts), and securities in bearer form. For non-U.K. residents it is usually 1% of the price paid for the security. All transactions are also subject to a "contract note fee" of 10p if the transaction is above £100 but below £500, 30p if it is between £500 and £1,500, and 60p if above £1,500.

SOURCES OF INFORMATION

One of the advantages of being a native speaker of English (or, in this case, a native *reader*) is the wealth of financial information and reporting available. There are excellent newspapers and magazines with syndicated columns, newsletters, and, of course, *The Wall Street Journal.* However, the *Financial Times* of London is without doubt the most comprehensive financial daily in the world with respect to international coverage. Not only are there the London listings you would expect, but there are the complete NYSE and AMEX listings and a large number of other foreign securities quotations. United States subscribers receive issues the same day as publication—that is, one does not have the usual wait for international mail. However, a year's subscription is $420, a bit steep for most investors. If you live in a large metropolitan area, look for it at large newsstands—it is a distinctive light peach color. An occasional copy would be well worth your while. (See the next section for instructions on how to read security price quotations in the *Financial Times.*)

Another source of information about U.K. investments is, presumably, the companies themselves. However, in the United Kingdom, as in the rest of Europe, reporting is required only twice a year, so don't expect quarterly financial statements.

Last but not least is the information provided by your broker. Major U.S. brokerages are undertaking an increasing amount of analysis of foreign companies. English brokers have provided such information as a matter of course for years. Reports from U.K. brokers will include analyses of other major markets, foreign currencies, and specific companies. (See "Useful Addresses" at the end of this chapter.)

HOW TO READ THE FINANCIAL TIMES QUOTATIONS

An entire section of the *Financial Times* is devoted to non-British companies, and another to international markets. Non-British quotations are divided by country and include Canada, Austria, Belgium/Luxembourg, Denmark, France, Germany, Italy, The Netherlands, Norway, Spain, Sweden, Switzerland, Australia, Hong Kong, Japan, Singapore, and South Africa. Listings of British stocks are divided into sections such as "Chemicals," "Plastics," "Electricals," "Food, Groceries," "Industrials," etc. Figure 4 is a sample, with interpretation as follows:

- The high and low may reflect prices as far back as fifteen or sixteen months if the quotation appears in the early part of the calendar year (e.g., in March the high and low will cover the entire preceding calendar year as well as the three months of the present year). A switch to the current year occurs in spring.
- If an amount immediately follows the company name it is the nominal (par) value of the security. If no value is given it is 25p.
- Figures in the price column are closing prices in pence unless they are marked in pounds.
- The "+" or "−" is the price change in pence so that ½ means one-half pence.
- The dividend is "net," that is, after 52% British corporate taxes have been paid. You may apply for exemption and have only 15% withheld. In order to calculate approximately what your dividends will be in pence, multiply the figure by 1.77.
- The "C'vr" stands for "cover," which is the number of times funds available for dividend payments exceed the expected gross dividend amount. Basically, it's an indication of how safe the dividend is. Thus, a cover of 2.1 means that the dividend is more than twice covered by available funds.

Hire Purchase, Leasing, etc.

1983 High	1983 Low	Stock	Price	+ or −	Div. Net	C'vr	Y'ld Gr's	P/E
267	140	✦Baltic Leasing 5p	253xd	−7	g2.8	φ	1.6	φ
32	23½	Cattle's (Hdgs) 10p	27	......	†h1.28	2.1	6.8	8.5
£32	£19¾	Cie B'cre Fr.100.	£30	......	gQ15%	—	4.5	—
*51	30	Lnd.Scot.Fin.10p	43	......	§2.5	2.8	8.3	7.8
31½	18	Moorgate Merc. 10p	29	+½	d1.1	1.7	5.4	(13.0)
160	114	Prov. Financial.	145	......	†8.0	1.9	7.9	9.6
102	86	✦Sthn.Bus.Leasg.10p...	100	......	bg1.75	3.2	2.5	(13.9)
10	4½	Sturla Hldgs. 10p	6#	......	—	—	—	—
168	130	Utd Leasing 20p..	165	......	1.5	4.2	1.2	28.0
56	39	Wagon Finance	42	......	2.31	0.4	7.9	44.1

Figure 4. Source: The Financial Times

- "Y'ld Gr's" is not applicable to nonresidents. It represents yield to U.K. investors after the average 30% tax is withheld.
- The PE is calculated on a "net" basis after tax.
- There are quite a number of miscellaneous symbols, all of which are more or less defined in the paper. A few that appear in our example are:
  "Maltese cross" = Company not a regular listing or subject to regulation
  xd = Ex-dividend
  Φ = Awaiting data
  There is no symbol for bankruptcy since bankrupt companies are delisted.

It is also important to point out what the quotations *don't* show. In the case of stock quotations, there is no volume given. Perhaps of more importance to the average investor, however, is the absence of daily price ranges. The daily highs and lows can obviously be helpful in detecting trends and in making sell decisions.

In Monday issues there is some variation in the usual format. The highs and lows are replaced by the dividend payment dates, and the price change column is replaced by the last ex-dividend date. Other examples of *Financial Times* quotations are given in the following sections on mutual funds and bonds.

MUTUAL FUNDS

Mutual funds are called "unit trusts." A wide selection is available with a variety of investment goals, such as income or growth, and a wide variety of instruments in which they invest, such as gold shares, insurance, gilts, etc. You may purchase shares directly from the company or through British banks (in the United Kingdom). Prices are quoted in a separate section of the *Financial Times.* The listings give the complete address of each fund, and even their phone number: write or call several funds for a prospectus before you decide to invest. Tax-free funds in the United Kingdom will not, of course, be tax-free in the United States. There is a charge for opening an account (2% to 8%) and an annual fee of ½% to ¾%. Unit trusts are an excellent way to begin an international investment portfolio if you do not have the funds for diversification. In particular, watch for buying opportunities when the dollar is high against the pound. That way you have the added possibility of future currency exchange rates increasing your earnings. Figure 5 is an example of unit trust quotations from the *Financial Times.*

- The letters following the trust's group name refer to footnotes.
- The third and fourth lines are telephone numbers.

- The funds are grouped under general types such as "Sector Specialist Funds." Among them are a commodity fund, a gold fund, and an international technology fund. The numbers in the first column mean bid price; in the second column, ask price; in the third column, change in bid price in pence; and in the fourth column, yield (in all but a few cases) showing the annualized rate of net asset value increase.

Britannia Gp. of Unit Trusts Ltd. (a)(c)(g)
Salisbury House, 31, Finsbury Circus, London EC2
01-638 0478/0479 or 01-588 2777
Britannia Viewpoint 01-673 0048

UK Specialist Funds			
Assets	151.9	163.8	−0.8	3.46
Recovery	57.0	61.5xd	−0.4	3.11
Smaller Cos	87.0	93.8xd		1.78
Spec. Mkt. Sits.	72.2	77.8xd	−0.3	1.52
UK Blue Chip	50.3	54.2		3.19
High Income Funds			
Nat. High Inc.	101.6	109.5xd	−0.4	6.82
Extra Inc.	41.6	44.9		8.72
Inc. & Growth	108.5	117.0	−0.3	5.91
Gilt	26.9	28.3	+0.1	9.30
Pref. Shares	17.0	18.3xd	+0.1	11.85
Sector Specialist Funds			
Commodity Shares	142.5	153.6	−0.4	1.46
Financial Secs.	143.2	154.4	−0.2	3.34
Gold & General†	25.7	27.9	+0.3	3.23
Inv. Tst. Shares.	89.6	96.6	−0.1	1.61
Prop. Shares	26.5	28.6xd		2.41
Univ. Energy	64.5	69.5	−1.0	0.99
World Tech.	51.5	55.5	−0.1	—
Overseas Funds			
American Growth	67.5	72.8	+0.1	1.84
Am. Smaller Cos.	23.2	25.0	−0.1	0.20
Am. Spec. Sits	68.8	74.2	−0.3	1.29
Australian Growth	66.1	71.3xd	+0.3	1.22
Far East	33.6	36.2xd	+0.3	1.48
Hong Kg. Perfmnce	12.6	13.6	+0.6	4.91
Intl. Growth	103.0	111.1	+0.2	1.60
Japan Perf. Tst	30.1	32.4	+0.3	—
Japan Smlr Cos Tst	9.5	10.2		—

Figure 5. Source: The Financial Times

ABOUT BONDS: GOVERNMENT AND CORPORATE

Corporate bonds are traded on The Stock Exchange but the market is relatively thin, and, strangely enough, first-class bonds of the most creditworthy companies often yield *less* than gilts of comparable maturities. To make a complicated story very short, this is because a tax break for institutions makes the interest from corporate bonds worth up to 50% more to institutions than it is to private investors. And with institutions ready and willing to buy bonds at the lower rates there is not much incentive to raise them.

If you purchase U.K. bonds you should know some terminology differences. "Debentures" are *secured* by assets of the company while "unsecured loan stocks" are not. (In this country a debenture is an unsecured bond.) Also, some bonds amortize the principal over the life of the bond. Be sure you have a full description of any bond you are considering: its type, dates of dividend payments, and whether it is callable. (Callable bonds are common in the U.K.) You must also depend on your broker or bank for evaluation of the bond. There are no rating companies in the United Kingdom (like Moody's or Standard & Poor's). Corporate bonds pay interest semiannually and are generally available in denominations of £100.

Government bonds are the most widely traded instrument in the United Kingdom, and there is a deep and liquid market. They are issued by the Bank of England and guaranteed (interest and principal) by the government. They are in registered form and available in denominations of £100. Interest is paid semiannually and, in certain instances, without withholding tax. They are available in a large variety of maturities and coupon rates.

Gilts account for 90% of the value of fixed-interest securities and 80% of the value of all securities traded in the United Kingdom. However, since investors tend to hold them longer than other types of securities, they constitute only 20% of the volume of all securities traded.

Quotations for medium-term gilts (five to ten years) and long-term gilts (longer than ten years) include the accrued interest (unlike bond quotations in the United States), while short-term gilts (under five years) are quoted independently of accrued interest. The issues are referred to by the issuing agency (e.g., Treasury, Exchequer, etc.), the coupon rate, and the year. Figure 6 is an example from the *Financial Times*.

BRITISH FUNDS

1983			Price	+ or	Yield	
High	Low	Stock	£	−	Int.	Red.
Five to Fifteen Years						
$96\frac{1}{2}$	$90\frac{3}{4}$	Treas. $9\frac{1}{2}$pc '88........	$94\frac{3}{4}$	......	10.40	11.76
$94\frac{1}{4}$	$91\frac{7}{8}$	Treas $9\frac{1}{2}$pc '88 'A'....	$92\frac{3}{4}$	......	10.38	11.73
$104\frac{5}{8}$	$95\frac{3}{4}$	Treasury $11\frac{1}{2}$pc 1989...	$98\frac{1}{2}$xd	......	11.71	11.95
$97\frac{5}{8}$	$94\frac{1}{4}$	Treas $10\frac{1}{2}$pc 1989....	$96\frac{7}{8}$	......	11.19	11.98
$83\frac{1}{4}$	$76\frac{3}{4}$	Treasury 5pc '86-89..	$77\frac{5}{8}$	$-\frac{1}{8}$	6.60	10.46
$112\frac{1}{2}$	103	Treasury 13pc 1990‡‡..	$106\frac{1}{8}$	......	12.45	11.96
$108\frac{1}{4}$	$100\frac{7}{8}$	Exch. $12\frac{1}{2}$pc 1990....	$101\frac{5}{8}$xd	......	12.21	11.99

Figure 6.   Source: The Financial Times

The first bond in the above example would be called the "Treasury 9½%, due in 1988"; the last one, the "Exchequer 12½%, due in 1990." The rest of the quotations are as follows:

- The high and low are a fifty-two-week high and low.
- The price is in pounds per each bond so that the fractions are literally fractions of pounds.
- The fractions in the "+ or −" column are also fractions of pounds (not fractions of the par value, as in the United States) so that −⅛ is −12½ pence.

- Under "Yield" the first column, "Int." (interest) is the annual interest rate.
- The second column, "Red." (redemption) is the total yield if the bond is held to redemption (including capital appreciation or depreciation depending on whether the bond is trading above or below par).

Sometimes issues are distinguished by letters, as in the case of the second bond listed above, "Treasury 9½%, 'A', due in 1988" (obviously, it has to be distinguished from the first 9½% due in 1988). Note that the third bond from the bottom has two redemption dates, indicating that it is redeemable in 1986 at the earliest or 1989 at the latest. Two of the bonds are ex-dividend on the day of the quotation ("xd" in the price column).

On Mondays the format of quotations is changed somewhat. The highs and lows are replaced by the two dividend payment dates. The second of these dates is the final redemption date in the year of maturity (which is shown in the name column).

New issues of gilts may be subscribed through a bank or broker. Sometimes the same issue is available over a long period of time (called a "tap basis"). If you buy gilts on the secondary market and there is less than five years until maturity, there will be accrued interest added to the purchase price. In all gilt purchases you must verify that the issue pays interest without withholding tax. (There are a few that don't.) If not, you must apply for exemption. Commissions are negotiable but, in general, are relatively small. Gilts are never called early.

INTEREST RATES

Interest rates affect all sectors of an economy but in few places is that effect felt as immediately as in the area of fixed-income instruments such as bonds. New instruments are always priced to yield an amount that is in line with the interest rates current at the time. If those rates are higher than the rates in effect when earlier instruments were issued, then there is an automatic decrease in the value of the earlier instruments (because they won't yield as much as the new ones), and, of course, the relationship works in reverse, too.

For almost ten years the Bank of England regulated interest rates by means of an interbank rate called the "minimum lending rate" (MLR). In Figure 7, regulation is clearly seen until August of 1981. Since that time, market conditions have been allowed to establish interest rates with only limited intervention from the government.

The interest rate you are most likely to see mentioned in the press is the "base rate" (which is usually quite close to the three-month interbank rate shown in Figure 7). The commercial rate the banks give their most credit-worthy customers (what we think of as the prime rate) is usually about a point above the base rate. Retail lending rates are, of course, higher still. Almost all interest rates in the United Kingdom are calculated from the base rate. As in this country, each bank may set its own, but in practice the base rate established is almost always the same among all the banks.

Figure 7. **Interest rate movements in the United Kingdom. Prior to August 1981, MLR is shown; thereafter, the 3-month interbank rate on the last day of the relevant month.**   Source: *The Stock Exchange*

TREASURY BILLS

Treasury bills are ninety-one-day instruments issued by the Bank of England in initial denominations of £50,000 and increments of £5,000 above that. They are issued weekly in bearer form and tenders may be made through a London bank, a money broker, or a discount house. There is an active secondary market where, of course, all maturities are available up to ninety days.

BANKS

If you wish to open a bank account in the United Kingdom you will deal with a retail bank (technically called a "clearing bank"). The four largest are Barclays, National Westminster, Lloyds, and the Midland (see "Useful Addresses" at the end of the chapter). The services offered include savings accounts denominated in foreign currencies. Banks in the United Kingdom, as mentioned before, can also purchase securities and manage portfolios. The commissions are generally the same as those of a broker. There are, however, hefty minimum investments for portfolio management (i.e., discretionary accounts). The amounts vary from bank to bank.

Another thing you should know about foreign bank accounts in general is that interest earned must be declared annually for U.S. tax purposes, even though you may not have converted any of the currency back into U.S. dollars. Gains or losses from currency exchange, however, need not be declared until the time of conversion.

WITHHOLDING TAX

Dividends are paid after corporations have paid a 52% tax, called an "advance corporation tax" (ACT), on all earnings. As a U.S. citizen you may receive a reduction of this amount to 15% (but see below). Interest on corporate bonds is free of withholding, and there is no withholding on many gilts provided they are held at least one month (but verify the specific issue with your broker).

Tax, in general, is complicated in the United Kingdom, and more changes are now being considered by Parliament. Currently, some reductions in withholding require an application from the investor. Your broker can take care of these applications which require, among other things, a statement of previous or anticipated periods of residence in the United Kingdom. To obtain reduced withholding and tax credit (which most companies on the London exchange will provide), it may be necessary to have your shares held by a nominee company approved by the Inland Revenue. United States brokers normally make use of such nominees, so the process is fairly automatic.

OPTIONS

There are two kinds of options: "traditional" options and "traded" options. Traditional options have been available for about a hundred years and are very different from the options to which U.S. investors are accustomed. Whether they are puts or calls, they may only be *bought*, they cannot be sold, and the purchaser has only the choice of exercising them or allowing them to expire. They are issued only in maturities of three months. Their price, set by the jobbers, is usually about 10% of the price of the underlying stock. Once the price is set it usually holds for the entire week. Prices (premiums) are quoted in the *Financial Times* under "Options, Three Month Call-Rates." Puts are not quoted in the paper.

With these restrictions, one's strategy is fairly simple. In the case of a call, unless the price of the underlying security rises more than 10% within three months, there is no point in exercising the option. Remember, exercising the option means buying or selling the shares, *not* buying or selling another option to close out your position as is done in this country. If you were not interested in holding the security you would have to buy and then immediately sell the underlying stock. (Incidentally, in this situation one would not have to pay commission on the sale; see "Settlement and Fees.") Investors are always the purchasers so they are never in danger of an option being exercised against them, and the total at risk is never greater than the premium paid plus the commission.

"Traded" options resemble options in this country. They may be bought and sold at any time (i.e., an investor can close out his or her position by trading another *option,* not by trading the underlying security). Traded options are available on about twenty-five companies and are quoted daily in the *Financial Times* under "London Traded Options." Prices vary daily (and more widely than traditional options) and expiration dates, called "expiry" dates, are available for three, six, and nine months.

Prices quoted for both traditional and traded options are on a per-share basis. All option contracts are for 1,000 shares (no less) of the underlying security, so the price is determined by multiplying the per-share price by 1,000. For example, if British Petroleum calls at 420 (the exercise price) in October where quoted at 18, then the premium for one option would be £180. The high contract size sounds as if it would make the premium quite high, but stocks in the United Kingdom are generally lower-priced than in the United States so the premiums are not as high as 1,000 shares would seem to make them.

BRITISH INVESTMENT JARGON

accounting period: The two-week period for which all transactions must be paid one week later on the account day. Thus, for all transactions between, for example, March 14 and March 25, the account day would be April 4. Two account periods during the year are three weeks long.

bargain: A transaction. Nothing is intended concerning the level, appropriateness, or "cheapness" of the price.

building society: Similar to the U.S. savings and loan.

contango: An extension of time for the payment of a security from one account day to the next account day two weeks later.

consideration: The monetary value of a transaction without the commission, duties, etc.

debenture: A secured bond backed by assets of the company.

expiry date: Last date on which an option can be exercised.

gilts: Government bonds, sometimes called government stock.

investment trust: Mutual fund.

jobber: Person on the floor of the London exchange with whom stockbrokers must make all transactions. There are at least two jobbers handling transactions in every listed security.

loan stock: Bond.

marking name: Roughly like "street name" in the United States.

option: See traded options and traditional options.

pence: Smallest unit of U.K. currency. There are 100 pence in the pound.

pound: Standard unit of U.K. currency; its symbol is £. There are 100 pence to the pound.

preference stock: Preferred stock.

quid: Slang for pound.

roll-up fund: A fund where all income is reinvested.

shares: The usual term for stocks, that is, equity instruments as opposed to bonds.

stocks: Usually used to mean bonds or fixed-income securities.

traded options: Options that can be bought or sold after the original transaction. Thus, they resemble options in this country.

traditional options: Options that only may be bought and either exercised or allowed to expire (i.e., they may not be sold after purchase).

unit trust: Mutual fund.

unsecured loan stock: Unsecured bonds.

USEFUL ADDRESSES

THE LONDON STOCK EXCHANGE

The Stock Exchange
London EC2N 1HP

COMPLAINTS
If you have a complaint in an area
where the exchange or U.K. authorities
would have jurisdiction, write to the
Secretary of the Council of the Stock
Exchange at the above address.

TWO LEADING U.K. BROKERS

Vickers da Costa & Co. Ltd.
Regis House
King William Street
London EC4R 9AR

Hoare Govett Ltd.
Heron House
319-325 High Holhorn
London EC3P 3BS

LEADING FINANCIAL NEWSPAPER

Financial Times
75 Rockefeller Plaza
New York, NY 10019

LEADING RETAIL BANKS

Barclays Bank, Ltd.
54 Lombard Street
London EC3P 3BS

Lloyds Bank, Ltd.
71 Lombard Street
London EC3P 3BS

Midland Bank, Ltd.
27–32 Poultry
London EC2P 2BX

National Westminster Bank, Ltd.
41 Lothbury
London EC2P 2BP

8

THE TORONTO STOCK EXCHANGE

Courtesy of the Toronto Stock Exchange

A NEW WORLD-CLASS STOCK EXCHANGE

Most people in the United States would be surprised to learn that just across Lake Ontario is the fourth largest national stock exchange in the world (with respect to market value of listed shares). In volume, it was fifth in 1982, after New York, Tokyo, London, and Zurich, easily outdistancing such notables as Paris and Frankfurt.[1]

On May 9, 1983, the Toronto Stock Exchange completed its move

---

[1]Both these rankings exclude U.S. exchanges other than New York. However, the performance of the "smaller" U.S. exchanges has been quite impressive. According to statistics compiled by the Frankfurt Stock Exchange, the ranking by volume in 1982 of all exchanges in the world would be New York, Tokyo, American, Midwest, London, Zurich, Pacific, Toronto, Paris, Frankfurt, Amsterdam, Hong Kong, Milan, Johannesburg, and Sydney.

THE TORONTO STOCK MARKET AT A GLANCE

Capitalization:
Market value of all shares in U.S.$*........................... 390.5 billion
Market value of domestic shares (only) in U.S.$*.............. $140.1 billion
Percent of total share capitalization of domestic companies
  represented by ten largest domestic companies................... 25.3%
Volume:
Average daily volume of shares .... 9.7 million
Percent of total volume represented by ten most active shares......... 15%
Listings:
Total equities... 1,316
PE ratio (average for TSE 300 Composite Index) 19.32
Price (average price per share).................................... C$12.37
Rank in the world:
Capitalization 4th
Turnover/shares... 5th

*Exchange rate at year end 1983: $1 = C$1.24.
Source: The Toronto Stock Exchange, *Fact Book,* 1984.

---

into a new exchange building. The floor is divided into five large trading posts for stocks, and three trading posts for options. Actually, the posts are long double-sided counters, as you can see in the above picture, the tops of which look something like dugout canoes. Futures are traded in two traditionally styled trading pits. As is the trend in progressive stock exchanges, the trading of a wide variety of instruments is integrated into one modern facility. Only bonds, curiously enough, do not trade on the Toronto Stock Exchange. In Canada, bonds generally trade over the counter.

The Toronto exchange is the largest of five Canadian exchanges and accounts for about 75% of the total dollar value of stocks traded in Canada. The other exchanges are the Montreal Stock Exchange, the Vancouver Stock Exchange, the Alberta Stock Exchange (in Calgary), and the Winnipeg Stock Exchange. Each exchange is regulated by various provincial securities acts and by a provincial securities commission. Most of the securities acts are patterned after the one in Ontario.

Only brokers may be members of the Toronto exchange, and there were seventy-nine in 1983. All are Canadian brokers except three Canadian subsidiaries of U.S. firms (Bache Securities, Inc.; Dean Witter Reynolds, Inc.; and Merrill Lynch Royal Securities, Ltd.).

Currently, there are about 100 Canadian shares listed on various U.S. exchanges. Most Canadian shares not listed on a U.S. exchange are available in the U.S. over-the-counter market through NASDAQ or the pink sheets.

U.S. INFLUENCE

The U.S. and Canadian economies are highly interdependent; each country accounts for at least one-half of the foreign direct investment of the other. Over 50% of Canadian foreign trade is with the United States, and our trade with Canada is greater than our total trade with all of Europe and Japan combined.

Obviously, the economies of two such countries cannot help but influence one another. Concern has been expressed in Canada, however, that the domination of such an enormous economic power as the United States keeps Canada from developing an independent monetary policy of its own. This concern is well founded. For instance, if there are high interest rates in this country, Canada usually increases its own interest rates whether or not there are internal economic reasons for doing so. If it didn't, Canada would have to impose strict currency exchange controls or watch an immediate flight of Canadian dollars to the United States. A currently popular saying in Canada is "when the U.S. sneezes, Canada catches cold."

Despite the influence of this country, Canada has considerable strengths, the potentials of which it has yet to realize. With only a small population, Canada has an enormous supply of every known energy resource. It is the world's largest producer of nickel, silver, and zinc; and possesses huge deposits of cobalt, copper, iron, lead, oil, and gas. Canada is the world's fourth largest exporter of agricultural products and has a highly developed lumber and paper industry. With a reasonable amount of protectionism, Canada should be able to profit from an increasing demand in world marketplaces for these resources. These are also the areas of most interest to the nonresident investor.

HISTORY

The Toronto Stock Exchange was founded by twenty-five local businessmen on October 25, 1861. Trading sessions, held at various members' offices, were only a half hour long. A "seat" was $5 and the list of securities, at its height, never exceeded eighteen. After seven years of daily meetings, the volume of trading became so light (sometimes only two or three transactions) that sessions were cut back to one a week, and then in 1869 meetings ceased altogether.

Although the initial attempt at an organized exchange proved to be premature, some important first steps were taken. A code of ethics was agreed upon (which included, among other things, that no broker could act as agent on both sides of a transaction). A commission schedule was established, and a price list was published regularly.

Part of the reason for closing the exchange was a steadily degenerating business climate which culminated in the failure of three major banks. Two years later, however, after a significant expansion of authorized bank capital, the Toronto Stock Exchange was re-formed as a partnership. The members were business firms, and the price of a partnership was $250. Seven years later, in 1878, the exchange became a nonprofit corporation.

Trading, at first, was by roll call twice a day (a procedure imitated from the New York Stock Exchange) except on Saturdays, when it was called only once. In the early years, order was not always easy to maintain, and exchange rules provided for fines from 25 cents to $5 for disrupting the proceedings.

By 1901 the number of companies that listed their securities was almost 100. Trading had switched to a continuous auction market, and a seat on the exchange had risen to C$12,000.

At the outset of World War I the exchange closed for three months (as did the New York Stock Exchange) for fear of a financial panic. When trading resumed, stocks were not allowed to change hands at prices lower than those before the closure. About this time, stock and bond dealers united in their most ambitious undertaking: to sell C$150 million in victory bonds. To everyone's astonishment the initial subscription totaled C$566 million and before the war was out they had raised C$1.8 billion.

The success of the victory bond issues was partly the result of all manner of mass marketing techniques, including sidewalk stalls. One out of every eight persons in Canada had been willing to invest his or her savings in government bonds. It was by this effort that the foundation was laid for a modern capital market in Canada.

From 1921 to 1929, probably the era of greatest speculation in Canada, the total value of mining shares went from C$5.6 million to C$688.3 million. The price of a seat on the Toronto exchange went from C$50,000 to C$220,000 (the highest price ever).

The world depression affected Canada as severely as it did the United States. The stock index of the Dominion Bureau of Statistics fell from 235.4 in 1929 to 38.6 in 1932. The sole comfort during this period was the performance of gold-mining shares, the index for which more than doubled. It is significant to note that despite severe financial problems, no member firm of the Toronto exchange defaulted on its obligations to clients. In 1934 the Toronto Stock Exchange merged with the Standard Stock and Mining Exchange, although it was not until 1937 that the merged exchanges shared a common trading floor. The final amalgamation was between 1948 and 1952 when the major bond houses joined the stock exchange and brought their equity transactions to the trading floor.

In recent years, a number of new securities have been added to the Toronto exchange. The first call options began trading in 1976. Options had traded previously in Canada, but terms were negotiated between brokers, and due to the lack of standardization of the contracts there was almost no secondary market. Put options began exchange trading in 1976. In 1980 financial futures were added, and, three years later, bond and silver options.

OTHER CANADIAN EXCHANGES

Montreal is the second largest exchange in Canada. In 1976 it was in a strong second place with a healthy 21.34% of the total value of share volume in Canada. In 1977, however, the language law was passed, making French the official language of the Province of Quebec. Gradually, banks and other financial institutions began relocating their headquarters to Toronto. Volume on the Montreal Stock Exchange fell steadily until 1980, when it stood at 10.1%. It regained .1% the following year and stood at 12.9% in 1983. Talks have been under way to allow English back into Montreal, but there is no assurance that Montreal can regain its former share of the securities market.

The options market on the Montreal Stock Exchange suffered a fate similar to that of its equities market. From a 47.7% share of the total Canadian options market, the Montreal percentage fell to 12.9% in 1981. By 1983 it had recovered to 23.9%.

The Vancouver Stock Exchange (VSE), founded in 1907, styles itself as a venture market for the resource industry. In 1983, over C$100 million was raised by VSE-listed companies. These were small "junior" companies mostly: highly speculative (many have no earnings records) and engaged in mining (particularly precious metals), oil, or gas.

The listing requirements are less stringent on the Vancouver exchange. Quarterly reports are required, and trading is closely supervised. The shares of junior companies characteristically trade between C$.25 and C$5.00 and are analogous to penny stocks in this country.

They represent investment with a high degree of risk and should not be purchased without professional guidance and the resources to obtain a reasonable diversity.

During the 1983 fiscal year, volume on the VSE was an incredible 3.1 billion shares, making it second in the world only to the New York Stock Exchange. The average price per share was C$1.21. Currently there are over 2,000 issues listed.

In recent years a number of new securities have been introduced on the VSE including silver and Canadian currency options. Equity options are scheduled to trade as part of Trans-Canada Options in cooperation with the Toronto and Montreal exchanges. Also, gold options are offered in partnership with the Montreal and Amsterdam exchanges. Talks are under way to include the Sydney Stock Exchange in the gold option network so that the combined exchanges would constitute a twenty-four-hour market.

The Alberta Stock Exchange lists mostly regional securities and junior resource companies. The Winnipeg Stock Exchange resembles the Cincinnati Stock Exchange in that it has no trading floor. Brokers trade by phone—mostly oil, mining, and energy-related stocks.

CANADIAN CURRENCY AND EXCHANGE RATE WITH U.S. DOLLAR

The unit of currency is the Canadian dollar, which contains 100 Canadian cents. In print it appears C$5.17 (five dollars and seventeen cents, Canadian), except, of course, in Canadian publications, where simply the dollar sign is used.

The Canadian dollar floats freely with respect to other currencies, and the government occasionally intervenes in the currency markets to stabilize fluctuations with the U.S. dollar.

As you can see from Figure 1, the exchange rate with the U.S. dollar closely paralleled that of world currencies until 1981. Since then, although it has fallen somewhat against the dollar, it has appreciated slightly against most other currencies. Room is left for you to continue graphing the dollar exchange rate if you like. Regular charting is not necessary, but a dot here and there as you observe the exchange rates may be useful to you later.

SECURITIES TRADED ON THE TORONTO EXCHANGE

stocks: Common and preferred are both available. The distinction between these two types is the same as it is in the United States. Both Canadian and U.S. securities may be held in street name.

rights: Normally granted to current shareholders. It usually requires more than one right (four to ten) to purchase a new share at the lower-than-market price. Rights are usually listed automatically on the exchange and expire in three to four weeks.

warrants: Often attached to bonds or preferred stock for the purchase of common stock. Similar to rights, they usually expire in one to three years.

options: Both put and call options are available on about forty Canadian stocks. Options on silver are also available. Interestingly enough, they are quoted and settled in U.S. dollars.

futures: Interest rate futures are available on the ninety-one-day Canada Treasury Bill, and the eighteen-year Canada Bond. Also available are futures on silver, the TSE 300 Composite Index, and U.S. dollars.

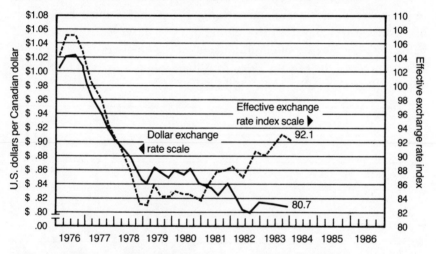

Figure 1. **Exchange rate of the Canadian dollar with the U.S. dollar and the effective exchange rate with other major currencies.**
Source: *Federal Reserve Bank of St. Louis*

It is interesting to note that bonds are not in the above list. As mentioned before, bonds in Canada are usually traded over the counter.

Dividends for Canadian stocks are usually somewhat smaller than for comparable securities in this country. Among those that pay the highest dividends, however, are the provincial telephone companies. Yields in 1982 for some of these companies were B.C. Telephone Co. (9.25%), Island Telephone Co. (9.18%), New Brunswick Telephone Co. (9.22%), Quebec Telephone Co. (10.34%), and Bell Canada Enterprises (8.53%).

There is also an active over-the-counter market. Investors normally buy from the inventories of brokers and so pay the asked price for the security, and no commission. This includes bonds. Brokers who engage exclusively in over-the-counter securities are not as closely regulated as those that deal in listed securities. There are approximately 2,000 unlisted Canadian securities that trade over the counter.

THE TSE 300 COMPOSITE INDEX

The Toronto Stock Exchange 300 Composite Index (Figure 2) is made up of 300 listed issues from fourteen major industry groups. It is calculated from a base of 1,000 in 1975. The majority of shares constituting the index must be the common stock of Canadian-based companies (a few preferred shares are permitted). These shares must have been listed on the exchange for three consecutive years with a quoted market value of C$3 million (not counting controlling blocks of 20% or more). The volume for the previous year must have been at least 25,000 shares with a minimum value of C$1 million.

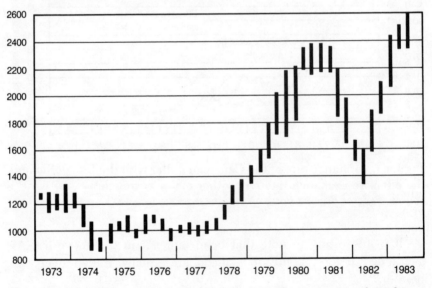

Figure 2. **TSE 300 composite index.**   Source: *The Toronto Stock Exchange*

This index replaced a 108-share index and a mathematical averaging system, the latter of which dated from 1934. Since it is one of the simpler indexes of a major stock exchange, the formula is given below.

Excluded from calculations are controlling blocks of shares, and allowances are made for additions, deletions, and other modifications.

Formula for the TSE 300 Composite Index:

$$\text{Index value} = \frac{\text{aggregate quoted market value}}{\text{base value}} \times 1,000$$

The combined industry groups of mining (including gold), oil, and gas account for 30.8% of the index. The largest single industry percentage, however, is financial services, which accounts for 16.38%. Financial services, of course, includes banks.

BUYING CANADIAN SECURITIES IN THE UNITED STATES

Purchasing Canadian securities in this country is practically as easy as buying domestic securities. One can even obtain Canadian securities through a discount broker. Ordinarily, one cannot buy foreign stocks through a "discounter" unless the shares are traded as ADRs, or the actual certificates are available in the United States. In the case of Canadian issues, most are available on a U.S. exchange (see the next section) or over the counter in their original share form. In those few cases where the shares are not available in this country a discount broker can go to a Canadian broker and purchase the shares from their inventory. In such a case, the shares would be obtained at the "asked" price as in any over-the-counter transaction. There would be a currency conversion cost, usually under 2%, and the discount brokerage commission. Unfortunately, this opportunity does not usually exist for the securities of other countries, so that, normally, discount brokers can only be used to purchase ADRs. This may not be such a disadvantage in the long run because foreign securities are best bought with the advice of a knowledgeable full-service broker. You should use a discounter only if you are experienced and fairly confident of the soundness of your investment.

Getting quotes from Canadian securities can occasionally be a problem. Your broker may have to call another broker and then call you back with the price.

There is no need to have your brokerage account in Canada. In fact, there is even the possibility of regulatory problems for nonresidents. Any U.S. broker can trade in Canadian securities. You are best off, however, using a full-service broker that provides you with analysis of Canadian securities. There are a number of Canadian brokers with U.S. offices, but most U.S. branches are for institutional business, and do not accept retail accounts. An exception, however, is the Florida branch of Wood Gundy, Inc. Wood Gundy is, essentially, a U.S. full-service firm but also has the resources of its Canadian affiliate, Wood Gundy Ltd, Canada's largest brokerage firm. These include analyses, reports, and recommendations of foreign securities, primarily Canadian. Commissions are in line with U.S. rates, and individual accounts average about $50,000 (see "Useful Addresses").

There are more Canadian stocks listed on U.S. exchanges than securities of any other country. Quite a number of these, as well as issues available over the counter, are followed by major analysis services such as *Value Line*. Since, for all practical purposes, any Canadian stock can be purchased over the counter, only exchange-listed issues are given in the next section.

CANADIAN SECURITIES AVAILABLE ON U.S. STOCK EXCHANGES

The following stocks trade in their original share form (i.e., not as ADRs) on one of the two major U.S. exchanges. As exchange-listed securities, they issue quarterly financial statements and report to the SEC.

AVAILABLE ON THE NEW YORK STOCK EXCHANGE

Alcan Aluminum Ltd.—aluminum

Bell Canada—telecommunication services

Campbell Red Lakes Mines Ltd.—mining

Canadian Pacific Ltd.—natural resources and transportation

Carling O'Keefe Ltd.—breweries

Dome Mines Ltd.—mining

Genstar Ltd.—building

Hudson Bay Mining & Smelting, Co.—mining

Inco Ltd.—mining

MacMillan Bloedel Ltd.—forest products

Massey-Ferguson Ltd.—agricultural machines, diesel engines

McIntyre Mines Ltd.—mining

Northern Telecom Ltd.—telecommunication equipment

Northgate Exploration Ltd.—mining

Seagram Co. Ltd.—distilleries

Walker, Hiram-Gooderham & Worts Ltd.—distilleries

Westcoast Transmission Co., Ltd.—natural gas distributor

AVAILABLE ON THE AMERICAN STOCK EXCHANGE

Asamera, Inc.—oil, gas, and mining

Banister Continental Ltd.—oil and gas

Bow Valley Industries Ltd.—oil and gas

Brascan, Ltd., class "A"—investment company

Campbell Resources, Inc.—mining, oil, and gas

Canadian Marconi Co.—radio and electronic equipment

Canadian Occidental Petroleum, Ltd.—integrated oil

Chieftain Development Co., Ltd.—oil exploration and production

Cominco, Ltd.—mining and smelting

Dome Petroleum, Ltd.—oil explorations and production

Domtar, Inc.—forest products and chemicals

Ford Motor Co. of Canada, Ltd.—automobiles and parts

Giant Yellowknife Mines, Ltd.—gold mine

Gulf Canada, Ltd.—integrated oil

Husky Oil, Ltd.—integrated oil

Imperial Oil, Ltd., class "A" convertible—integrated oil

Inter-City Gas Corp.—gas utility

Lake Shore Mines, Ltd.—gold mine

North Canadian Oils, Ltd.—oil and gas

Numac Oil & Gas, Ltd.—oil and gas

Page Petroleum, Ltd.—oil and gas

Placer Development, Ltd.—mining

Prairie Oil Royalties Co., Ltd.—oil development

Redlaw Industries, Inc.—manufacturing and distributing

Rio Algom, Ltd.—uranium and coal

Scurry-Rainbow Oil, Ltd.—oil and gas

Texaco Canada, Inc.—integrated oil

Westburne International Industries, Ltd.—plumbing, heating, and electrical supplies

Wright-Hargreaves Mines, Ltd.—gold mine

There are also two Canadian bonds traded on the American exchange: the Maple Leaf Mills 11% debenture of 1998 and the Page Petroleum 10% debenture of 2000.

THE TEN LARGEST CANADIAN STOCK ISSUES

The ten Canadian issues with the greatest market value make up a total of 25.3% of the total market value of Toronto-listed stocks (Table 1). This relatively low percent (the NYSE percent is 18.1%) indicates that the Toronto exchange has reasonable market breadth and that the bulk of the market capitalization is not concentrated in only a few issues.

Table 1

THE TEN LARGEST CANADIAN STOCK ISSUES ON THE TORONTO STOCK EXCHANGE

COMPANY	MARKET VALUE IN MILLIONS OF CANADIAN DOLLARS
1. Bell Canada Enterprises Inc.—telephone	7,088.3
2. Imperial Oil Ltd., class "A"—integrated oil	5,676.8
3. Northern Telecom Ltd.—telecommunications equipment	5,518.0
4. Texaco Canada Inc.—integrated oil	5,008.4
5. Alcan Aluminium Ltd.—aluminum	4,764.6
6. Seagram Co. Ltd.—distillery	4,056.1
7. Gulf Canada—integrated oil	3,981.0
8. Canadian Pacific Enterprises Ltd.—holding and investment	3,694.5
9. Canadian Pacific Ltd.—transportation	3,601.0
10. Noranda Mines Ltd.—mining	3,375.5

Source: The Toronto Stock Exchange, *Fact Book,* 1984.

Table 2

THE TEN MOST ACTIVE STOCKS ON THE TORONTO STOCK EXCHANGE

COMPANY	VOLUME IN MILLIONS OF SHARES
1. Bell Canada Enterprises Inc.	44.3
2. Dome Petroleum	42.6
3. Nova Alberta	35.6
4. Transcan Pipelines	26.0
5. Ranger Oil	24.0
6. Drummond	24.0
7. Nu-West Group	23.8
8. Asamera Inc.	23.7
9. Toronto Dominion Bank	23.6
10. Gulf Canada	22.8

Source: Official Trading Statistics, 1983.

NEW ISSUES

Perhaps because of our proximity to Canada one hears more frequently of Canadian new issues than of the new issues of other countries. However, there are restrictions pertaining to new foreign issues of which the U.S. investor should be aware. The SEC forbids solicitation of new issues that have not been registered with the SEC. Furthermore, such issues cannot be sold in the secondary market across state lines for ninety days following their issue. Many new issues in Canada *are* registered with the SEC but for those that are not, even your written request for a prospectus will not be honored for fear of "soliciting" in violation of SEC regulations. New issues must "settle" (i.e., wait ninety days) before they can be sold in this country.

TORONTO TRADING FLOOR OPERATIONS

It is likely that your broker will obtain your Canadian securities over the counter in the United States. Nevertheless, some idea of trading floor procedures in Toronto may be helpful.

Commissions charged in Canada formerly ranged from 3% if the per-share price of the stock were under C$5.00 to 1% plus C$.20 per share if the per-share price were over C$15.00. However, in 1982 fixed commissions were discontinued. After nine months of deregulation, a study by RAMA, a Toronto-based research firm, showed that commissions dropped an average of 17%. Unfortunately, this has mostly benefited institutional investors. Commissions on small transactions (under C$5,000) actually have risen slightly.

A board lot is the Canadian equivalent of a round lot. The size depends on the per-share price of the security (Table 3). Obviously, most stocks trade in board lots of 100 shares. For those issues, an odd lot would be any number of shares from one to ninety-nine. On ex-

Table 3

BOARD LOT SIZE FOR CANADIAN STOCKS

PER-SHARE PRICE	BOARD LOT SIZE
Up to C$1	500 shares
C$1–100	100 shares
Above C$100	10 shares

change trading there is usually a price differential of ⅛ to ¼ point for odd lots.

The types of orders available on the Toronto Stock Exchange include the following (most are the same as their U.S. counterparts):

market order: Same as in this country.

limit order: Same as in this country. This type of order may also be given with a limited price discretion available to the broker.

day order: As in this country. All orders are considered day orders unless otherwise specified. Week and month orders are also possible.

good till canceled (also called an open order): A limit order away from the current market price may be given a time limit (a week, month, etc.) or specified as "good till canceled." Your broker will probably require that you reconfirm or cancel such an order if not executed in sixty or ninety days.

good-through order: Cancel if not executed by a specific date.

stop order: As in this country.

contingent order: A combination of two orders which must both be executed.

switch order: An order to buy one security from the proceeds of the sale of another.

delayed delivery order: Delivery of the security sold will not take place until a specified date after normal settlement.

either/or order: A combination of two orders such that the execution of one cancels the other.

any-part order: An order indicating that it may be filled by any combination of odd or board lots.

all-or-none order: Order is not considered filled unless a specified minimum (perhaps the total) amount of shares is traded.

Margin orders are permitted on shares with a market price of a minimum of C$1.50. At least 50% margin is usually required. Short sales are also permitted.

Settlement for stocks, rights, and options is five business days. Over-the-counter securities, including bonds, settle also in five business days.

Brokers on the Toronto exchange serve as individual members, although they may represent firms. Members may deal for their own accounts or for the firms they represent. Some brokers, however, only act as intermediaries.

ABOUT BONDS: GOVERNMENT AND CORPORATE

As mentioned before, all bonds in Canada, including government bonds, are traded over the counter. There are two bond rating services, the Canadian Bond Rating Service, and the Dominion Bond Rating Service, Ltd. They describe, analyze, and rate all bond issues. Government bonds, of course, receive the highest rating, with provincial bonds considered almost at the same level. Ratings are particularly important for corporate bonds and municipal bonds, whose ratings can vary considerably. Before buying a Canadian fixed-interest security, you should know how it is rated by at least one of the above rating services.

The usual denomination of Canadian bonds is C$1,000 or a multiple thereof. Maturities within three years are considered short-term, three to fifteen years medium-term, and over fifteen years, long-term bonds. Accrued interest is always added to the price of a bond, paid by the buyer and received by the seller.

Both registered and bearer-form bonds are available. Interest is paid semiannually. When a bond is registered, interest is mailed to the owner automatically. Bonds registered as to principal but not interest have dated coupons like bearer bonds which must be cashed at a bank for the interest payment. The certificate, however, contains the owner's name, and must be presented to the issuer for return of the capital amount.

Corporate bonds resemble bonds in this country and come in categories such as mortgage bonds, collateral trust bonds, debentures, and notes. Bonds may be convertible, redeemable by sinking fund, participating, etc. Mortgage bonds may be ranked in terms of their claims on a company's assets.

Most municipal bonds are serial bonds—parts of which mature at different times. They are normally not callable. Municipals in Canada are not tax-exempt for Canadian citizens, therefore their yields are commensurately higher than municipals in the United States.

Extendable and retractable bonds are issues which allow the investor to hold the bonds and collect interest past maturity (extendable) or to redeem bonds early (retractable).

MUTUAL FUNDS

A wide variety of mutual funds is available in Canada. As in the United States, their shares are not listed on an exchange, but are available from banks, some brokers, or from the funds themselves. Their shares often sell slightly above the net asset value, whereas closed-end funds and Canadian holding companies frequently sell at a discount. Of particular interest to nonresident investors are those funds specializing in energy or natural resources. In this country the leading mutual fund that specializes in Canadian stocks is the Canadian Fund, Inc. The minimum initial deposit is only $1,000 (see "Useful Addresses").

BANKS

Any U.S. citizen may open a bank account with a Canadian bank and transfer funds to and from Canada without restriction. Banks may be used to purchase and sell most types of securities (even gold), and, for a small charge, they also provide safekeeping for your securities.

Chartered banks in Canada provide all banking services. The five largest account for over 90% of the total assets of the banking industry. They are the Royal Bank of Canada, the Canadian Imperial Bank of Commerce, the Bank of Montreal, the Bank of Nova Scotia, and the Toronto Dominion Bank. Among the reasons for such a concentration of capital in a few banks is that in Canada it is common for a bank to have many branches. In 1982 it was estimated that there were over 7,000 Canadian branch banks.

A variety of high-yielding Canadian bank accounts are available with minimum investments of C$5,000 or C$10,000. Interest is subject to the 15% Canadian withholding tax (for which you can get U.S. tax credit). Term deposits in foreign currencies (with guaranteed rates of return) are also available and are *not* subject to withholding tax. Typical minimum deposits for three-, six-, or nine-month accounts are DM 20,000, ¥2,500,000, £5,000, and SFr 20,000. Such deposits, however, are not insured by the Canada Deposit Insurance Act, or any of the provincial insurance boards.

TAXES

Taxes on Canadian securities are very complex. If you require income from securities with less than the standard 15% withholding from dividends or interest, you should make your requirements known to your broker. The following can serve only as a general guideline. There are many exceptions, and, of course, tax laws change frequently.

Interest from deposits in a Canadian chartered bank is exempt from withholding if both deposit and interest paid are in non-Canadian currencies. Thus, U.S. dollar accounts are exempt.

Dividends from Canadian companies are subject to 15% withholding. There are some exceptions in the case of substantial holdings in companies of which Canadian residents hold at least 25% and have 25% representation on the board of directors. In this case withholding is only 10%.

Withholding on interest from Canadian bonds is generally 15% but there are many exceptions. If the following bonds were issued after April 15, 1966, and before 1983 they are exempt:

1. Government, provincial, and municipal bonds, or bonds of their agencies. These bonds are quite popular with nonresidents.
2. Bonds of corporations over 90% owned by a province or municipality.
3. Certain hospital or educational institution bonds whose interest is guaranteed by the government or province.

Interest from corporate bonds is exempt if the issue was after June 23, 1955, and before 1983, and if not more than 25% of the principal is amortized in less than five years from issue. Also exempt are bonds issued after 1960 that are denominated in non-Canadian currencies. Treasury bills of the government, a province, or a municipality are also exempt.

GOLD

Gold is the traditional long-term hedge against inflation, and no well-diversified portfolio should be without gold or gold-related securities at some time. Nonresidents of Canada may freely buy, sell, or export gold. Bullion and the one Canadian gold coin, the maple leaf, may be bought through Canadian banks. As mentioned earlier, silver and gold options are available on the Toronto and Vancouver exchanges, respectively.

Since the price of gold stocks tends to increase faster than the price of the metal itself, gold shares are often thought to be a better way of "holding" gold than possessing bullion or coins. In addition, one has the extra advantage of dividend return while waiting for the price of gold to appreciate. Gold itself, alas, pays no dividends.

Canada is the second largest producer of gold in the free world (although that is still only 4% of the world output), and there are many reasons for considering Canada for the purchase of gold securities. The two most important are:

1. Canada is closer, safer, and has none of the political or ethical encumbrances of South Africa.

2. Canadian gold mines are diversified into other metals and resources such as silver, copper, zinc, oil, and gas. (Canada, incidentally, is the world's leading producer of silver.)

A disadvantage of Canadian shares over South African shares (or "kaffirs" as they are called) is that Canadian gold shares do not pay as handsome a dividend. However, with greater return comes greater risk. If serious civil disturbances in South Africa were to close the mines, it would devastate the value of South African gold-mining shares while at the same time precipitating an enormous increase in the price of gold and other gold shares throughout the world.

SOURCES OF INFORMATION

There is probably more information available in this country about Canadian securities than the securities of any other country. *The Wall Street Journal* and *Barron's* have more coverage of Canadian securities than they have for the securities of any other foreign country. In addition, leading U.S. newspapers carry quotations for the most active stocks listed on the Toronto and Montreal exchanges. The Canadian daily newspaper with the best financial coverage is *The Globe and Mail* in Toronto. However, keeping track of your investments through a foreign daily is expensive. There are two excellent weekly papers, *The Financial Post* and *The Financial Times,* that provide in-depth coverage of companies, markets, the economy, and political developments. In addition, they include end-of-the-week security quotations.

The exchanges publish data, statistics, indexes, and the price charts of listed companies. The best of these is *The Exchange Review,* published by the Toronto Stock Exchange. It is available monthly by subscription for $102.20 (U.S.) a year.

USEFUL ADDRESSES

STOCK EXCHANGES

The Toronto Stock Exchange
2 First Canadian Place
Toronto, Ontario
Canada M5X 1J2

The Vancouver Stock Exchange
536 Howe Street
Vancouver, B.C.
Canada V6C 2E1

U.S. BRANCH OF LEADING
CANADIAN BROKER

Wood Gundy, Inc.
50 North Tamiami Trail
Sarasota, FL 33577

CANADIAN MUTUAL FUND

Canada Fund, Inc.
1 Wall Street
New York, NY 10005

FINANCIAL WEEKLIES

The Financial Post
481 University Avenue
Toronto, Ontario
Canada M5W 1A7

The Financial Times
920 Yonge Street, Suite 500
Toronto, Ontario
Canada M4W 3L5

OTHER SOURCES OF INFORMATION

Investment Dealers Association of
Canada
33 Yonge Street, Suite 350
Toronto, Ontario M5E 1G4

Investment Funds Institute of
Canada
70 Bond Street
Toronto, Ontario M5B 1X3

9

THE FRANKFURT STOCK EXCHANGE

Courtesy of the Frankfurt Stock Exchange

FROM MEDIEVAL TRADE FAIR TO MODERN STOCK EXCHANGE

Most West German stock exchanges trace their origins to the great German trade fairs of the Middle Ages. For over 800 years such fairs played an important role in the German economy, and today they flourish in large cities such as Frankfurt-am-Main, Dusseldorf, and Munich. There are fairs for building materials, the plastics industry, fashion, waste disposal, books—almost every sector of German industry.

At the early fairs, a few days' trading could generate a large number of financial obligations (mostly bills of exchange[1]) and merchants would meet frequently, both during the fairs and after, to settle, trade, or set

[1]A written instruction to one's banker to pay the bearer a stated amount of money at a specified time. Such bills are negotiable until they mature.

THE FRANKFURT STOCK MARKET AT A GLANCE

Capitalization:

Market value of domestic shares in U.S.$*............... $73,389.9 million

Nominal value of domestic bonds in U.S.$*.............. $147,815.3 million

Volume:

Total yearly volume of shares in U.S.$* .... $16,538.6 million

Total yearly volume of bonds in U.S.$* .... $17,353.0 million

Listings:

Domestic shares 227

Domestic bonds 4,847

Foreign shares... 181

Foreign bonds... 598

Rank in the world:

Capitalization 5th

*Exchange rate as of Dec. 30, 1983: $1 = DM2.7602.
Source: Frankfurt Stock Exchange, *Annual Report,* data for 1983.

---

off those obligations against one another. In order to facilitate such transactions, currency exchange booths began appearing at fairs in the early fifteenth century (1402 in Frankfurt). Gradually, as financial instruments were traded with increasing independence from the commodity transactions that generated them, new instruments, such as bonds and notes, began to be traded. Stocks, latecomers to the German financial market, were not introduced until the beginning of the nineteenth century.

As with most stock exchanges, trading was originally outdoors. In Frankfurt, it is generally accepted that organized trading began in 1558. The first indoor exchange was in the house "Braunfels" (brownstone) on the Liebfrauenberg. The "Old Exchange" opened in 1843, and the "New Stock Exchange" (the present exchange building) opened in 1879.

Despite the fact that Berlin was the capital of the various German "Reichs," Frankfurt maintained a prominence among the German exchanges. Before World War I it listed about 1,500 securities, fifty-one of which were foreign stocks and 388 of which were foreign bonds. Foreign securities, however, were confiscated in World War I so that the exchange forfeited all international trading. The world depression of the 1930s closed the exchange for a short period in 1931, and the foreign exchange controls that were later imposed almost paralyzed the newly restored trading of international securities.

In 1944 an air raid came close to demolishing the floor of the exchange, and trading shifted to some small rooms in the basement. After the fall of the Third Reich the Frankfurt Stock Exchange was closed for six months. Reopened in September 1945, it conducted only a modest volume of business.

The recovery of the German economy after World War II is a success story comparable only to Japan's spectacular growth during the same period. The stabilization of the deutschemark was a major achievement for which the banks must be given a great deal of credit. The Frankfurt exchange, responding to the renewed vigor of new financial markets, rebuilt its trading floor in 1957, and a separate bond floor was opened in 1966.

Today the Frankfurt exchange is the largest in Germany, usually accounting for about 50% of all securities turnover. While that represents half of securities trading, Frankfurt does not completely dominate the country's securities market as does the principal exchange in other countries such as Japan, the United Kingdom, and France. According to the Frankfurt Stock Exchange, the Frankfurt percentage of the total securities volume on all German exchanges in 1983 was as follows: 44% of the turnover of German shares, 48% of domestic bonds, 57% of foreign shares, and 87% of foreign fixed-interest securities.

The Frankfurt exchange has also regained its international perspective. There are no restrictions on foreign ownership of German stock, and revenues from securities transactions may be repatriated freely. Of the stocks listed in Frankfurt, 45% are foreign, and of the ninety-two exchange members, twenty-two are branches of foreign banks or stockbrokers.

The other exchanges in West Germany are in Düsseldorf (the second largest), Berlin, Bremen, Hamburg, Hanover, Munich, and Stuttgart. Together they form the Association of German Stock Exchanges. The rules and regulations of each exchange are subject to approval of the state. Frankfurt is in the state of Hesse.

HOW DIFFERENT IS THE GERMAN STOCK MARKET?

From the perspective of the U.S. investor, the most obvious difference in the German stock market is the apparent absence of stockbrokers. In Germany, brokerage services are provided by banks, and only banks may become members of the stock exchanges.[2]

[2]Foreign brokerage firms can obtain a German banking license and are thereby subject to the German Banking Act.

There is, however, another activity of German banks that is far more important than brokerage services in the shaping of German financial markets, and that is the freedom of commercial banks to engage in investment banking.[3] What this means is that German banks may underwrite new issues of stock. In the United States, investment banks may or may not be stockbrokers, but they cannot be banks. The Glass-Steagall Act of 1933 prohibits commercial banks in this country both from dealing in securities (with a few exceptions) and from underwriting securities.

Banks in Germany are quick to point out the advantages of this system. They feel that close contact with customers through banking services makes it easier for them to convert savings deposits into investments in securities. They also feel that their substantial assets and diversity make them more stable than institutions confined solely to investment banking or brokerage services.

However, providing banking services and bringing out new securities are two different industries, typically requiring two different approaches. Banks, viewing their operations as return on credit, are appropriately the more cautious of the two. Investment bankers, on the other hand, view their operations as return on risk and, under ordinary circumstances, are willing to take a slightly greater degree of risk for the possibility of higher return. For instance, it is not unusual for investment bankers in the United States (such as some of the major brokerage firms), after spreading their risk among a reasonable number of new issues, to average as much as 25% greater return on equity than U.S. commercial banks.

The "banker's" approach to the securities industry in Germany has resulted in a conservative equities market that, some would say, borders on the stagnant. The most obvious sign of difficulty is that so few companies are brought public each year. This means that the country's equity market is in danger of becoming solely a secondary market. The opportunity for businesses to raise needed capital becomes limited to bonds and other debt instruments. For those companies already public it means that the amount of their equity financing may be quite small in relation to their total capitalization. According to the Bundesbank (the central bank), equity capital of the average corporation at the beginning of 1983 fell to only 18.5% of corporate assets.

[3]The term "investment banker" is, in fact, a misnomer. Investment banks are not banks in the usual sense—they do not accept deposits or provide savings accounts or checking account facilities. An investment bank conducts only one type of activity: it helps corporations raise money through the marketing of securities.

But what does all this mean to the foreign investor? Probably the most significant fact is that there is somewhat less risk on such a market and, to a corresponding degree, less upside potential. There are fewer issues, but the companies that *are* public are usually well-established, solid institutions. Interestingly, some have a relatively small amount of stock trading because of large family-held blocks or large bank holdings. This may increase the volatility of their prices should there be a sudden change in demand for any of those securities. One fact, however, remains inescapable: if you are interested in new issues then you had best look to another market.

WEST GERMAN CURRENCY AND EXCHANGE RATE WITH THE U.S. DOLLAR

The German currency is the deutschemark (pronounced with three syllables) and the pfennig. It appears in print, for example, as DM 7.23 (seven deutschemark, twenty three). West Germany participates in the European Monetary System, and the central bank will intervene on the Frankfurt Currency Exchange to keep the exchange rate within EMS guidelines. The Frankfurt Currency Exchange is the central exchange in West Germany, and is affiliated with the stock exchange.

After Germany recovered from the war, its currency eventually became the most stable and sought-after in Europe. Low inflation and steady increases in the GNP made the German economy a model for the rest of Europe. In the late 1970s the oil crises, balance of payment deficits, and inflation began to catch up with Germany and have an adverse effect on exchange rates. Recently, however, the deutschemark has rebounded from new lows against the U.S. dollar.

Figure 1 shows the exchange rate of the deutschemark to the U.S. dollar and its effective exchange rate (see p. 40) with a basket of seventeen other major currencies. Despite the mark's dramatic rise and fall against the dollar, it has, in general, gradually appreciated against other world currencies. As in previous exchange-rate graphs, room is left for you to continue plotting the rate against the dollar.

SECURITIES TRADED ON FRANKFURT EXCHANGE

stocks (common and preferred): Most are common stocks and in bearer form. Insurance stocks are usually registered. Dividends are annual. About 5% of German stocks are preferred: they are usually participating, nonvoting, and cumulative.

bonds: Mortgage bonds and commercial bonds constitute the greatest number of issues. Turnover is greater, however, in public sector issues of the government or government agencies. Convertible bonds are available, as are bonds with warrants. All are in bearer form. Interest is paid semiannually or annually.

warrants: Fairly long-lived warrants are traded. They are usually issued only with bonds.

dividend rights certificates (Genusscheine): These are certificates with no par value and represent no equity in the issuing company. They entitle the holder only to receive dividends from certain specified revenues that are expected by the issuer. They have expiration dates, and are not issued frequently.

rights: These trade for only a brief period, ten days on average, before expiration.

options: Both puts and calls are available (see section entitled "Options").

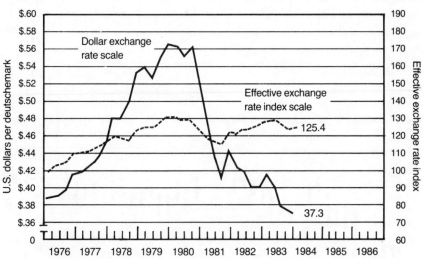

Figure 1. Exchange rate of the deutschemark with the U.S. dollar and the effective exchange rate with other major currencies.
Source: *Federal Reserve Bank of St. Louis*

Bearer-share certificates are printed with numbered dividend coupons, and dividends are paid upon submission of coupons. Your broker or bank will provide this service for you. New dividend sheets are sent when the last dividend coupon is used. Today, most security transfers are electronic; the actual certificates are held in a depositary (such as the Frankfurt Central Depository), and you need not worry about sending in the coupons yourself.[4]

Any number of shares may be purchased but those shares subject to continuous trading, as are many of the larger companies (see "Frankfurt Trading Floor Operations"), are traded in lots of fifty.

All transactions are in cash (no margin) and settlement is in two days. Your U.S. broker may also require two-day settlement. Prices for shares are quoted in deutschemarks; those for bonds are quoted in percent of par value.

THE FRANKFURT STOCK EXCHANGE SHARE-PRICE INDEX

There are a number of different stock exchange indexes for securities listed in Frankfurt. The Frankfurt Stock Exchange Share-Price Index was formed to show quarterly highs and lows (Figure 2). This is an index maintained by the exchange which contains all listed shares. Calculated from a base of 100 in 1968, it is the most broadly based of all the indexes.

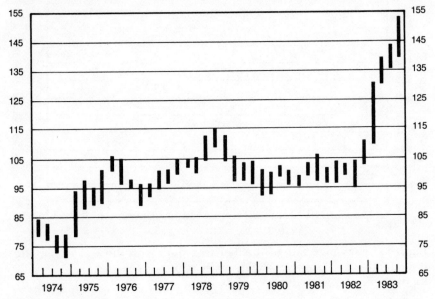

Figure 2. Frankfurt Stock Exchange share-price index, showing quarterly highs and lows.   Source: *The Frankfurt Stock Exchange*

[4]In fact, the central depositary doesn't physically send in the certificates either. The coupons are simply canceled (called "depreciated") in their vaults and the dividend amounts applied for, received, and credited to the customer's account.

GERMAN SECURITIES AVAILABLE IN THE UNITED STATES

There are no German securities available on the New York or American Stock Exchange. The following list is of German stocks available over the counter as ADRs. They are grouped by industry, and the industries shown are listed in the order of their share of nominal capital in Germany. The chemical industry, listed first, makes up over 20% of the total capital value of the German stock market.

CHEMICAL INDUSTRY

BASF

Bayer

Hoechst

AUTOMATIVE

Volkswagenwerk

COMMERCIAL BANKS

Bayerische Vereinsbank

Commerzbank

Deutsche Bank

Dresdner Bank

ELECTRICAL

AEG

Siemens

FRANKFURT TRADING FLOOR OPERATIONS

The exchange is officially open for trading only two hours a day, 11:30 A.M. to 1:30 P.M., Monday through Friday. All sessions are supervised by at least one member of the Board of Governors. His intervention is expected only in cases where a severe imbalance of the supply or demand of a security makes rationing a necessity or when the security's price is in danger of exceeding the limit allowable on the exchange. Like a few other stock exchanges, there are limits beyond which a security's price may not vary from one day to the next. Stocks may not rise or fall more than 5% of their price on the preceding day, and bonds may not vary more than 1.5%. In cases where these limits are exceeded a member of the Board of Governors is called upon to decide how trading will proceed.

There are three types of member firms on the Frankfurt Stock Exchange as regards function:

• *Enterprise (bank) members* conduct security transactions for their clients and their own accounts. These are domestic banks and foreign brokerage firms with a German banking license that offer brokerage services to the public.

- *Kursmakler members* are floor brokers who arrange transactions between members and are responsible for the daily setting of official prices. They are restricted with respect to their own accounts. They are also responsible for reporting all transactions in securities assigned to them. As brokers they receive commissions from the banks. Each *Kursmakler* is usually assigned to securities within specific industry sectors. In the photo at the beginning of the chapter it is the *Kursmaklers* who are in the middle trading ring.
- *Freie Makler members* are floor brokers who arrange transactions between members. They are not allowed to set official prices. The *freie Maklers* are primarily engaged in unofficial trading.

The types of orders available on the Frankfurt exchange include:

limit order: The bank is not to sell below or make a purchase above a specified limit.

at best or *at bottom:* This is, in fact, a market order. The bank is instructed to sell at the highest price or buy at the lowest.

The increments by which the price of a stock may move depend on its price. Stocks below DM 1 will be quoted in increments of DM .01, from DM 1 to DM 20 increments of DM .05, and above DM 20 increments of DM .10.

WHEN YOUR BROKER TRADES IN FRANKFURT

The commission schedule shown in Table 1 applies to the Frankfurt exchange. Should your U.S. broker purchase securities for you on the Frankfurt exchange, the interbroker fee will be less but you will also have your own broker's commission. Branches of some U.S. banks are members of the Frankfurt exchange but their U.S. offices do not offer

Table 1

COMMISSION SCHEDULE FOR FRANKFURT EXCHANGE

	COMMISSION TO *KURSMAKLER* ON FLOOR OF EXCHANGE	COMMISSION TO BANK
Shares	.1%	1% with minimum fees
Rights	.1%	1% with minimum fees
Bonds:		
Nominal value up to DM 50,000	.075%	.5% with minimum fees
Nominal value from DM 50,000 to DM 100,000	.05% with minimum of DM 37.5	.5% with minimum fees

brokerage service. You may, of course, choose to have an account with a bank in Germany. There is also a securities turnover tax. For public sector bonds and mortgage and commercial bonds it is .1%, and for shares and all other bonds it is .25%.

For shares, the total of the above charges amounts to 1.3%; for government bonds it is .7%, and for corporate bonds it is .8%. The securities turnover tax applies both to purchases and sales. Nevertheless, the rate is low by U.S. standards.

When you use a U.S. broker the price of a German security will usually be quoted net, which means it will already contain the (German) broker and bank commission. Only the securities turnover tax will be

Table 2

THE TEN LARGEST STOCK ISSUES ON THE FRANKFURT STOCK EXCHANGE

COMPANY	PRICE PER SHARE IN DM (END OF 1983)	MARKET VALUE IN MILLIONS OF DM (END OF 1983)
1. Daimler Benz	649.80	22,051.3
2. Siemens	382.80	16,466.4
3. Deutsche Bank	337.20	9,145.8
4. Bayer	172.20	8,713.3
5. Hoechst	181.00	8,519.3
6. Allianz-Versicherung	793.00	7,936.3
7. Rhein.-Westf. Elektrizitätsw.	179.00	7,805.1
8. B.A.S.F.	172.00	7,607.6
9. Allianz-Levensversicherung	3,200.00	6,336.0
10. Volkswagenwerk	218.90	5,253.6

Source: Frankfurt Stock Exchange, *Annual Report,* data for 1983.

Table 3

THE TEN MOST ACTIVE STOCK ISSUES ON THE FRANKFURT STOCK EXCHANGE

COMPANY	TURNOVER IN MILLIONS OF DM
1. Siemens	3,177.1
2. Daimler Benz	1,762.6
3. Deutsche Bank	1,731.0
4. Volkswagenwerk	1,698.4
5. Bayer	1,341.1
6. Bayer. Motoren-Werke	1,315.5
7. B.S.S.F.	1,308.9
8. Hoechst	1,168.6
9. Mercedes-Automobil-Hldg.	1,035.0
10. Rhein.-Westf. Elektrizitätsw.	1,019.6

Source: Frankfurt Stock Exchange, *Annual Report,* data for 1983.

listed separately, as will your U.S. broker's commission. German stocks are, on the whole, more expensive than U.S. stocks.

HOW PRICES ARE SET

Many exchanges throughout the world make use of a mechanism whereby prices are set by a specialist, either at the beginning of trading or at some point during official hours. Such an operation is called "fixing."

The process is more or less the same on all exchanges. In Frankfurt, the *Kursmakler* (who deals only with other brokers) collects all buy and sell offers up to the time of the fixing (about 12:15) which could not yet be executed and have therefore accumulated, including all odd-lot orders. He then selects a transaction price that will accommodate the most orders. Obviously, there is no one price that can perfectly balance them all, so he may enter into the transactions himself, buying or selling so as to balance the buy and sell orders insofar as possible. Each price set by this method is arrived at as a compromise of the opposing forces of supply and demand. From 12:15 on, he continues to match buy and sell orders and adjust the price.

A price set by a fixing may hold for the entire trading period; it is also the price usually published in the press. On the Frankfurt exchange, if your odd-lot order reaches the trading floor before noon you have a legal right to buy or sell at that price.

There is one serious problem with a system such as the one just described. It is impractical to have the price of a security remain fixed for an entire trading session if that security also happens to be listed on *another* exchange where its price is not fixed. A difference will invariably develop between the prices of the security at the two different exchanges, and arbitrageurs will immediately step in, simultaneously buying and selling the security on the two different exchanges, reaping instant profits. Therefore, those securities traded on other exchanges, particularly foreign exchanges, are subject to continuous trading on the Frankfurt floor (i.e., the orders are not accumulated; they are executed as they come in, and the price may continually fluctuate).

THE THREE TYPES OF SECURITY TRADING

There are three types of security trading in Germany, applicable to both stocks and bonds:

official dealing: Trading is on an exchange; the transaction prices are published in the Official List and in the press; the requirements for listing are high; mostly larger companies, government bonds, and foreign securities are listed. Official prices are set by the *Kursmakler.*

regulated unofficial dealing: Trading is between banks and/or *freie Maklers* on an exchange; prices are published by the *freie Maklers;* requirements for listing are not so severe as for official dealing; mostly government bonds with a maturity up to four years and some smaller or new companies.

unregulated unofficial dealing (also called telephone dealing): Trading is not limited to the stock exchange or stock exchange hours; trading is between banks and/or *freie Maklers;* there is no supervision of listing; prices are published by the *freie Maklers;* and many of the securities traded are foreign stocks which, for various reasons, are not traded officially.

The nonresident should concentrate on stock subject to official dealing. Not only are the listing requirements for those stocks the highest but the required financial reporting is closely regulated and scrutinized. Even the banks and the personnel responsible for compiling the prospectus can be held liable for any inaccuracies or misrepresentations. Annual reports are, of course, required, and most larger companies publish interim reports as well.

While considering forms of trading it should be mentined that unregulated, unofficial dealing is sometimes referred to as over the counter. However, in Germany there are literally transactions that are "over the counter"—over a bank counter, that is. The transaction is in cash, and the customer leaves with the actual certificate. Such a procedure is practical only when the certificates are in bearer form. In the United States this kind of trading may only take place with bearer certificates such as those used at one time for municipal bonds. The term "over the counter" does not imply a higher-than-normal degree of speculativeness on the part of the security. The bluest of blue-chip German stocks can be bought this way if the bank happens to have a bearer certificate of the stock desired.

Official dealing prices in the Official List will always appear with the following abbreviations that explain the circumstances under which the individual prices were fixed:

b (bezahlt): All orders were executed at the price indicated.

bG (bezahlt Geld): Not all the purchase orders that had been limited by the established price could be executed.

bB (bezahlt Brief): Not all the sell orders that had been limited by the established price could be executed.

ratG (rationiert Geld): All purchase orders—including unlimited orders—had to be rationed.

ratB (rationiert Brief): Sell orders—including unlimited orders—had to be rationed.

exD: Ex-dividend.

exBr: Ex-rights.

ABOUT BONDS: GOVERNMENT AND CORPORATE

Prior to 1980 nonresidents could not purchase domestic bonds with maturities of less than five years. The intention was to restrict the flow of foreign capital into Germany because the subsequent increase in the money supply would put upward pressure on exchange rates. Germany maintained a remarkably stable currency through the 1960s and 1970s. However, the balance of payment deficits eventually weakened the deutschemark, and the restrictions were lessened. Today, all restrictions of that kind have been abolished.

Not surprisingly, bonds of financial institutions and banks make up 75% of domestic bonds outstanding. Mortgage bonds, in particular, are popular and are issued with maturities as long as fifteen years.

All public sector bonds are listed on exchanges, and many are available directly from banks. The secondary market is quite active. The rates of such bonds are only fractionally lower than other bonds. Most are backed by the West German government and considered to be among the safest in the world.

Corporate or industrial bonds constitute only 1% of the total domestic bond market, and they do not enjoy the liquidity of bank or public sector bonds. Industrial bonds supply, on the average, only about 2% of a corporation's financing. Far larger amounts come from various bank obligations. As it turns out, however, capital from bonds reaches corporations anyway (although indirectly) since the funds borrowed from the bank are in turn raised through bonds sold by the banks.

BANKS

A great deal has already been said about banks, so the present discussion will be quite limited. The Deutsche Bundesbank in Frankfurt (usually referred to as the Bundesbank) is the central bank of West Germany, and is responsible for regulating the value of the deutschemark. Besides directly intervening in the money market and exchange market, it sets reserve requirements and establishes discount facilities for all German banks.

The "big three" private commercial banks in Germany (Deutsche Bank, Commerzbank, and Dresdner Bank) are also major stockholders in German businesses. It is estimated that the three control 36% of the shares in the seventy-five largest corporations in Germany.

All services of German banks are available to nonresidents, including call and time deposits in any major currency, securities transactions, investment advice, and portfolio management. You may write to any of them at the addresses given at the end of the chapter.

MUTUAL FUNDS

Almost every major bank in Germany manages its own mutual funds. The "big three" banks and their funds are listed below. All are well-managed, solid funds. Although they may not advertise in this country (they are not registered with the SEC) you may purchase them if you approach one of their U.S. bank branches. Their annual reports and six-month interim reports are excellent sources of information on foreign markets. The address of the management company is given if you wish to write to them directly.

Deutsche Bank is the majority shareholder and custodian bank of DWS Deutsche Gesellschaft für Wertpapiersparen mbH, a mutual fund management company. All the funds are open-ended. The two most well known are:

Investa: The largest fund investing exclusively in German equities, with shares usually held in approximately fifty companies.

Intervest: Invests in equities throughout the world.

Other funds include those that reinvest all income for maximum growth, bond funds, natural resource and energy funds, and technology funds. There is a 5% sales charge for purchases. The redemption price, as it is for most German funds, is the net asset value. You can get information from Deutsche Bank, including its U.S. branches, or write directly to DWS Deutsche Gesellschaft für Wertpapiersparen mbH, Postfach 2634, D-6000 Frankfurt 1.

Commerzbank is majority shareholder in ADIG Investment, which manages a group of funds whose combined market share equals 20% of all investment companies in Germany. A few of the funds are:

Adifonds: An income-oriented fund that invests primarily in German shares, although some foreign shares, including those of the United States, are included.

Adirenta: A bond fund acquiring both German and foreign bonds.

Fondis: Investment emphasis on international blue-chip stocks.

Other funds include a growth fund and a European stock fund. You can obtain information from U.S. branches of Commerzbank or write directly to ADIG, Neue Mainzer Strasse 37–39, 600 Frankfurt 1.

Dresdner Bank's Deutscher Investment-Trust manages two funds:

Concentra: a diversified fund.

Internationales Rentenfonds: an international bond fund.

You can obtain information from a U.S. branch of Dresdner Bank or write directly to Deutsche Investment-Trust, Gesellschaft für Wertpapieranlagen mdH, Mainzer Landstrasse 11–13, D-6000 Frankfurt.

OPTIONS

Frankfurt is the leading exchange in Germany for options. Both puts and calls may be bought or sold in contracts of three, six, and nine months. The "expiry" dates (dates of maturity) are always on the fifteenth of the month.

Option contracts are for fifty shares. The exercise price (the price at which the option enables one to buy or sell the security) is usually close to the market price of the underlying security on the day of the option transaction. As in the United States, exercise prices must be set at specified increments. If the share price is higher than DM 100 then the increment of the exercise prices must be DM 10 (e.g., DM 110, DM 120, DM 130, etc.).

Options can either be exercised or allowed to expire if it is not in the purchaser's interest to exercise them. As of April 1983 there has been an active secondary market so that option positions can be closed out at any time. On the Frankfurt exchange, options are available on about forty West German securities and on ten foreign securities.

WITHHOLDING TAX

Dividends from investment funds are free of withholding tax. Capital gains are not subject to withholding nor are the proceeds from the sale of rights or bonus shares (shares or rights dividends).

Withholding from dividends for stocks can be reduced from 25% to 15% and for bonds from 25% to 0% by applying to the German tax authorities, the Bundesamt für Finanzen (Friedhofstrasse 1, D-5300 Bonn 3). The forms may also be obtained from that office. You have four years after the year of the applicable refund to apply, so if the amount is relatively small you may want to let the refund accumulate a few years before applying. You may receive credit on your U.S. income tax for foreign withholding you do pay.

GERMAN INVESTMENT JARGON

Börsenmakler (independent broker): Broker for the unofficial market.

Bundesbank (Deutsche Bundesbank): The central bank of West Germany.

cash quotation: A quotation set by a fix.

dividend rights certificate: Permits one to receive dividends from a specified and expected source of income to the issuer. It does not represent equity, and it will have an expiration date.

Kursmakler (official broker): Broker assigned to stocks in official dealing; sets prices, reports all transactions in securities to which assigned; a broker's broker.

over the counter: Sometimes refers to unregulated, unofficial dealing. More correctly refers to the purchase or sale of bearer-form certificates at a bank for cash where there is no client account.

Vinkulierte Aktie: Shares that cannot be transferred without the consent of the issuing company.

SOURCES OF INFORMATION

There is not as much inforation in English about German securities as one would like. The best sources are reports published by the banks, particularly the big three (see "Useful Addresses"). These are difficult to get, however, unless you have an account with those banks, and sometimes their investment account minimums are rather high.

As far as annual reports are concerned, some are provided in English. The accounting is similar but not exactly the same as in the United States. One general rule is that earnings are sometimes underestimated. As mentioned earlier, annual and interim reports of investment companies can be particularly helpful.

Non-German sources of information on specific securities include

English and Dutch brokers. If you have an account with them (or an international U.S. broker) you will often receive excellent investment information on German securities.

Among German publications probably the *Handelsblatt* is the most respected, and the smaller *Börsen Zeitung*. London's *Financial Times* publishes a Frankfurt edition. Unfortunately, the daily papers in Germany tend to carry a relatively small amount of financial news.

USEFUL ADDRESSES

THE FRANKFURT STOCK EXCHANGE

Frankfurter Wertpapierbörse
Informationsdienst
6 Frankfurt a.M.
Postfach 2913

LARGEST COMMERCIAL BANKS

Deutsche Bank
10–14 Grosse Gallus Strasse
P.O. Box 2631
6000 Frankfurt a.M.

Commerzbank
32–36 Neue Mainzer Strasse
6000 Frankfurt a.M.

Dresdner Bank
Jürgen-Ponto Platz
P.O. Box 110661
6000 Frankfurt a.M.

THE ZURICH STOCK EXCHANGE

Courtesy of Credit Suisse

A MAJOR FINANCIAL MARKET

Switzerland occupies a position of importance in free world markets that belies its geographic size. Because finance, particularly international finance, has been developed into a major industry, there are now more banks per capita in Switzerland than in any other country in the world. Among European markets, the stock exchange in Zurich enjoys a turnover second only to London, and more gold is traded through Switzerland than through any country outside the communist bloc.

There have been many reasons put forward for Switzerland's financial success, such as its well-known neutrality, its liberal economic policies, and its ability to maintain a sound currency. However, one must also add a more prosaic reason: being in the right place at the right time. Switzerland was one of the few countries with a healthy, functioning banking system left intact at the end of World War II. With the deposits, currencies, and securities of surrounding countries decimated by the war, it is easy to see why Europeans and investors in other parts of the world turned to Switzerland for a safe financial haven.

There are seven stock exchanges in Switzerland; Zurich is the largest. The others are in Basel, Geneva, Berne, St. Gall, Neuchâtel, and Lausanne. Each is under the direct control of the canton (state) in which it is located.

Contrary to assumptions, there are no commodity exchanges in Zurich; neither gold nor currencies are traded on the exchange. Such transactions are between banks without the interpolation of an exchange. In fact, even the exchange trading of securities is not required in Switzerland. Stocks and bonds are traded on exchanges out of convenience, but banks are also free to trade among themselves, and they often do, particularly for large transactions.

THE ZURICH STOCK MARKET AT A GLANCE

Capitalization:
Market value of listed Swiss shares in U.S.$*............... $44,071.0 million
Nominal value of domestic and foreign bonds in U.S.$* .... $61,701.5 million
Percent of total share capitalization represented by ten largest
   companies†.. 60.8%
Volume:
Value of total annual turnover in U.S.$* .... $122,060.8 million
Listings:†
Domestic equities.. 184
Domestic fixed-interest securities................................ 1406
Foreign shares... 170
Foreign fixed-interest securities 635

*Exchange rate as of Dec 30, 1983: $1 = Sfr 2.18.
†1982.
Source: The Zurich Stock Exchange, Annual Report, data for 1983.

At the beginning of 1984 Zurich listed 2,395 securities, 354 of which were stocks. The turnover for the previous year was typically 40% bonds and 60% stocks.

A BRIEF HISTORY

Three cantons formed the first military alliance in 1291. Present-day Switzerland, however, was formed in 1848 by the alliance of twenty-five cantons. Another canton was created in 1978 so that the Confederation of Switzerland is now constituted of twenty-six cantons. It was in 1873 that the Zurich Stock Exchange was founded. There has been some controversy about the exact year (the exchange centennial was celebrated in 1977), but 1873 now seems to be the official year. Zurich, incidentally, was not the first; the Geneva Stock Exchange predates Zurich by twenty years.

Organized security trading in Zurich dates from the middle of the seventeenth century when a body called the Sensale (an organization of brokers and business intermediaries) began meeting regularly on the "lower bridge." Their first set of regulations, which established official guidelines for the conduct of its members, was adopted in 1663.

It is interesting to note that since the seventeenth century repeated attempts to make trading on an exchange compulsory failed to be ratified by the cantonal high authorities. Such a regulation was seen as an intrusion on personal liberty. Regulations could not be entirely avoided, however, and in 1884 the exchange members struck for three months over the requirement of a broker's license and the appointment of an exchange commissioner.

In comparison with other Swiss cities, Zurich was definitely not progressive. Stocks and bonds, for instance, had been accepted in Geneva and Basel long before they were considered proper to own in Zurich.

During World War I the exchange was closed for almost two years. As mentioned earlier, it remained open during World War II, but that period is known as the period of affidavits. Proof of ownership in the form of an affidavit was required for trading. This was to keep the Axis powers from using the Swiss stock exchanges to raise funds.

The Zurich exchange has had a variety of homes in its history, including a converted music hall. The present building, strikingly modern (built in 1928) is now too small, and a design for a new building has been ratified.

The premises for the exchange are provided by the canton of Zurich. In return, the canton receives the listing fees from the corporations whose securities are traded on the exchange.

SWISS CURRENCY AND EXCHANGE RATE WITH THE U.S. DOLLAR

The standard units of Swiss currency are the Swiss franc and the centime. There are a hundred centimes to the Swiss franc. In print it appears variously as SFr 7.13 or Sfr 7.13 (seven Swiss francs, thirteen). Because of periodic strong demand for the Swiss franc, there have occasionally been exchange restrictions imposed if it seemed demand would destabilize the currency or the internal economy. The National Bank, for example, has the authority to charge a commission on deposits in Swiss francs; it also may restrict purchases of Swiss securities by nonresidents as was done from February 1978 to January 1979.

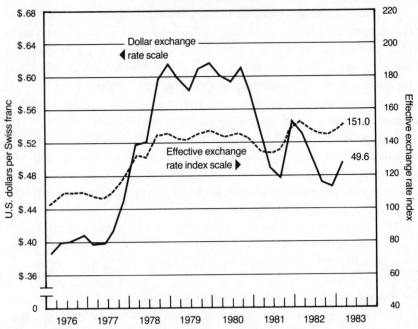

Figure 1. Exchange rate of the Swiss franc with the U.S. dollar and the effective exchange rate with other major currencies.
Source: *Federal Reserve Bank of St. Louis*

The solid line on the graph in Figure 1 shows the exchange rate of the Swiss franc with the U.S. dollar. As with earlier currency exchange graphs, this simply shows the relationship between the two currencies. The broken line shows the effective exchange rate against the combined currencies of seventeen other major nations (also taking into account their relative trade flows, domestic costs, etc.). This obviously comes closer to representing some kind of "absolute" value of the Swiss franc than solely its exchange rate with the U.S. dollar. As you can see, in relation to world currencies the franc has not been as volatile as the rate with the U.S. dollar would imply.

SECURITIES TRADED ON THE ZURICH EXCHANGE

stock: Issues often consist of both bearer form and registered form. Usually, only bearer form is available to nonresidents. Dividends are usually paid annually. There are currently no preferred shares.

bonds: Issued in bearer form. Interest is paid annually; some denominations are as low as Sfr 1,000. Maturities are up to twenty-five years. Some are convertible and some issued with options to buy shares. There are also a larger number of foreign currency issues.

rights: Also called share subscription rights. They are issued to current shareholders and are usually good for a couple of weeks.

warrants: Usually issued with bonds, may be good for up to several years. They usually state whether they are good for bearer or registered stocks.

certificate of participation: These are, in effect, nonvoting shares.

mutual fund shares: Shares of some mutual funds are quoted on the stock exchange (especially those of the Union Bank of Switzerland). Their price is usually the net asset value.

When a bank purchases shares for a nonresident investor, the shares must usually be in bearer form. This allows the companies themselves to decide the percentage of foreign ownership they will permit. If your broker trades regularly in Swiss securities he or she will know if the company whose shares you are considering has such a limit and if registered stocks are available.

As mentioned earlier, the same issues of stock may be made up of both bearer and registered shares, and, frequently, the registered shares are issued at a lower par value than the bearer shares. In this country, par value of common stocks is of no concern to the investor, but par value affects Swiss stock in two important ways. First of all, the dividend is declared as a percent of par value (although you may see it quoted in francs). This means that a higher par value registered stock will pay a higher dividend than a lower par value bearer-form stock. It also means that the registered shares will sell for a higher price (since the dividend is higher).

Rights issuance is more common in Switzerland than in the United States. However, when purchasing stocks through rights you should know that you may not make use of an odd number of rights. For example, if you own fifty-five shares (and thus receive fifty-five rights) and it takes ten rights to purchase one additional share, then you must purchase five extra rights to have enough to purchase six new shares.

MAJOR STOCK INDEXES

The leading share-price index for the Zurich exchange is the Swiss Bank
Corporation General Share Index, usually labeled the SBV Index
(Schweizerischer Bankverein). Other major banks issue indexes but this
is the one most likely to be quoted in the media. It should be pointed
out that indexes and other accoutrements of technical analysis are not
as popular in Switzerland as in the United States. While this broadly
based index can be helpful as a gauge to past market performance, it
is debatable whether the fact that it is not closely watched makes it
more or less reliable in terms of technical analysis. Figure 2 shows only
the yearly closing values from 1958.

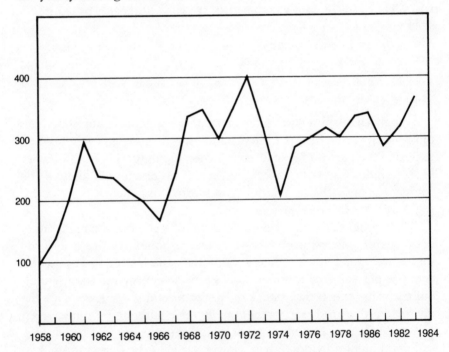

Figure 2. **SBV General Share Index (yearly closing prices).**
Source: *Swiss Bank Corporation, Zurich*

BUYING SWISS SECURITIES

There are no Swiss stocks available in the United States as ADRs, so your
broker must purchase them in Switzerland. If your broker is a Swiss

bank then you will discover that commissions are quite low. For shares, warrants, investment funds, and certificates of participation:

PER-SHARE PRICE	COMMISSION
Under Sfr 150	1% of the total price
Over Sfr 150	⅝% of the total price

The minimum commission is Sfr 10.
For bonds:

PER-SHARE PRICE	COMMISSION
Swiss bonds	⅜% of the market price
Foreign bonds	½% of the market price

Accrued interest must be added to all bond transactions.
Other charges on the Zurich exchange are as follows:

1. Federal stamp tax of .75% of the market price of all Swiss securities; 1.5% if the security is foreign.
2. Canton of Zurich charge of Sfr .10 for every Sfr 1,000 of the transaction.
3. Stock Exchange Association charge of Sfr .05 for every Sfr 1,000 of the transaction.

A typical transaction might look like this:

Purchase of fifty shares of Swiss XYZ at Sfr 100 =	Sfr 5,000.00
Brokerage of ⅝%	31.25
Federal stamp tax of .75%	37.50
Canton tax of .1%	5.00
Stock Exchange Association charge	.25
Total	Sfr 5,074.00

Thus, as you can see, the average charge is about 1.5% for securities transactions on the Zurich exchange.

As on many other exchanges, the size of the trading lot varies depending on the price of the security. For bonds, the normal trading lot is par value of Sfr 5,000. For stocks it is as shown in Table 1.

The increments by which a stock's quotation may move also depend on the price of the security (Table 2).

There are a variety of different orders available on the Zurich exchange:

at best: Market order. Most orders are given with this instruction.

limit price: An instruction not to buy above or sell below a stipulated maximum or minimum.

approximate limit order (circa order): A price will be given with a boundary within which it can vary. For example, an order to sell at Sfr 500 circa 5 means that a sale between 495 and 505 Swiss francs is acceptable.

stop-loss order: Same as in this country. Sell if the price reaches a specified low point or buy if it breaks through a specified high point.

ordre lié: A combination of two orders which must be executed in sequence, usually the sale of one security followed by the purchase of another.

Table 1

STOCK PRICE IN SWISS FRANCS	TRADING LOT SIZE
0–5	1,000
5–10	500
10–50	100
50–200	50
200–500	25
500–2000	10
2,000–5000	5
5,000–10,000	2
Over 10,000	1

Table 2

SECURITY PRICE, IN SWISS FRANCS	INCREMENT BY WHICH IT CAN MOVE, IN SWISS FRANCS
Less than 10	.05
10–100	.25
100–300	.50
300–2,000	1.00
Over 2,000	5.00

SOME EXAMPLE STOCKS

Despite the fame of the Swiss financial market, Switzerland itself is a small country, and for that reason nonresidents are best advised to invest only in large international Swiss companies or the largest domestic companies.

The annual report of the Zurich Stock Exchange lists the following companies as the twenty largest on the exchange in terms of the market value of their shares (Table 3). For an additional perspective, the percentage of the total Zurich stock market that these securities represent is also shown. The prices given are for bearer-form shares (Table 3).

Table 3

THE TWENTY LARGEST STOCK ISSUES ON THE ZURICH STOCK EXCHANGE

COMPANY	MARKET VALUE OF SHARES IN MILLIONS OF SWISS FRANCS	% OF TOTAL SWISS SHARES IN ZURICH	SHARE PRICE ON JAN. 1, 1983, IN SWISS FRANCS*
1. Schweizerische Bankgesellshaft (Union Bank of Switzerland)	9,866.0	12.8	3,280
2. Nestlé	8,137.9	10.5	3,850
3. Schweizerischer Bankverein (Swiss Bank Corporation)	6,794.5	8.8	322
4. Schweizerische Kreditanstalt (Credit Swiss)	6,192.5	8.0	1,905
5. Ciba-Geigy	4,975.3	6.4	1,610
6. (Zurich) Versicherungen (Insurance)	3,054.1	4.0	16,850
7. Sandoz	2,354.7	3.0	3,025
8. (Winterthur) Versicherungen (Insurance)	2,034.5	2.6	3,025
9. Schweiz. Rückversicherungsges. (Reinsurance)	1,901.9	2.5	7,125
10. Elektrowatt	1,683.0	2.2	2,550
11. Oerlikon-Bührle	1,572.6	2.0	1,200
12. Interfood	1,510.0	1.9	5,400
13. Schweiz. Volksbank	1,166.0	1.5	1,295
14. BBC Brown Boveri	981.9	1.3	955
15. Bank Leu	979.8	1.3	4,025
16. Swissair	951.7	1.2	725
17. Holderbank	912.6	1.2	670
18. Pargesa	868.0	1.1	1,240
19. Alusuisse	816.9	1.1	1,240
20. Banca della Svizzera Italiana	750.6	1.0	3,025

*At the time, the Swiss franc was valued at about U.S. $.50.

Combined, the twenty stocks listed in Table 3 constitute almost 75% of the market value of all the shares listed in Zurich. The nonresident investor should be aware that the Swiss market is thus narrowly based and invest accordingly (i.e., never, except on expert advice, invest in any but the largest companies).

When checking Swiss stock quotations be sure that you have the price for bearer-form (and not registered-form) shares. For instance, the above list shows the bearer-form share price for the Union Bank of

Switzerland as Sfr 3,280. On the same day the price of registered shares was only Sfr 585. As mentioned before, the par value of the two forms of stock is usually different. In this case, par value of the bearer shares is Sfr 500 while par value of the registered shares is only Sfr 100; thus the dividend (which is declared as a percent of par value) for bearer shares is five times greater than that of registered shares. Also, because of the high price of the shares, the size of the standard trading lot is only five shares.

ZURICH TRADING FLOOR OPERATIONS

Banks in Switzerland perform all brokerage and investment banking services in addition to their other banking activities. Only banks are members of stock exchanges, and the twenty-four banks that are members of the Zurich exchange are called "ring banks" because their membership entitles them to a seat around each of the three trading rings.

Official trading hours are 10:00 A.M. to 1:00 P.M. Monday through Friday. However, the actual closing time depends on the volume of business. The pre-bourse trading is conducted from 9:30 to 10:00 A.M. This session is primarily for stocks which are not officially listed or for new bonds which must trade pre-bourse until their certificates are printed and distributed (what we would call "when issued" in this country).

There are two kinds of settlement, cash and time. Cash (or spot) settlement is within five business days. Time (or forward) transactions require payment and delivery on the last day of the month, either of the current month or of one of the next two following months.

While there are no options on the Zurich exchange there is a contract that functions somewhat like an option. It is called a "premium contract" (or "option contract"). It is a type of time contract with a special twist: it allows traders to "get out" of a contract four days before settlement (i.e., four days before the last day of the month). There is, of course, an extra charge (called a "premium") for this kind of contract. If the traders elect to cancel the contract they pay the premium only. If they go through with the purchase they must also pay the premium in addition to buying the security. There are also premium contracts for the selling of securities, but they are very rare.

It is estimated that on the Zurich exchange almost all bond transactions and 70% of stock transactions are traded on a cash basis. Of the forward contracts only a small number are premium contracts.

As on the London exchange, settlement can be extended to the following settlement day, a month later, by a carry-over transaction (also called "contango" or "backwardation"). It is a bit complicated because the bank must purchase the security for the investor on the original settlement day and immediately "borrow" it from him or her. The investor does not have to put the cash forward until taking possession of the security one month later. Short selling is also permitted under these same guidelines with covering required at the end of the month (unless extended).

HOW BIDDING TAKES PLACE

At the opening of official trading the exchange clerk calls out the name of each security, one at a time, thereby opening the trading in each issue individually. The order of the securities is alphabetic but by industry. When a security's name is called all accumulated trading takes place. After trading in one security is finished the clerk goes on to the next stock. Traders may go back to a former security so long as they are still in the same industry group. Once all the securities within a single industry group are finished, traders may not go back. Stocks are read through twice a day in this manner and bonds once.

As everyone knows, trading on a stock exchange can get heated and quite noisy. In a description of trading published by Credit Suisse it is described as follows: "Securities are not traded on a stock exchange in a conversational tone of a tea-party. . . ." In French, the "system" is called *à la criée,* that is, by open outcry. Such a method is more than simple expediency, it is also the law. Security quotations must be called out by the exchange traders loud enough for all other traders in the ring to hear clearly. When the bedlam makes that impossible, the outcries are to be supplemented with hand signals.

On all stock exchanges, order is made from seeming chaos, in part, by the conventions of bidding and trading. While practices vary from country to country, there are basically two formats to trading: one where all securities are traded continuously and simultaneously (orders are brought in person or electronically to a specific area and executed at once), and one where each security is traded, in turn, during a kind of roll call. The second system is not used in the United States. In fact, it is quite inappropriate for large markets such as the New York and Tokyo exchanges. (It is interesting to note, however, that the roll-call method was used in the early days of the New York exchange, when it met in the Tontine Coffee House.)

The Zurich exchange uses the roll-call system. Since this procedure is unfamiliar to U.S. investors a brief example is given below. In the bidding, two German words are used: *Geld* (which literally means money) and *Brief* (which literally means paper, that is, certificates).

Exchange clerk: "Swiss XYZ!" This is shouted loud enough for all traders around the ring to hear. The trading in Swiss XYZ Company has thereby been opened. No volume is given so a standard-sized trading lot is assumed.

Bank A trader: "25 Geld!" "Geld" (money) means he wants to buy Swiss XYZ for Sfr 625. Since all the ring traders know the approximate range within which the security has been trading, the first number is usually left off.

Bank B trader: "35 Brief!" "Brief" (paper) means the trader has the certificates and wants to sell. Again, the "6" is left off, so his asking price is Sfr 635.

Bank A trader: "30 Geld!" Trader A has increased his bid by Sfr 5.

Bank B trader: "30 bezahlt" ("Bezahlt" means "paid.") Trader B has accepted trader A's offer and with this statement obligates them both to the transaction.

Exchange clerk: "30 bezahlt!" As a matter of form the exchange clerk repeats the transaction price while recording it to make sure there has been no misunderstanding.

If there are no further offers to buy or sell Swiss XYZ then the exchange clerk announces the next security which is thereby opened for trading.

Two words which are avoided on the exchange because of the ease with which they could be mistaken for one another are the German words for buy and sell, *kaufen* and *verkaufen.* Any transaction in which those two words were confused would probably be costly for the traders. For that reason, the French words for buy and sell, *acheter* and *vendre,* are used.

There is an interesting aspect of trading on the Zurich floor that comes quite close to fulfilling the "casino without music" description sometimes used for stock exchanges. It is a special device called an "electronic allotting system." In the event that two or more traders accept another trader's bid or asked price and there is not enough stock or demand to accommodate everyone, then the electronic trading system determines which trader gets the transaction. For instance, one trader might bid a certain price for 100 shares, and three traders accept the bid simultaneously. The important point is not the imbalance of supply and demand, but the fact that three traders accepted the bid (i.e., wanted to sell) *at the same price.* When this happens, the bank making the initial offering pushes a button which turns on the electronic allotting system. Then the traders who wish to be considered for the placements push a button indicating same. Their names immediately appear on the cluster of four TV monitors hanging in the middle of the ring. (If you refer to the picture at the beginning of this chapter you will see the monitors hanging from the ceiling, looking something like a square chandelier.) A computer then randomly selects which trader may sell the stock to the bidder, and his name begins to flash on the screen. Afterwards, trading resumes for the other traders seeking to sell the stock but the price will doubtless have fallen.

TRANSFER OF BEARER-FORM SECURITIES

Just because Swiss shares bought by nonresidents must be in bearer form does not mean that you should have the share certificates shipped to you. Even investors in Switzerland rarely take delivery of bearer-form shares. You can, of course, insist on delivery, but there will be extra charges and delays, and there will be the same charges and delays when you sell.

What usually happens is that the certificates are held in a Swiss central depository (SEGA). These certificates serve as a collateral basis for the electronic transfer of ownership which is accomplished simply by debits and credits to the proper institutional bank accounts. For example, investor A calls in a buy order to Bank A. Bank A goes through the purchase process on the exchange and then instructs the Swiss National Bank to debit (add to) its account the amount of the securities purchased. Bank B, whose customer sold the security, will meanwhile instruct the Swiss National Bank to credit its account. Meanwhile, the actual share certificates remain deposited in the various accounts of the ring banks in the central depositary. The result is simply the transfer of ownership in the banks' accounts. The customer, of course, will receive confirmation notices.

This process is diagrammed in Figure 3. A number of steps have been left out, but it is a fair representation of the overall process.

It should be pointed out that this is a simpler process than that necessary for the transfer of registered securities (even when a depositary is used) because additional transfers do not have to take place on the books of the companies.

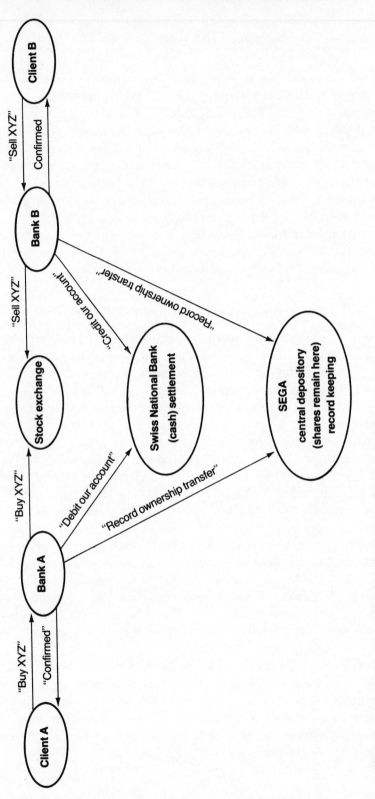

Figure 3. Transfer of ownership for bearer-form securities.

ABOUT BONDS: GOVERNMENT AND CORPORATE

As stated before, the bond market in Switzerland is large. Both domestic and foreign borrowing needs are usually accommodated. It is estimated that about 10% of the GNP is represented by share and bond issues. Bonds are in bearer form, in minimum maturities of eight years, and in denominations of Sfr 1,000 and up. Interest is paid once a year.

Government bonds are called "confederation bonds" and issued by the Swiss National Bank. They are often callable; they may amortize the capital, and maturities are up to fifteen years. In 1980, a tender system was initiated; small investors can submit noncompetitive bids (that is, without a price) and get the same purchase price as institutions. Noncompetitive bids may not exceed Sfr 20,000.

Bonds issued by the cantons are not guaranteed by the confederation government although, with the Swiss record for fiscal responsibility, they can be considered quite safe. They are issued under terms similar to government bonds and yield approximately .25% higher interest.

A variety of banking and financial institution bonds are available with yields about half a percent higher than cantonal bonds. Denominations are Sfr 1,000, 5,000, and 10,000. The *Pfandbrief* are bonds issued by mortgage bond houses and secured by mortgages.

Corporations issue three types of bonds—straight bonds, convertible bonds, and option bonds. Maturities are up to fifteen years, and they are denominated as low as Sfr 1,000. The yields are 1.5 to 2% greater than government (confederation) bonds.

WHAT ABOUT NUMBERED SWISS BANK ACCOUNTS?

First of all, bank secrecy is not the sole domain of Switzerland. You may open, for instance, a numbered bank account in The Netherlands. The fame of such accounts stems partly from the survival of Switzerland during World War II and the assumption that in future world conflicts Switzerland will again be safe. That may be true. It is claimed by some that Swiss banks have contingency plans whereby, in case of nuclear attack, they would transfer all accounts outside the country in a matter of hours. (However, it is not clear what this would mean if it were solely a transfer of records.) It is claimed by others that Switzerland is safe because Russian leaders have secret bank accounts there. More likely, Switzerland would be safe because it would be useful. It contains one of the world's most efficient financial and banking systems while occupying a relatively small amount of land containing a relatively small population. Participants in a future war could also be relatively sure that Switzerland would maintain its neutrality unless its own borders were violated.

But to go back to numbered accounts. Access to bank accounts by number is common in many countries. In Switzerland, however, only a few bank personnel will know the names associated with those numbers. Violation of Swiss banking secrecy is punishable by fine and imprisonment. The banks will not reveal even the existence of a numbered account, much less more detailed information, either to Swiss or foreign authorities, unless reasonable suspicion is demonstrated of criminal offense. Tax evasion, by the way, is only a civil offense; tax fraud, however, is criminal.

One of the thorniest problems for U.S. authorities has been the use of numbered Swiss accounts to cover insider security transactions. An individual privy to insider information concerning any company could buy or sell securities of that company through a Swiss bank without those transactions ever being traced back to him or her. This is because trading on insider information is not illegal in Switzerland.

Times, however, are changing. The Swiss Ministry of Justice is currently consulting with cantonal governments and major banks in preparation for the drafting of a bill that would make insider trading illegal. The earliest such a bill could pass Parliament would be late 1984 for enactment in 1985. But in the meantime, banks in Switzerland have begun to require a disclosure agreement with their clients (U.S. or otherwise) who trade on U.S. exchanges. It states that bank secrecy will be forfeited for any individual against whom insider trading has been established.

All manner of services are available through a Swiss bank account. You may have portfolio guidance for your security transactions should you meet the minimum investment requirement. Both time and foreign currency deposits are available, and shares in mutual funds (managed by your bank or other banks) are offered. You may set up trust funds; and safe deposit boxes are available.

Minimums vary greatly for different types of accounts, and they, of course, sometimes vary from year to year. If you are interested in a Swiss account, write to several banks (see "Useful Addresses") for specific information on the services they offer. Unlike financial institutions in some other countries, Swiss banks are prompt in answering foreign inquiries. Most will send a variety of brochures and booklets in English describing the accounts and, very important, the minimum balances required. You can correspond in English, and you can make deposits by check, cashier's check, money order, or whatever. You can denominate your deposits in U.S. dollars and leave the conversion to them.

In order to open your account you will have to have a signature verification by a U.S. bank or notary public. You may also, if you wish, grant power of attorney for the account. Since power of attorney in Switzerland continues after the death of the person holding the account, you should probably give power of attorney to an heir or to the executor of your will. The individual with power of attorney after your death controls the account. In case of an inactive account, bank officials will eventually inquire as to the whereabouts of the account holder.

MUTUAL FUNDS

As one would expect, there are many mutual funds in Switzerland with almost every investment goal imaginable. The largest fund manager is *Intrag,* a subsidiary of the Union Bank of Switzerland (Schweizerische Bankgesellschaft). Currently, Intrag manages thirteen stock funds, five bond funds, and three real estate funds. Among stock funds you may select from those that invest separately in Swiss, Canadian, Spanish, French, German, Italian, Japanese, and South African stocks. Separate bond funds concentrate on fixed-income instruments worldwide, in Europe, or in the Pacific, or on companies that specialize in raw materials and energy.

One may purchase mutual fund shares through a bank. To get the best possible price you may want to request purchase only of funds listed on the stock exchange. Those funds tend to have a smaller spread between the bid and ask price.

As is the case with most foreign mutual funds, Swiss mutual funds are not registered in this country with the SEC. This means that you must purchase shares directly from Switzerland. Do not bother writing the U.S. branches of Swiss banks; they cannot sell you the shares (see "Useful Addresses").

WITHHOLDING TAX

Through a tax treaty with the United States, withholding for U.S. citizens on Swiss securities is reduced to 5% on interest and 15% on dividends. As with most foreign withholding, however, one must apply for the reduction; otherwise it is 35%. Capital gains from Swiss securities is taxable only in the United States.

GOLD

There are no restrictions on purchases or sales. There is a 5.6% sales tax if you take physical possession of the gold, but not if you simply hold it in your account. Most purchases are cash transactions. Bars and gold coins of most countries are available.

SWISS INVESTMENT JARGON

Aktien: Shares

Anlagefonds: Bond and share funds, both open-ended and closed-ended.

Inhaberaktie: Bearer shares

Namenaktie: Registered shares

Obligationenfonds: Bond mutual funds

Partizipationsschein: Participation certificates

Pfandbrief: Mortgage bonds

USEFUL ADDRESSES

THE ZURICH STOCK EXCHANGE

Bleicherwege 5
CH-8021 Zurich

BANKS

Union Bank of Switzerland
(Schweizerlische Bankgesellschaft)
Bahnhofstrasse 45
CH-8021 Zurich

Swiss Bank Corporation
(Schweizerische Bankverein)
Paradeplatz 8
CH-8021 Zurich

Credit Swiss
(Schweizerische Kreditanstalt)
Paradeplatz 8
8021 Zurich

11

THE SYDNEY STOCK EXCHANGE

Courtesy of the Sydney Stock Exchange

THE STOCK EXCHANGE DOWN UNDER

In terms of market capitalization, the Sydney Stock Exchange is the seventh largest stock exchange in the world and the largest in the southern hemisphere. Australia, referred to as the land "down under," has six stock exchanges, one in each of the state capitals: Sydney, Melbourne, Adelaide (whose exchange has recently been rebuilt after having been destroyed by fire in September of 1982), Brisbane, Perth, and Hobart. Combined, they form the Australian Associated Stock Exchanges.

The Sydney Exchange, located in the state of New South Wales, is the largest, partly because of its volume in options. The Sydney and Melbourne exchanges together conduct about 95% of the total stock trading in Australia. An interesting new development is the initiation of talks to explore their possible merger. In such a case, however, both trading floors would be maintained. The two exchanges currently have extensive quotation and computer links and share services such as portfolio analysis and daily valuation services.

The twenty-five to thirty years following World War II saw the maturing of Australian industry and commerce. Australia is enormously rich in natural resources. It has the world's largest reserves of aluminum oxide, titanium oxide, and zirconium silicate. It has the second-largest reserves of uranium and lead, and the third-largest reserves of silver, zinc, and iron ore. Not surprisingly, Australia accounts for 20% of the world trade in iron ore, 23% of the world trade in aluminum, and 25% of coal. It is also a major exporter of beef, wheat, wool, dairy products, and sugar. Its major trading partners are Japan and the United States.

The Sydney Stock Exchange opened in 1871, charging a membership fee of 5 guineas. For about fifty years prior to that, however, there had been trading of Australian colony stock. Then, as now, trading was dominated by mining shares. The Melbourne exchange predated Sydney by twelve years. Both were originally profit-making corporations. Sydney was not incorporated as a limited liability nonprofit company until 1964, Melbourne in 1970. Sydney, as of December 1983, has 252 member brokers.

Australia is one of the few uncrowded places left in the world. Its current population of 15 million is small in comparison to the island continent's 4.8 million square miles. Only about 10,000 of the native

---

THE SYDNEY STOCK MARKET AT A GLANCE

Capitalization:
Market value of shares in U.S.$* .... $51.4 billion
Percent of total share capitalization represented by ten largest
    companies. 26%
Volume:
Average daily volume in U.S.$* .... $19.5 million
Listings:
Listed corporations (including foreign)† 1,000
Average price per share (industrial) .... A$2.28
Average price per share (mining and oil). . . . . A$0.66
Rank in the world
Capitalization 7th

*Exchange rate as of July 1, 1983: $1 = A$1.167.
†Deleting foreign stocks and Australian issues for which Sydney is not the home exchange, the
    total is 396.
Source: The Sydney Stock Exchange Ltd., Annual Report, 1984.

Australians (aborigines) remain; the rest of the population is a homogeneous blend of various European ancestries.

As far as foreign investment in Australia goes, the government encourages it, but also keeps a close eye on domestic markets. In the past it has been protective of its money markets and, like Japan, has restricted nonresidents from purchasing debt instruments or timed deposits of less than six months' maturity. However, this ban was lifted in 1978, and in 1983 further internationalization began with negotiations to establish an operational branch (for settlements, not for trading) of the London stock exchange in Sydney.

Currently, the Sydney exchange is the home exchange for 413 securities, with Melbourne carrying 236. However, listing on any exchange in Australia guarantees availability on all others. Total volume for the last fiscal year was 3,267 million shares, up from 2,144 million shares the year before. Most of the turnover was in mining shares, and the metals and minerals price index was up 59% from the previous year. Bonds accounted for 45.4% of the total volume.

Although all industry types are listed on the Sydney exchange, it is the resource and mining stocks which have stirred the most interest on the part of foreign investors. One-third of all shares on the Sydney exchange are mineral and oil issues. These shares are also among the most volatile. If an investor acquires energy issues at the beginning of an economic upturn their performance may be truly spectacular. Capital gains in excess of 100% are common, particularly with the more speculative issues. However, the investor is also cautioned not to hang on to falling stocks, because the downside risk of mining stocks can be equal to their upside potential if sentiment changes or commodity prices begin to fall. Should your holdings in these issues decline by 20%, then it is best to cut your losses and wait for a better time to invest.

The individual exchanges actively promote education in finance, economy, and investment training, both in the schools and among the general public. One particularly appealing event is The Share Game, an evaluated investment contest for high school seniors. The 1983 prize was won by members of a syndicate from The Armidale High School in New South Wales. They called themselves the "Tricky Sam Syndicate."

AUSTRALIAN CURRENCY AND EXCHANGE RATE WITH THE U.S. DOLLAR

The currency is the Australian dollar, which contains 100 cents. In writing you will see variously "A$10.00" (ten dollars Australian), "Aus

$10.00," and other variations. The Australian dollar floats freely with respect to all other currencies. The Reserve Bank has the right to intervene in currency markets only to smooth over extreme fluctuations in exchange rates. Exchange controls have been lifted both for nonresident investors and for Australians who wish to invest overseas. Table 1 shows the midpoint exchange rate for each year as calculated by the International Monetary Fund.

Table 1

**MIDPOINT EXCHANGE RATE OF
THE AUSTRALIAN DOLLAR**

YEAR	AUSTRALIAN DOLLARS PER U.S. DOLLAR
1975	A$0.79
1976	A$0.92
1977	A$0.88
1978	A$0.87
1979	A$0.90
1980	A$0.85
1981	A$0.88
1982	A$0.93
1983	A$0.86

Interest rates are also the result of marketplace supply and demand. The Reserve Bank sets a discount rate at which it agrees to rediscount money market instruments, but a more important factor in establishing interest rates is probably the rates at which treasury notes are sold weekly.

SECURITIES TRADED ON THE SYDNEY STOCK EXCHANGE

stocks (both common and preferred): Almost all publicly traded companies list their stock on an exchange. Dividends are paid semiannually in most instances. As in the United States, preferred shares have priority with respect to dividends, and may be cumulative, participating, and convertible.

rights: As in most European countries, Australian companies usually make additional issues of stock available first to present shareholders in the form of rights. One right is usually issued per each share held, and it normally takes four or five rights to purchase one share of stock. Rights trade for about a month.

options: The Sydney exchange trades stock options. Expirations are up to nine months, and both puts and calls are available. There are plans to introduce an option on the All Ordinaries index (see p. 161).

bonds: Both government and corporate bonds are listed. Small transactions are usually conducted on the exchange. Denominations are as low as A$100. Interest is paid semiannually.

investment companies: Companies resembling closed-end investment companies are listed on the stock exchange. They are called closed-end mutual funds.

Ordinarily, the price of Australian securities seems low to the U.S. investor; however, the trading lots depend on the price of the security so that lower-priced issues are not as cheap as they at first seem (if you are purchasing round lots). Odd lots are available but your U.S. broker may not allow it.

According to the Sydney exchange, the average share price is currently A$1.84 per share, down from A$2.03 last year. In mining and oil the average is A$.64, down from A$.71. Total turnover in 1983 (fiscal) was more than 6 billion dollars Australian. Liquidity is generally good, at least for the large national companies. Shares are popular financial instruments in Australia and constitute a major part of the nation's financial market.

As with many other foreign companies you may have difficulty getting financial reports, or they will arrive after some delay. If you hold ADRs in an unsponsored account you should request financial reports from the depositary bank. Most companies issue annual reports four months after the end of the fiscal year, June 30. The fiscal year for banks, however, ends September 30, and some major companies use different dates, such as Broken Hill Proprietary, which uses May 31. Semiannual reports are also required, and usually a preliminary report to the annual report. The preliminary reports are made available to the press and public through the stock exchange.

A separate futures market was established in Sydney in 1978. Contracts are available for gold, U.S. and Japanese currencies, and Australian financial instruments. Futures on the All Ordinaries index were recently introduced. Expiration dates available are anywhere from one to eighteen months.

MAJOR STOCK INDEXES

New indexes, collectively called the Australian Stock Exchange Share Price Indexes, were created in 1980. The most widely quoted is the ASE All Ordinaries Index, found in most newspapers (Figure 1). "Ordinaries," short for ordinary shares, is the Australian term for common stock.

The All Ordinaries Index is calculated from a 1980 base of 500. It includes the trading of both the Sydney and Melbourne exchanges and some data from other exchanges. About 90% of Australian equity trading is represented.

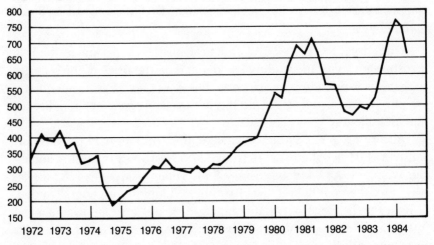

Figure 1. Australian Stock Exchange's All Ordinaries Index (quarterly closing prices).   Source: *Sydney Stock Exchange*

AUSTRALIAN STOCK TRADED IN THE UNITED STATES

There are no Australian securities listed on the New York or American Stock Exchanges. However, the number of ADRs available over the counter, about seventy-five, is second only to the number of Japanese ADRs. There is thus a large number of Australian shares from which investors in the United States can choose.

It is common, unfortunately, for issues of Australian ADRs to appear and disappear with some frequency. It is therefore best to stick to the companies that have the largest capitalization or those that are the most frequently traded. At most risk are the ADRs for shares of small resource and mining companies. (See Tables 3 and 4 and their descriptive text, below.)

WHEN YOUR BROKER TRADES IN SYDNEY

There are four Australian brokers with branch offices in this country: A.C. Goode & Co., Potter Partners, J.B. Were & Sons, Cont., and Ord Minnett. As a rule, however, they require a large minimum for individual accounts. A full-service U.S. broker would probably be more convenient. Banks also purchase and hold securities for individual investors.

There are a number of general limitations on securities purchased by nonresidents. For instance, foreign ownership is limited to 10% of banks, 25% of uranium mines, 20% of broadcasting, and 15% of television stations. Also, permission of the Foreign Investment Review Board is required for companies with as much as 15% under the control of a single foreign investor, or with a *total* nonresident ownership amounting to 40%.

The exchanges themselves do not restrict nonresident trading, and income and capital may be freely repatriated. Despite usually active turnover, the shares of smaller companies can sometimes be difficult to sell in a down market.

Standard transaction sizes (round lots) are determined by the price of the shares (Table 2).

Table 2

PRICE RANGE	ROUND LOT SIZE, SHARES
A$0.01–0.25	2,000
A$0.26–0.50	1,000
A$0.51–1.00	500
A$1.01–10.00	100
A$10.01 or over	50

Quotations may move in increments set according to the price of the security—stocks up to A$5 by 1 Australian cent, up to A$10 by 2 Australian cents, etc.

COMMISSIONS AND FEES

In April 1984 fixed commissions were completely abolished. Formerly, commissions ranged between 1% and 2 ½%, depending on the size of the transaction. It is expected that negotiated commissions will not be far below this amount.

The various states apply their own stamp tax. The state of New South Wales, in which Sydney is located, charges .3% of the total transaction, both to the buyer and the seller. Stock dividends granted by Australian companies are called bonus shares. Thus, the qualifier "XB" in Australian quotes means the security that day is trading ex-bonus shares.

The stocks shown in Table 3 represent 25.5% of the total capitalization of the Sydney Stock Exchange. All are available as ADRs from

Morgan Guaranty Trust and a few other banks.

All the stocks listed in Table 4 are available in the United States as ADRs except those marked with an asterisk.

Table 3

THE TEN LARGEST STOCK ISSUES ON THE SYDNEY STOCK EXCHANGE

COMPANY	% OF TOTAL MARKET CAPITALIZATION
1. The Broken Hill Proprietary Company Limited	6.5
2. CRA Limited	3.7
3. Westpac Banking Corporation	2.4
4. M.I.M. Holdings Limited	2.1
5. Carlton and United Breweries Limited	1.9
6. Australia and New Zealand Banking Group Limited	1.9
7. CSR Limited	1.9
8. Santos Limited	1.8
9. National Commercial Banking Corporation of Australia Limited	1.7
10. Western Mining Corporation Holdings Limited	1.6

Source: Sydney Stock Exchange, data as of June 30, 1984. Excludes companies with greater than 33% of their capital held by another public company.

Table 4

THE TWENTY MOST ACTIVE STOCKS ON THE SYDNEY STOCK EXCHANGE

COMPANY	TURNOVER VALUE IN MILLIONS OF AUSTRALIAN DOLLARS
1. The Broken Hill Proprietary Company Limited	626.8
2. Carlton and United Breweries Limited*	215.7
3. CRA Limited	186.3
4. CSR Limited	162.7
5. Santos Limited	149.2
6. Australia and New Zealand Banking Group Limited	135.9
7. Western Mining Corporation Holdings Limited	127.6
8. Westpac Banking Corporation	114.1
9. M.I.M. Holdings Limited	100.5
10. Peko-Wallsend Limited	91.2
11. Bougainville Copper Limited	74.8
12. Elders IXL Limited	72.1
13. Hookers Corporation Limited	64.2
14. The Adelaide Steamship Co. Limited*	63.5
15. Bridge Oil Limited	62.0
16. Thomas Nationwide Transport Limited	58.2
17. Woodside Petroleum	53.7
18. National Commercial Banking Corporation of Australia Limited	53.4
19. Pioneer Concrete Services Limited	51.2
20. Umal Consolidated Limited*	47.2

*Not available as ADRs in the United States.
Source: Sydney Stock Exchange; data for the year ended June 30, 1984.

SYDNEY TRADING FLOOR OPERATIONS

The Sydney exchange makes use of the trading post system; specialists, however, are not used (the only exception being the odd lot specialists). Membership is open to brokers only, who conduct transactions among themselves at the post assigned to the particular stock they are trading. Brokers (called "sharebrokers") may not transact business for their own accounts, only for those of their clients.

When the exchange opens in the morning the clerks write the opening prices of the shares they trade on their respective posts in chalk. (These clerks, appropriately enough, are called "chalkies.") After the initial transaction the price of each security is erased and brokers conduct the rest of the day's trading by means of a two-way auction system similar to our own. There are two sessions daily, 10:00 A.M. to 12:00 noon, and 2:00 P.M. to 3:00 P.M., Monday through Friday. Trading activity is constantly reported on a ticker, and there are no limits set by the exchange for overall price movement. Some trading after hours, called "off" trading, is permitted.

INVESTMENT COMPANIES AND MUTUAL FUNDS

Investment funds, such as the Australian Foundation Investment Company, are listed on the stock exchange. Major commercial banks in Australia administer these types of funds. One of the best is ANZ Managed Investments Ltd., managed by the Australia, New Zealand Banking Group. A number of different funds are available and the bank also offers managed portfolios. Another bank-managed group of funds is the Wales Financial Services Ltd., managed by the Westpac Banking Corporation. Write to both of them for prospectuses (see "Useful Addresses").

ABOUT BONDS: GOVERNMENT AND CORPORATE

Government bonds are regulated by the Australian Loan Council, whose members include the Prime Minister and the premiers of each state. Commonwealth government bonds are issued on a tender basis, as in the United States. They may have maturities that range up to thirty-five years, although between two and ten years are the most common. These bonds are usually in registered form, and the secondary market is active. The minimum for an initial purchase is A$5,000, although they are in denominations of A$1,000. More than a hundred issues are currently available, and most smaller transactions, those for individual investors, are handled by an exchange. Interest is paid semi-annually. Australia's ten Eurobonds are listed on the London and Luxembourg exchanges. Trading is not very active.

There are three types of corporate bonds. *Debentures* are secured (unlike those in this country) with the specific or general assets of a company. Bondholders' interests are watched over by a trustee company. Maturities are from seven to thirty-five years, and the secondary market is moderately active. Yields are from ¾% to 2% higher than government bonds. They are seldom amortized; capital is paid in full at maturity, and interest is paid semiannually. *Unsecured notes* are issued with up to fifteen years' maturity and traded on the stock exchange. *Convertible notes* are like convertible bonds in the United States.

The smallest denomination of Australian corporate bonds is A$100. The commission is 1% up to the first A$10,000, and .5% above that.

TREASURY BILLS

Treasury bills are called "treasury notes" and issued weekly by the Reserve Bank of Australia. They are sold at discount as in the United States. The secondary market is quite active, and notes can also be redeemed at the Reserve Bank. The maturities are thirteen and twenty-six weeks, but almost any maturity is available on the secondary market.

In order to buy treasury notes you must register with the Reserve Bank; but that is only a formality which your broker can handle for you. The minimum denomination is usually A$10,000. They are in registered form.

BANKS

Nonresidents may open any type of bank account with Australian commercial banks, often called trading banks. Some have offices in this country, but generally these handle only corporate business.

Money and banking systems are regulated by the Reserve Bank of Australia, the lender of last resort to Australian companies. Banks and financial institutions are major holders of securities, and it is estimated they control about half of the securities in Australia.

WITHHOLDING TAX

The rules are simple: 15% on dividends, 10% on interest, and no withholding on capital gains.

AUSTRALIAN INVESTMENT JARGON

bonus shares: A stock dividend. The qualifier "XB" in the quotations means ex-bonus.

debentures: Secured bonds. See "About Bonds: Corporate and Government."

ordinary shares: Common stock.

pty: Abbreviation for "proprietary," which, in Australia, is equivalent to a corporation or company.

sharebrokers: stockbrokers.

SOURCES OF INFORMATION

As with all Pacific-area markets, *The Asian Wall Street Journal* and *The Asian Wall Street Journal Weekly* are excellent sources of information. Special reports on companies, business trends, earnings, politics, law, and extensive securities quotations make both papers extremely useful tools. There are also reports on government data, and major financial indicators.

An investment advisory letter published in the United States that specializes in Australian stock is the *Australian Newsletter.* It began publishing in 1981, and the subscription price is $150 for twelve monthly issues.

The various financial reports of Australian companies, mentioned earlier, are, of course, a source of information. However, there are some accounting differences, such as the occasional reevaluation of fixed assets and the occasional reporting of property without depreciation.

Any analytic reports you may receive from brokers will probably be very reliable and insightful. The Australians have over the years developed sophisticated methods of financial analysis and comprehensive financial models. Analysts are often trained by the Securities Institute of Australia, one of the best institutions of its kind.

The Australian Financial Review is a daily financial newspaper. Weeklies available include the *National Times* and the *Bulletin. Personal Investment* is a monthly magazine that incorporates the *Aus-*

tralian Stock Exchange Journal (see "Useful Addresses"). Among the books available for technical analysis are two from the Sydney Stock Exchange bookshop: *The ASE Index Chart Book,* and the *Computer Investor Services Pty. Chart Book.*

USEFUL ADDRESSES

THE SYDNEY STOCK EXCHANGE

20 Bond Street
Sydney, Australia

or: Box H224
Australia Square
NSW 20000

NEWSLETTER

The following is a United States–based newsletter that specializes in Australian stocks.

Australian Newsletter
P.O. Box 524
Mentor, Ohio 44060

INVESTMENT TRUSTS AND MUTUAL FUNDS

ANZ Managed Investments Ltd.
GPO 517AA
Melbourne, Australia

Westpac Banking Corporation
The Wales House
66 Pitt Street
Sydney, Australia

FINANCIAL PERIODICALS

Personal Investment
GPO Box 55A
Melbourne, Victoria 3001

Australian Financial Review
1500 Broadway
New York, NY 10036

National Times
Jones Street and Broadway
Sydney, Australia

Bulletin
P.O. Box 4088
Sydney, Australia

COMPLAINTS

Write to the exchange or to:

National Companies and
Securities Commission
GPO 5179AA
Melbourne 3001
Australia

12

THE PARIS STOCK EXCHANGE

Courtesy of the Paris Bourse

THE PARIS BOURSE

The Paris Stock Exchange (Paris Bourse) completely dominates securities trading in France. Although there are seven stock exchanges (the others are in Bordeaux, Lyon, Marseilles, Nancy, Nantes, and Toulouse) about 99% of all securities trading is conducted through Paris. Compared to other countries, the market in equities is sixth in the world: about the same size as Switzerland.

For a variety of reasons, the most important being favorable banking regulations, companies often prefer bank loans when seeking new capital, to issuing stocks or bonds. Thus, the equity market in France is small compared to the country's industrial base. It is also common for those companies that do list stocks to have relatively thin floats, which

---

THE PARIS STOCK MARKET AT A GLANCE

Capitalization:
Market value of domestic shares in U.S.$*.................. $38,223 million
Nominal value of bonds in U.S.$* .... $102.7 billion
Percent of total share capitalization represented by ten largest
    companies.. 25%
Volume:
Total 1983 volume in U.S.$*............................. $12,537.2 million
Listings:
Domestic equities (including French zone stocks)..................... 655
Domestic bonds 1,696
Foreign equities 278
Foreign bonds... 160

*Exchange rate as of Dec. 31, 1983: $1 = Ff 8.33.
Source: Paris Stock Exchange, *Annual Report,* figures for 1983.

---

can lead to erratic price movements. Nevertheless, there are over 2,500 securities listed on the Paris Stock Exchange, about a third of which are stocks. In volume, stocks and bonds are usually about equal. Liquidity is good although that, in part, is because of the removal of major companies from the marketplace through nationalization (thus creating fewer stock issues).

The stock market in France has been frequently misunderstood—even mistrusted—by the French themselves. Today it is a market hindered by outmoded regulations, and, even more troublesome, a market subject to powerful state controls. Unfortunately, the political objectives of such controls seldom include a stable marketplace.

There are, however, at least two positive signs for the future. The first is that after numerous studies—and numerous recommendations—new regulations are being introduced that will greatly enhance exchange efficiency (such as electronic transfer of ownership). Secondly, the stock market has proven more resilient to a socialist government than was previously expected. Even the nationalization of a large number of major companies has not been the kiss of death to the equity markets that was anticipated. (See "The Paris Stock Exchange Under Socialism.")

Nonresidents may open accounts with French banks (those that permit such accounts) or French brokers, and purchase or sell French securities (or foreign securities listed in Paris) through these accounts. Securities may be transferred out of the country through the foreign department of an authorized bank, although it is easier to have them held in France. Gold, if bought in France, is best held there, too; at various times its export is not permitted.

A CHECKERED HISTORY

As one might expect, securities trading in Paris has a long and colorful history. In 1141, Louis VII consolidated much of the trading activity of his day by establishing it in houses on a bridge that crossed the Seine. (Bridges were considered prime locations since they were bottlenecks for transportation.) Security trading was confined to houses on the "up-stream" side, and the downstream houses were occupied primarily by gold- and silversmiths. Unfortunately, close proximity did not make for amicable relations, and, frequently, one side would goad the authorities into expelling the other. In 1621, both sides lost when the bridge burned down.

Until the bridge was rebuilt, various places were designated for trading, but frequently it simply took place in the streets. This provoked many complaints from the populace and continual harassment from the local authorities. Lack of regulation encouraged many abuses. Money was lent by the hour, speculation was rampant. Shares in the famous Compagnie des Indes, which traded for 20,000 livres in 1719, traded for 5 livres a year later. Security transactions were depicted at the time as being conducted in "hovels" by "vagrants." However, before 1768 (when the bridge burned down again) a "respectable" center for some exchange trading had finally been established in the Palais du Justice.

During the revolution, securities trading continued intermittently at a number of locations. At one point, stock market activity was conducted in the apartments of Anne of Austria at the Palais du Louvre.

After the revolution, in 1797, trading reopened for some securities in a nationalized church (today, the Notre Dame de Victoria). Under Napoleon, securities trading was merged with the Tribunal de Commerce, and trading began in a newly constructed building in 1827. This was the first time that all exchange trading was effectively combined under one roof.

A STOCK MARKET UNDER SOCIALISM

It was feared, both in France and abroad, that when the Socialists came to power in the elections of 1981 the stock market would not only lapse into a serious decline but might even cease to function as a viable marketplace. As promised, the new government nationalized a number of important companies including, in 1982, thirty-seven banks. And, as if to add insult to injury, the presidents of all the nationalized banks were replaced by political appointees (hardly an encouragement to management).

During 1981, the leading stock price index fell about 33%; however, the predicted collapse of the market did not materialize. Some of the nationalized companies had been on the brink of failure anyway, and state-owned banks were already commonplace. The "big three" commercial banks (the Banque Nationale de Paris, the Credit Lyonnaise, and the Societé General) had been state-owned since the end of World War II.

By 1983, the stock price index had broken through its 1980 highs and continued on to set a new series of records. Such a positive development caught many people by surprise. How does one account for a thriving stock market under a Socialist government? This was a combination that was not supposed to work.

The answer lies in state regulation. First of all, the government deliberately set out to encourage investment. Capital gains tax was cut significantly; for some, the cuts amounted to more than 50%. The government was also more generous than expected in the reimbursements for the shares of nationalized companies such as Cie. Générale d'Electricité and Rhône-Poulenc S.A. The removal of such companies from the equities market had the double effect of freeing large chunks of investment capital and at the same time reducing the number of stocks available to investors. Fewer stocks and an increase in available funds are a combination almost guaranteed to stimulate a rise in security prices.

The reason for such solicitous treatment of investors was the need to attract money to industry. Jobs on a mass scale can only be provided by factories, and factories must have the capital to refurnish and modernize if they are to compete effectively in world markets. Although many major shareholders felt that their compensation was inadequate, the reimbursements went a long way toward quieting investors' fears about the safety of their capital. The clear implication was that if future nationalizations were to take place, shareholders would be reasonably compensated.

In another move, not aimed at pleasing investors but having a positive effect on the market anyway, new exchange controls were put into place to stop the flight of money to foreign investments. Under the new regulations, French citizens must pay premiums on foreign exchange that amount to as much as 30% above the commercial rate *if* the currency is to be used to purchase foreign securities. On the positive side, investors *receive* that premium if they sell foreign securities and repatriate the revenues. With those regulations, investors have few choices but to look for domestic investments.

There are some other interesting factors. The French are traditionally hoarders of gold. New legislation now requires that all purchases and sales be reported to the government. The loss of anonymity and the recent slump in the price of precious metals has caused many French investors to begin liquidating their holdings. The money generated from these sales, of course, has to go somewhere.

Real estate, also a traditionally popular investment for the French, is now subject to new Socialist-backed legislation that favors tenants. (For instance, evictions are now much more difficult.) This has begun to bring about the liquidation of real estate holdings, and, again, the money needs a place to go.

The unusual partnership of capitalism and socialism seems to be working well for the present. Some analysts even suggest now that a defeat of the Socialist Party would precipitate a disastrous *drop* (!) in the stock market. Whether or not that is true is difficult to anticipate. Certainly, stock markets can react very negatively to change.

It is clear that the key factor in the market's rise has been direct state intervention. (Historically, that seems to be the way of things in France.) While not all the regulations were put in place to cause stock prices to rise they nevertheless had that effect.

Now, one must consider the government's future course of action. In particular, what happens when the economy recovers and industry gets back on its feet? Will a Socialist government continue to treat investors so kindly when it no longer needs their money? What kind of adjustment will be necessary if the Socialists are voted out of office? (Controls, like Band-Aids, can be painful to remove.) When will market conditions be allowed to guide the course of the French marketplace? These and other questions are going to make the Paris exchange an interesting place to watch for the next few years.

FRENCH CURRENCY AND EXCHANGE RATE WITH THE U.S. DOLLAR

The currency is the French franc and centime. It appears in print as Ff 57.36 (fifty-seven francs, thirty-six). France is a member of the European Monetary System, and the Bank of France (Banque de France) will intervene to keep exchange rates within the margins established by the EMS.

The exchange rate with the U.S. dollar (shown in Figure 1) does not, of course, reflect the value of the franc with other currencies. However, as you can see from the effective exchange rate, the franc's dollar exchange rate has closely paralleled that of the average of other world currencies for the last five years.

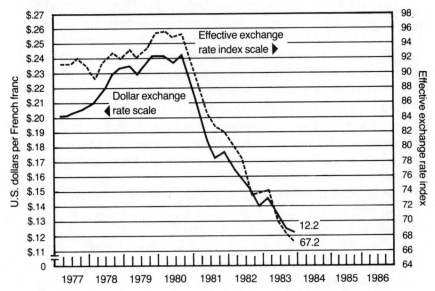

Figure 1. **Exchange rate of the French franc with the U.S. dollar and the effective exchange rate with other major currencies.**
Source: *Federal Reserve Bank of St. Louis*

SECURITIES TRADED ON THE PARIS STOCK EXCHANGE

Nonresidents may purchase or sell French securities freely on both the *cote officielle* (the "official" market) and the *hors-cote* (roughly equivalent to the over-the-counter market in the United States). The one restriction is that a nonresident is not allowed to own more than 20% of the capital of any listed French company without permission from the Ministry of the Economy.

stocks: Both bearer form and registered form are currently available.

bonds: Straight, floating-rate, and convertible bonds are available, usually in bearer form. Interest may be paid either annually or semiannually. Some may amortize the principal over all or a part of the life of the bond. Index-linked bonds, a special feature of the Paris exchange, link the interest or principal (often amortized) to gold, currencies, and even utility revenues.

options: Both puts *(option de vent)* and calls *(option d'achat)* are available in expirations up to nine months. (See *marché à options* under "Paris Trading Floor Operations.")

rights: These are common on the Paris exchange; all secondary offerings are made through the issuance of rights.

gold: Both coins and bars are traded on the exchange. Nonresidents must obtain authorization from the Banque de France before exporting either.

Exchange trading is restricted to stockbrokers *(agents de change)* who may not buy or sell for their own account, only for their clients. All brokers belong to the National Broker's Association (Compagnie des Agents de Change) whose regulations are legally enforceable by the Minister of the Economy. The executive branch of the Broker's Association, the Chambre Syndicale des Agents de Change, is responsible for publishing the daily official list which contains quotations and other market information. The Commission des Opérations de Bourse (COB), is the French equivalent of the SEC. It is the duty of the COB to assure that:

1. Listed companies publish all information that is legally required of them.
2. Corporate insiders do not trade securities on the basis of confidential information.
3. Complaints are properly processed.

THE LEADING STOCK INDEX

The Compagnie des Agents de Change (CAC) publishes the broadly based CAC General Index. Figure 2 shows this index calculated back to 1979 from a base of 100 on January 31, 1981. In addition to the CAC General Index there are indexes published on industrial stocks only, nine industry segments, and thirty-five industry subsectors.

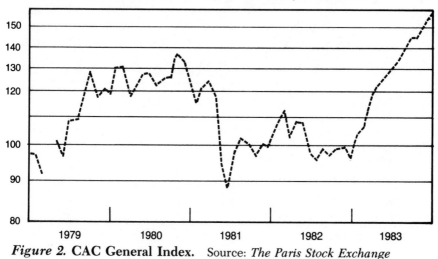

Figure 2. **CAC General Index.**   Source: *The Paris Stock Exchange*

BUYING FRENCH STOCKS IN THE UNITED STATES

No French securities are listed on the NYSE or the AMEX. The stocks listed below are traded in this country as ADRs. The depositary bank is shown in parentheses after the security name, and the ratio of shares to ADRs is also given. Note that, as in the case of the first security, L'Air Liquide, one ADR may only represent a fraction of an underlying share (e.g., one-fifth). This is the opposite of the ratio typical, for example, of Japanese or Australian shares.

L'Air Liquide (Morgan Guaranty Trust) 1:5

Compagnie des Machines Bull (Morgan Guaranty Trust) 1:1

Compagnie Generale Maritime French Lines (Chase Manhattan) 1:1

Fiat France S.A. (Citibank) 1:1

Peugeot-Citroen S.A. (Morgan Guaranty Trust) 1:5

Société Anonyme Francaise Feroda (Citibank) 1:5

Société Nationale Elf Aquitaine (Morgan Guaranty Trust and Citibank) 1:5

Source Perrier S.A. (Morgan Guaranty Trust and Citibank) 1:5

The ten stocks listed in Table 1 were the largest stock issues, with respect to total capitalization, listed on the Paris Stock Exchange as of the beginning of 1984. The market share of each is indicated. The total market value of these stocks was exactly 25% of the entire capitalization of the Paris exchange. This indicates relatively good market depth. By contrast, the ten largest stocks in Amsterdam totaled over 80% of the exchange capitalization. In New York the ten largest companies

Table 1

THE TEN LARGEST STOCK ISSUES ON THE PARIS STOCK EXCHANGE

COMPANY	MARKET VALUE OF STOCK IN MILLIONS OF FRANCS	% OF MARKET VALUE
1. Elf-Aquitaine	15,541	4.8
2. L'Air Liquide	11,932	3.7
3. L'Oréal	9,241	2.9
4. BSN-Gervais Danone	8,940	2.8
5. Moët-Hennessy	6,839	2.1
6. Pernod-Ricard	6,413	2.0
7. Cie. Gle des Eaux	6,183	1.9
8. Esso	6,138	1.9
9. Sanofi	4,982	1.5
10. Avions M. Dassault-Bréguet	4,447	1.4

Source: Paris Stock Exchange, *Annual Report,* 1983.

constitute about 18% of the total exchange capitalization.

The ten most active stock issues on the Paris Stock Exchange as of the beginning of 1984 were as follows:[1]

1. Générale des Eaux
2. BSN-Gervais Danone
3. L'Air Liquide
4. Elf-Aquitaine
5. Moët-Hennessy
6. Club Méditerranée
7. Pernod-Ricard
8. L'Oréal
9. Source Perrier
10. Michelin

Two well-known French stocks that do not appear among the ten largest or ten most traded issues are Bic (20th largest, 74th most active) and Peugeot (28th largest).

PARIS TRADING FLOOR OPERATIONS

Before describing trading on the Paris exchange it should be made clear that even the French are confused by their stock exchange. Its system of markets within markets has evolved seemingly in isolation from the other major exchanges of the world. However, long-overdue modernization now seems to be in progress, and much of the following explanation may soon be rendered obsolete. Currently, stock transfer is being computerized in order to do away with stock certificates. Continuous trading will begin for a few stocks in 1985, and beyond that, it is assumed that such trading will eventually be available for all exchange-listed securities, or at least those on the official market. Commissions are scheduled to change, and a number of other "back office" procedures will be completely revised.

Overall, the Paris Stock Exchange is divided into two "markets," the official market *(cote officielle)* and the unofficial market *(marché hors-cote).* The official market is further divided into:

marché au comptant: This is the cash or spot market. All officially listed securities except those listed on the "RM" market (see below) may be traded in any quantity (odd lots or round lots) for immediate payment and delivery.

"RM" market (marché a reglement mensuel): This is the newly revised (as of October 1983) forward market, formerly *marché à terme.* Over 250 stocks, both French and foreign, are listed here. Transaction prices (and quantities) are established as of the transaction date, but payment and delivery is on the settlement day, seven business days before the end of the month.

[1]Paris Stock Exchange, *Annual Report,* 1983.

Odd lots may be traded on the RM market but will be subject to an odd lot "differential" commission. Round lots will vary from ten, twenty-five, fifty, to 100 shares as decided by the Chambre Syndicale, depending on the per-share price. Immediate settlement (called "RI" settlement) is also available but subject to an early settlement commission.

Margin for securities purchased on the RM market must be put up by the investor according to the schedule in Table 2.

Table 2

MARGIN REQUIREMENTS OF RM MARKET

TYPE OF SECURITY THAT MAY BE USED FOR MARGIN	% OF PURCHASE IT MAY BE USED TO COVER
Cash or treasury bonds	20
French bonds or gold	25
Other securities	40

Margin requirements tend to change frequently, so the above requirements should be verified. Also, your broker may have more stringent margin requirements for foreign securities in general.

There is a "conditional" market *(marchés conditionnels)* on which most of the securities of the RM market can be purchased. There are two kinds of contracts available:

marché à primes: In English, these may be referred to simply as primes. The investor (always a buyer) may cancel the transaction on the day before settlement and pay only a fee called a "prime" to the seller. Settlements can be made on any of the next three settlement days, and only on those days.

marché à options: In English these are referred to simply as options. Both puts *(option de vent)* and calls *(option d'achat)* are available. As with options on other markets, the buyer has the right, but not the obligation, to buy or sell a specified number of shares at a fixed price at any time within the contract period (up to nine months).

Note that in the case of primes the seller receives the premium (and does not sell the stock) only if the buyer backs out of the contract, while with options the seller always receives the premium.

Put options are not traded as frequently as call options; their premiums are lower than call options, and they sometimes experience liquidity problems. Also, short-term options (less than three months) are seldom traded. For the short term, traders seem to prefer primes.

The unlisted securities market *(marché hors-cote)* is the other major division of the market. It consists of the securities in the "second" section, and in the "ordinary" section. Second-section securities were formerly companies in the process of trying to obtain listing on the official market. Most new issues still appear first in this market. Currently it is made up of over sixty stocks (including two foreign securities), and the trading is brisk. For securities in the "ordinary" section, even liquidity is not required. All transactions on the unlisted market are for cash. Obviously, purchases on the unlisted securities market should be undertaken only with expert advice.

The types of orders permitted on the Paris exchange include:

au mieux (at best, or *at the market price):* The equivalent of a market order. It will be executed at the opening price (if the order arrives in time) or at the next price quoted after the order reaches the floor.

cours limité (limit order): The investor specifies the highest buying price or lowest selling price.

premier ou dernier cours (opening or closing price): An opening price order will be executed at the opening price, if it arrives on the floor in time, or at the same price later, if possible. Otherwise it is canceled. The closing price order is appropriate only for orders on the forward market.

stop order: the investor specifies a buy only if a price rises above a specified limit, or a sell if the price falls below a specified limit.

Most orders are available *jour seulement* (valid for only one day) or *révocation* (good till canceled). "Revocation" orders expire on the last day of the month on the cash market and on the next settlement day on the forward market.

The hours for the Paris exchange are Monday through Friday, 10:30 A.M. to 12:30 P.M., trading in most government bonds and corporate bonds; 12:30 P.M. to 2:30 P.M., trading in stocks, convertible bonds, major government bonds, and securities on the "unofficial market." There is also a late session timed to coincide with the opening hour of the New York Stock Exchange when quotations for securities listed on the NYSE are set again.

COMMISSIONS, SETTLEMENTS, AND QUOTATIONS

Settlement for all stocks listed on the forward market (the RM market) is seven business days before the end of the month. However, in a process known as *marchés des reports* (or contango market) settlement may be delayed until the settlement day of the *following* month. What literally happens is that the purchase must be made, as contracted, on the regular settlement day, but on the following day the investor sells the security at a fixed price, and waits until the following settlement day to buy it back (at the fixed price). There is, of course, a fee for this service, called a "contango rate." Sellers may also avail themselves of the service (selling on the settlement day and buying back the next day), but, in practice, it occurs infrequently. In the United States, it will depend on the individual broker as to whether contango contracts are permitted.

Quotations for all stocks and some bonds, including convertible bonds and foreign-currency bonds, are in French francs. The minimum increments by which these quotations may fluctuate are shown in Table 3. Bonds quoted in francs will always include the accrued interest in the price. Most of the time bonds are quoted in percent of par, as in the United States.

Table 3

MINIMUM QUOTATION FLUCTUATIONS

FOR SECURITIES WITHIN THE PRICE	MINIMUM FLUCTUATION
Ff 0–5	Ff 0.01
Ff 5–100	Ff 0.05
Ff 100–500	Ff 0.10
Ff 500–5,000	Ff 1.00
Ff 5,000 up	Ff 10.00

Prices for securities are set (called "fixed") in a manner similar to that described for the Frankfurt exchange. Orders are accumulated and a price arrived at which will accommodate the largest number of orders. This price is called a "balancing" price. It is always the price which will allow the greatest number of bid orders and asked orders to be matched.

On the forward market, prices are established *à la criée* (by open outcry). An auctioneer opens the quotations at the closing price for the previous day. Prices are raised or lowered until a balancing price is reached. A number of prices may be established in the course of trading. The final price is the closing price.

As on many foreign exchanges, there are limits beyond which the prices of securities may not fluctuate in the course of a single day. Foreign securities are exempt from these limitations and allowed to fluctuate in accordance with the prices on their home exchanges.

On the forward market (RM market), trading is halted if the price varies from the closing price of the previous day by more than 8%. Brokers are asked to reconfirm their orders and cancel those that are not firm; trading resumes later within the same session.

On the cash market *(marché au comptant)* stocks are not allowed to open more than 4% to 5% from their previous closing prices, and bonds are not allowed to open more than 2% to 3% from their previous closing prices. If this limit is exceeded, the Chambre Syndicale establishes a price within 4% for stocks and 2% for bonds. If more than 24% of the orders cannot be accommodated by this process, trading is suspended for the day.

In the daily official list an "R" next to the closing price indicates that such a limit was imposed on the price. An "off" indicates trading was suspended because of an excess of sell orders, and a "dem" indicates trading was suspended because of an excess in buy orders.

When a takeover attempt is announced a number of regulations come into effect. Conditional transactions such as primes are not permitted, and the margin requirement is 100%. A tender offer must be good for one month. A shareholder may withdraw tendered shares up to ten days from the announced close of the offer. The offering company may withdraw if there is a competing offer. If a tender offer is oversubscribed, purchases will be on a pro rata basis.

The following commissions are currently applicable on the Paris exchange. For shares, convertible bonds, and rights:

PER-SHARE PRICE	COMMISSION, %
Under Ff 600,000	.65
Ff 600,000–1,100,000	.43
Ff 1,100,000–2,200,000	.325
Over Ff 2,200,000	.215

For bonds:

PER-SHARE PRICE	COMMISSION, %
Under Ff 6,000,000	.5
Ff 600,000–1,100,000	.33
Ff 1,100,000–2,200,000	.24
Above Ff 2,200,000	.165

A "TVA" tax (value added tax) is added which amounts to 17.6% of the brokerage commission. A stamp tax also is added on all transactions except for bonds that mature within seven years; it is .3% of the total transaction up to Ff 1,000,000 and .15% above that. For contango transactions, the stamp tax is a flat .15%.

ABOUT BONDS: GOVERNMENT AND CORPORATE

Bonds account for about 70% of the total market value of all listed securities in France, and of that number, about three-quarters are government issues. Bonds are identified by the name of their issuer, the coupon rate, and year of issue. For example, "Caisse Nationale de l'Energie, 17.40%, 1981" is the National Energy Fund (CNE) 17.4% bond issued in 1981.

Government bonds include only direct obligations of the government. They are popular with both resident and nonresident investors because they pay interest without withholding tax. First-category bonds include issues of government agencies and local authorities so long as they are guaranteed indirectly by the government, a government agency, or a municipality. Second-category bonds are corporate bonds. There is no real difference between the first two categories with respect to risk. Therefore, the nonresident investor may prefer government bonds to first-category bonds because of the exemption from withholding.

Do not assume that all the bonds from a single issuer are in the same category. An agency, in particular, may issue one bond in the first category and another in the second, depending on whether a government guarantee was obtained.

Maturities for government bonds may go up to fifteen years. Those of less than seven years' maturity (whether new or old issues) are known as "bankable" bonds and enjoy slightly more liquidity. (Otherwise, there is no significant difference between "bankable" and "unbankable" bonds as far as the investor is concerned.) There are both fixed-coupon bonds which pay dividends annually, and floating-rate bonds which pay dividends semiannually. Be careful to determine whether a bond you are considering amortizes the principal over all or part of the life of the bond. Interest is free of withholding tax for nonresidents. Some issues are denominated in Ff 1,000, but most are Ff 2,000 and Ff 5,000.

First-category bonds are similar to government bonds and issued in denominations of Ff 2,000. Interest is paid annually and is not free of withholding. First-category bonds include issues of nationalized institutions such as major banks, utility companies, and steel companies. Most are fixed-coupon and pay interest annually. Again, some amortize the principal over the life of the bond.

Corporate bonds, the second-category bonds, have maturities up to twenty years. Straight or convertible bonds are issued, and interest is paid annually. Yields are 1½% to 2½% higher than government bonds.

Indexed bonds are a unique feature of the French securities market. Either the principal or the coupon rate is linked to a commodity. At present, bonds linked to gold, oil, and a basket of currencies are available. Minimum yields are less than other bonds but investors will participate in a rise in the price of the commodity to which the bond is linked, either through an increase in interest or an increase in face value. There are no rating systems in France, like Moody's, so investors must rely on their bank or broker to evaluate the safety of second-category bonds. If the issue is marked "pari passu" it will not be subordinate to any other issue, either in competition for benefits or in case of liquidation.

A number of interesting bonds have been issued as indemnification of the nationalizations of 1981 and 1982. Among them are the *titres participatives* that are, in part, guaranteed by the government. For instance, Rhône-Poulenc has issued 10% minimum floating-rate bonds, 7% of which is guaranteed by the government. The 3% guaranteed by the company is a minimum, tied to company revenues, with no upper limit to its yield.

BANKS

Banks are an important link to French brokerages. More than 75% of all securities orders are transmitted to brokers through banks. Banks provide all support services required by the investor such as safekeeping, collection of dividends and interest, portfolio guidance, and mutual funds.

WITHHOLDING TAX

As mentioned before, interest from government bonds is paid without withholding tax. Interest from first-category and second-category bonds is 10%, although check with your broker; there are some exceptions.

Withholding from dividends is 15%. In France, dividends are paid at the source net of tax. As a resident of a tax treaty nation you may claim this amount, known as the *avoir fiscal,* which can be as much as 50% of your dividends, depending on the tax bracket of the company. The 15% withholding is then applied to that amount.

There is no capital gains tax for nonresidents.

FRENCH INVESTMENT JARGON

agents de change: Stockbrokers.

a mieux: At the market order.

*bankable bonds (*and *unbankable bonds):* A designation for many bonds of less than seven years' maturity. These bonds may be used to constitute part of a bank's reserve assets. That a bond is "unbankable" does not reflect on its quality. Bankable bonds are slightly more liquid than unbankable bonds.

bourse: Stock exchange.

Compagnie des Agents de Change: National Broker's Association.

cote officielle: Official market.

cours limité: Limit order.

fonds d'état: Government bonds.

jour seulement: Order valid for day only.

marché à options: Options market.

marché à primes: Conditional purchase which allows revocation of purchase on the day before settlement day.

marché à reglement mensuel: The RM market or forward market.

marché à terme: Former term for the forward market.

marché au comptant: Cash or spot market.

marché hors-cote: Unofficial market, somewhat analogous to the over-the-counter market except trading is on the exchange.

marchés conditionnels: Market constituting options and primes.

marchés des reports: Contango market.

option d'achat: Call option.

option de vent: Put option.

premier or *dernier cours:* Order to be executed at opening *(premier)* or closing *(dernier)* price.

primes: See *marché à primes.*

révocation: Order good until canceled.

"RI" settlement: Cash settlement.

unbankable bonds: See bankable bonds.

USEFUL ADDRESSES

THE PARIS STOCK EXCHANGE

Bourse de Paris
4, place de la Bourse, 4
75080 Paris Cedex 02

LEADING BANKS

Banque Nationale de Paris
16 boulevard des Italiens
Paris

Banque de L'Indochine et de Suez
96 boulevard Haussmann
Paris

Credit Lyonnais
19 boulevard des Italiens
Paris

Société Générale
29 boulevard Haussmann
Paris

SOURCE OF ADDITIONAL
INFORMATION

Chambre Syndicale des Agents de
Change
4, place de la Bourse, 4
75080 Paris Cedex 02

LEADING FINANCIAL NEWSPAPER

AGEFI (L'Agence Économique et
Financière)
108 rue de Richelieu
75002 Paris

13

THE SINGAPORE STOCK EXCHANGE

Courtesy of the Stock Exchange of Singapore

A MAJOR EXCHANGE OF ASIA

The Stock Exchange of Singapore Ltd. is the third largest stock exchange in Asia, with respect to market capitalization, after Tokyo and Sydney. In recent years, only in 1979 and 1980 did Hong Kong surpass Singapore. With respect to turnover, however, Hong Kong consistently outperforms Singapore.

At the beginning of 1984, 301 companies listed their securities in Singapore with a total market capitalization of $49 billion (U.S.). Volume was about $5 billion (U.S.)

The Singapore economy has been among the more stable in the world, with inflation in 1983 running at a mere 1.1%. The Singapore dollar rose against almost all other currencies in 1982 except the U.S.

dollar, against which it fell only 1.3%. The balance of payment surplus in 1983 was $2.2 billion (U.S.), and $2.5 billion (U.S.) the year before. The real GNP slowed to 7.9% after 6.3% the year before.

The Singapore Stock Exchange is self-regulatory with respect to its internal affairs, and managed by a five-member committee elected anew each year. Government regulation of the securities industry is based on The Securities Industry Act of 1973 (modeled after British law), which governs areas such as trading, record keeping, licensing of securities dealers, and financial reporting.

The exchange is organized as a not-for-profit joint stock company with a float of 2,000 shares, each with a par value of S$1. Becoming a member of the exchange entails buying one share, an act equivalent to buying a "seat" on other exchanges. The highest price paid for a share was in 1979 when one share was bought by a security company for S$2 million. Membership on the exchange also requires meeting a number of government requirements and the approval of the other members. Although a number of foreign security companies are licensed to trade in Singapore, they may not become members of the stock exchange; therefore, orders from foreign brokerages must be transacted on the exchange through a Singapore firm.

Many securities are dually listed on the stock exchange in Kuala Lumpur, the leading exchange in Malaysia. Listing requirements in Singapore are somewhat less stringent, but the paid-in capital required in Singapore, S$4 million, is twice that of Kuala Lumpur.

THE SINGAPORE STOCK MARKET AT A GLANCE

Capitalization:
Market value of shares in U.S.$* .... $43.9 billion
Nominal value of bonds in U.S.$* .... $5.5 billion
Percent of total share capitalization represented by ten largest
  companies. 28.8%
Volume:
Total turnover. .... 3.6 billion units
Value of total turnover in U.S.$* .... $5.6 billion
Listings:
Domestic and foreign equities 307
Government securities 39
Fixed-interest securities 128
Rank in the world:
Capitalization 10th

*Exchange rate as of Jan. 1, 1983: $1 = S$2.11.
*Source: Singapore Stock Exchange, *Fact Book 84*.

Geographically, Singapore is ideally located to link some of the major markets of the world. It is exactly twelve hours from New York. As the farthest west of the exchanges of the Pacific basin, its hours can overlap those of Tokyo, Hong Kong, and Sydney, as well as all the exchanges of Europe (see Appendix 1).

Although the government does encourage Malaysian ownership of Singapore securities, there is no exchange control for nonresidents nor are there controls for Singapore residents who invest abroad. Revenues from securities transactions can be freely remitted outside the country.

THE ISLAND CITY-STATE STOCK EXCHANGE

The city of Singapore was founded in 1819 by Sir Thomas Stamford Raffles of the East India Company. Located on the site of a Malay fishing village, it was to serve as a trade depot. It is both a city and an island on the tip of the Malay Peninsula. It guards the entrance to the strategic Strait of Malacca, and so served as the central naval base for the British Empire in Asia.

During World War II Singapore was occupied by the Japanese. In 1957, as part of the United Malay National Organization, it became independent of British rule. However, in 1959 Singapore became self-governing, partly because the racial mix was different from the rest of the Federation, being about 75% Chinese. In 1963, Singapore became completely independent for nineteen days, and then joined the Federation of Malaysia (which included Malaya and two Borneo states of Sabah and Sarawak). In 1965, Singapore left the Federation once again to become independent.

Singapore is now an independent republic, and a member of the British Commonwealth. Singapore Island, on which the city is located, is only 239 square miles. It is governed by a one-body parliament, and has a population of about 2.4 million.

The oldest stockbrokerage firm in the Far East, Fraser and Company, was established in Singapore in 1873 by John Fraser, a Scotsman. Most of the shares traded at that time were British-owned mines and plantations, many of which were listed on the London stock exchange.

A central marketplace for the trading of securities was not needed until 1910 when the rubber boom was in full swing. A bar and the pavement in front became the center for securities trading. After a few years, the rubber trade declined, and many stockbrokers went out of business. Securities trading, however, continued, located from time to time in various streets.

Singapore experienced enormous economic growth in the 1920s, partly due to a large influx of U.S. firms. However, the Wall Street crash of 1929 profoundly affected the Malayan economy. Ruthless competition among brokers necessitated some form of organization, and on January 23, 1930, fifteen brokerages founded the Singapore Stockbrokers Association. The intent was partly to regulate the conduct of its members and partly to close out other stockbrokers.

This was not an exchange as we would recognize it. Brokers would spend mornings and early afternoons traveling in rickshaws to visit their clients. At 4:00 P.M. they would congregate with their orders, and orders telegraphed from London, and set the day's prices.

In 1938, the name of the association was changed to the Malayan Share Brokers Association. During the Japanese occupation the exchange was closed, but it reopened in 1946 after the war.

In 1960, under the guidance of the president of the Sydney Stock Exchange, the Malayan Stock Exchange was founded by nineteen brokerage firms, and a year later two telephone-linked trading rooms were established in Kuala Lumpur and Singapore. A scoreboard system of trading was used.

Another name change, to the Stock Exchange of Malaysia, was effected when Singapore became a member of the Federation of Malaysia in 1963. In 1965, it became the Stock Exchange of Malaysia and Singapore.

Because of the inability of the exchange to enforce regulations, abuses abounded and the exchange remained highly speculative. The interchangeability of Malaysian and Singapore currencies was terminated by Malaysian authorities in 1973, and, as a result, the two exchanges finally split. The new name of the exchange in Singapore was the Stock Exchange of Singapore Ltd. (its present name); it began full operations on June 4, 1973. Close ties still remained between the exchanges (brokers generally deal on both). The Singapore government enacted the Securities Industry Act of 1973 which included regulations and enforcements based on British law.

The Singapore exchange has experienced steady growth, both in sophistication and size. In 1977, call options were listed. Singapore was, thus, the first financial center in Asia to have an organized option trading market. In 1979, the Securities Clearing and Computer Services began operations, providing clearing and computer services between the exchange and its member brokerage firms. An electronic trading board commenced operation in 1982 as did a new video display terminal system on the floor of the exchange.

SINGAPORE CURRENCY AND EXCHANGE RATE WITH
THE U.S. DOLLAR

The unit of currency is the Singapore dollar, which contains 100 cents. In print it usually appears as S$5.17 (five dollars, seventeen, Singapore).

As mentioned earlier, the Singapore dollar is quite stable. The government actively watches the exchange market and stabilizes the currency by purchasing Singapore dollars, usually from its assets of U.S. dollars. The government discourages speculation in the Singapore dollar and will require banks to report their currency exchange transactions on a daily basis (instead of monthly) whenever it wishes to keep close tabs on the exchange rates.

An effective exchange rate, as shown for the other major currencies, is not calculated for the Singapore dollar. Table 1, however, shows the average exchange rate with the U.S. dollar for each year since 1975.

Table 1

**AVERAGE YEARLY EXCHANGE
RATE WITH THE U.S. DOLLAR**

YEAR	UNITS PER U.S. DOLLAR
1975	S$2.49
1976	S$2.46
1977	S$2.34
1978	S$2.16
1979	S$2.16
1980	S$2.09
1981	S$2.05
1982	S$2.04

Source: International Monetary Fund.

SECURITIES TRADED ON THE SINGAPORE STOCK EXCHANGE

stocks: Ordinary and preferred available. Dividends are usually annual but some may be semiannual.

rights: Usual life about two months. There were eleven issued in 1982.

bonds: Government and corporate bonds are listed although there is a very small market in the latter. Bonds, in general, constitute only about 12% of the exchange's turnover. Interest is paid semiannually.

options: A small market in call options began in 1977 but there is almost no secondary market.

Those securities which constitute the largest percentage of the market's capitalization are issues of industrial and commercial companies, property and real estate companies, and finance companies. About 80%

of all Singapore stocks pay a dividend, and in 1983 forty-seven issues granted bonus shares.

Public placements and private offerings are both infrequent in Singapore. Normally, new shares are allotted to current shareholders at less than market price through rights issues.

The over-the-counter market is almost nonexistent in Singapore. Thus, bringing a company public is synonymous with exchange listing.

The following Singapore securities are available in the United States as ADRs. The depositary bank is Morgan Guaranty Trust, and the ratio of shares to ADRs is 1:1.

Bandar Raya Developments Berhad

Boustead Holdings Berhad

Genting Berhad

Kuala Lumpur Kepong Berhad

Perlis Plantations Berhad

Selangor Properties Berhad

Sime Darby Berhad

Supreme Corporation Berhad

LEADING STOCK INDEXES

There are two stock indexes that one will see quoted in the media. The Stock Exchange of Singapore (SES) Index is the most broadly based of the indexes, made up of six weighted indexes. The other is the Straits Times Index. ("Straits" refers to the Strait of Malacca; the *Straits Times* is the leading newspaper of Singapore.) The Straits Times Index is made up of six subgroup indexes, and the one which is usually used to represent the exchange is the industrial index. Shown in Figure 1, it is an unweighted average made up of thirty industrial stocks.

The ten companies shown in Table 2 are the largest on the Singapore exchange with respect to market capitalization. The ten companies shown in Table 3 had the greatest turnover in 1982.

TRADING OF SINGAPORE SECURITIES

Since 1975, stock market trading has been in two sections. First-section companies, which make up about 66% of exchange-listed stocks, must have:

1. S$5 million in paid-in capital
2. 500 shareholders

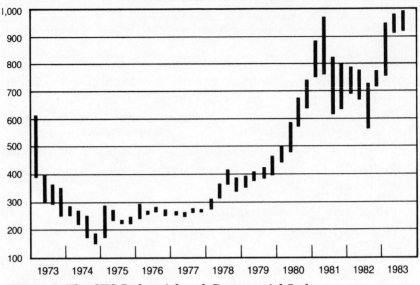

Figure 1. **The SES Industrial and Commercial Index.**
Source: *Singapore Stock Exchange*

3. A turnover of 5% of the paid-in capital per year
4. A 5% annual dividend (that is, 5% of the par value, not market value)

At its discretion, the exchange may grant exemption from some of the above requirements. All stocks that do not meet the first-section requirements are traded in the second section. The most significant difference between the two sections has to do with the type of settlement permitted.

Table 2

THE TEN LARGEST STOCK ISSUES ON THE SINGAPORE STOCK EXCHANGE

COMPANY	PRICE IN S$ AT THE BEGINNING OF 1984	MARKET CAPITALIZATION IN MILLIONS OF S$
1. Hong Kong Land	4.95	10,607
2. Overseas Chinese Banking Corp.	11.30	5,630
3. Development Bank of Singapore	10.20	2,331
4. United Overseas Bank	5.70	2,248
5. Sime Darby	2.65	2,075
6. ABN Bank (Netherlands)	269.00	1,960
7. Malayan Banking	9.30	1,674
8. Consolidated Plantations	3.42	1,605
9. Straits Trading	6.00	1,296
10. Overseas Union Bank	4.68	1,185

Source: Singapore Stock Exchange, *Annual Report*, 1984.

One of the most interesting features of the Singapore exchange is that trading is by means of an electronic trading board. Traders do not walk from post to post as they do on most stock exchanges. Here, orders are telephoned to trading-room clerks who relay instructions to the exchange computer and onto the electronic trading board. The highest bid and the lowest offer of each listed company are displayed. When bid and offer prices match, a transaction is made. The process resembles a NASDAQ system confined to one room. You will see in the photograph at the beginning of the chapter that there are no trading posts at which traders can congregate. Most of the brokers and dealer's representatives (called "remisiers") are seated in front of their terminals. On the right is a small part of the large electronic quote board.

Trading lots, called board lots, are set at 1,000, 2,000, and 3,000 shares, although for stocks priced over S$10.00 the trading lot may be set at 500 or 100 at the discretion of the exchange. As on other exchanges, there is a minimum increment by which the prices of securities may move (Table 4).

Table 3

**THE TEN MOST ACTIVE STOCKS ON THE
SINGAPORE STOCK EXCHANGE**

1. Faber Merlin—hotels
2. Malayan United Industry—industrial, commercial
3. Pahang Consolidated—mining
4. Promet—industrial, commercial
5. Arab Malaysian Dev.—industrial, commercial
6. United Overseas Bank—financial
7. Sime Darby—industrial, commercial
8. General Corporation—industrial, commercial
9. City Developments—property
10. Genting—industrial, commercial

Source: Singapore Stock Exchange, *Annual Report,* 1984.

Table 4

**MINIMUM PRICE INCREMENTS
FOR SINGAPORE STOCKS**

Up to S$1	S$0.005
S$1–3	S$0.01
S$3–5	S$0.02
S$5–10	S$0.05
S$10–25	S$0.10
S$25–100	S$0.50
Above S$100	S$1.00

There are three trading sessions daily on the Singapore Stock Exchange: 10:00 A.M. to 11:00 A.M., 11:15 A.M. to 12:30 P.M., and 2:30 P.M. to 4:00 P.M., Monday through Friday.

SETTLEMENT AND COMMISSIONS

Two different settlements are available: ready delivery and future delivery. Ready-delivery settlement means that all contracts are to be delivered and payments made by Tuesday of the following week. Usually, the majority of most transactions are settled in this manner.

Both first- and second-section stocks may be settled by ready delivery. However, first-section stocks may also be settled by future delivery, which means on the last Thursday of the month. Furthermore, settlement can sometimes be rolled over from month to month.

Strangely enough, no margin is required and no interest is charged by Singapore brokers for this service although the commissions for stocks under a dollar are fractionally lower. This constitutes 100% interest-free credit. Recently, speculation of future delivery has increased dramatically. Probably the biggest danger of such speculation is that a sudden drop in the market index could trigger panic selling in order to close investors' sometimes massive speculative positions.

However, neither the government nor the securities industry has shown an inclination to put a stop to the situation. Since its inception in 1974, the future delivery market has been closed only once, in 1981, because of the danger of a market crash.

The minimum commissions established by the Singapore Stock Exchange are shown in Table 5. Minimum commission is S$5. All securities quoted in foreign currencies are 1%. There is also a stamp tax of .2% on both sales and purchases.

Table 5

STOCKS AND RIGHTS PER SHARE	READY CONTRACTS	FORWARD CONTRACTS
Under S$.50	S$.005	S$.0075
S$.50–.99	S$.01	S$.0125
S$1 and over	1%	1%

ABOUT BONDS: GOVERNMENT AND CORPORATE

Although government bonds dominate the bond market, Singapore is in the odd position of having the majority of its bonds held by two semipublic institutions: a national insurance fund (CPF) and the Post Office Savings Bank. The growth of the bond market has thus been somewhat stifled.

Maturities of government bonds are as long as twenty years, and coupon rates go as high as 7.1%. Interest is paid semiannually. Government bonds are sometimes referred to by number (e.g., Loan 2, 1981). Most are in registered form (referred to as "registered government stock") although there are a few coupon-form issues.

Corporate bonds constitute a very small percent of the market, are not very liquid, and consequently are not of much interest to nonresident investors.

TAX

There is no capital gains tax and no tax on stock dividends. Cash dividends and interest, however, are subject to a whopping 40% withholding tax. There is also a .2% stamp tax for share transfer deeds.

SOURCES OF INFORMATION

As with all Asian markets, a prime source of information is *The Asian Wall Street Journal.* Also of particular interest are the periodic reviews of Asian markets in the *Financial Times* of London.

The Singapore Stock Exchange publishes the *Financial News,* a daily, for S$800 annually and a weekly version for S$234 annually. However, both are generally of more use to the institutional investor. Probably the best publication for the serious individual is the *Singapore Stock Exchange Journal.* It is a monthly, for a subscription price of S$52. (The Singapore dollar is around $.50 currently.) The *Journal* presents a summary of trading in all listed stocks, semiannual company reports, and financial articles of interest to the investing public. It may be ordered through the Singapore Stock Exchange, 16 Raffles Quay, #16-03, Hong Leong Building, Singapore 0104.

14

THE AMSTERDAM STOCK EXCHANGE

Studio Krimp Fotografie/Courtesy of the Amsterdam Stock Exchange

THE FIRST MODERN STOCK EXCHANGE

The Amsterdam Stock Exchange lays claim to being the oldest stock exchange in the world, but, as you can imagine, such a claim does not go uncontested. Earlier claims include the city of Venice, where state loan stocks (i.e., bonds) were traded as early as the fourteenth century; and Verona, which had a forward commodities market dating from about the same period.[1] Markets such as these in Italy and Spain met

[1] For more details of the history of exchanges see Fernand Brandel's *Les Jeux de l'Exchange,* translated into English by Siân Reynolds as *The Wheels of Commerce* (William Collins Sons & Co., Ltd., London, 1982, and Harper & Row, Publishers, Inc., New York, pp. 97–106).

and conducted business in public squares, the corners of palace por-
ticos, church steps, and even on bridges. Lucca, in northern Italy,
boasted a currency exchange as early as 1111. But if one included
money changing, the answer to the question of the oldest "exchange"
would indeed be shrouded in the proverbial mists of antiquity.

In Amsterdam, the old exchange association was founded in 1530,
and the new exchange in 1608, but these dates are not the real bases
for the Amsterdam claim—it was an event that took place in 1602. In
that year for the first time shares in a limited liability company were
offered for public subscription. That company was the Dutch East India
Company. The enormous success of that issue and others that followed
brought about what was for all intents and purposes the first stock
exchange.

Prior to that time government loan stock had traded in Amsterdam,
and there was even a separate corn exchange. But the Dutch East India
shares constituted ownership (they were not bonds); they were *written*
shares in a company (not a government), and those shares enjoyed one
of the most important features of securities trading, liquidity: they were
highly negotiable. Although the physical certificates *(actiën)* were at
first held by the company (they could be purchased only by inscribing
one's name in the company book), they were issued in bearer form soon
after the inception of trading.

Historically, the Dutch have enjoyed the roles of investor and spec-

---

THE AMSTERDAM STOCK MARKET AT A GLANCE

Capitalization:

Market value of domestic shares in U.S.$*	$33,366 million
Nominal value of bonds in U.S.$*	$41.7 billion
Percent of total domestic share capitalization represented by ten largest domestic companies	81%

Volume:

Average daily volume in U.S.$*	$159 million

Listings:

Domestic equities including funds	253
Domestic fixed-interest securities	1,345
Foreign shares	290
Foreign fixed-interest securities	140
PE Ratio (average)	8.4

Rank in world:

Capitalization	11th

*Exchange rate as of Dec. 31, 1983: $1 = Dfl 3.099.
Source: Amsterdam Stock Exchange, data for 1983.

ulator. It is estimated that 4,500 people jammed into the first exchange building, completed in 1631, for the purpose of trading and socializing. It was frequently so crowded that a contemporary wrote that one had "to be of the serpentine race to get in."

The concentration of capital in The Netherlands proved to be important in the early years of the United States. In 1782 the first loan to the new republic (actually, to the Continental Congress) was by public subscription in Amsterdam: a 5% bond. There were eleven such loans (the rest were at lower rates), and even loans to individual states.

Today, there are still strong ties between the United States and The Netherlands. The Amsterdam exchange lists 300 U.S. securities, more than any other foreign exchange. At least half the volume of foreign shares traded in Amsterdam is made up of U.S. shares. Since American stock certificates differ greatly from those of The Netherlands (Dutch stock certificates are in bearer form) the American certificates cannot be traded directly on the exchange. They are held by a depositary and transactions are simply by book entry. So efficient is this system, called American Shares Amsterdam System (ASAS), that there is never more than a quarter-point difference between the Amsterdam price and the NYSE price for the same share.

The Amsterdam exchange in itself is not a large exchange, but before World War II its volume of international trading made it the third largest stock exchange in the world. During the war it suffered greatly, closing for six months. It was, in fact, closed longer than the exchange of any other country taken by the Nazis. During the occupation, the trading of American securities was, of course, banned. In fact, this situation later brought about the only peacetime strike in the exchange's history. In 1946, after the war, the personnel struck in order to force the resumption of trading in U.S. securities.

Today, Amsterdam lists more than 2,000 securities, of which about 30% are stocks and 70% are bonds. In volume, however, stocks and bonds are about equal. Of the listed stocks, less than 50% are Dutch companies. There would be more domestic equities except for the tendency of Dutch companies to obtain financing through bank loans rather than through the issue of stocks or bonds. Shares of the larger Dutch companies are widely traded and have a high percentage of foreign ownership (30% to 50% average). Price-earnings ratios are attractive to the U.S. investor, the average being around 8.5%, although, of course, the norm varies from industry to industry.

Amsterdam is the official Netherlands exchange and lists all Dutch securities (except Eurobonds). At one time there were also smaller exchanges in Rotterdam and in The Hague, but those were closed in 1973. The Amsterdam exchange makes use of the *hoekman* system, which is similar to the system described for the London stock exchange. The *hoekman* makes a market in specific securities, and the broker and banker members of the exchange must conduct transactions through him. In that way he also resembles the specialist on the New York Stock Exchange.

DUTCH CURRENCY AND EXCHANGE RATE WITH THE U.S. DOLLAR

The currency is the Dutch guilder which contains 100 cents. In writing, the abbreviation for guilder (gldr.) is almost never used; the word is simply spelled out. Another term, "florin" or "Dutch florin," is also used, although not as much in this country. However, it is the various *abbreviations* for florin which are found most often in the press. For example, f 51.10, Fl 51.10, and DFl 51.10 all mean fifty-one guilders and ten cents or, to be idiomatically correct, fifty-one guilders, ten. The most likely confusion is to mistake "f" for franc. Nevertheless, the context usually makes the abbreviation clear.

The guilder is one of the currencies that participates in the European Monetary System (EMS), whose other members include West Germany, France, Belgium, Luxembourg, Italy, Denmark, and Ireland. The Dutch government is obligated to intervene in foreign exchange markets in order to keep the guilder within the EMS guidelines, which state that no member's currency will fluctuate a total of more than 2.25% against the currency of another member. In the past there has been a tendency to keep the exchange rate of the guilder in line with the deutschemark since The Netherlands conducts more trade with West Germany than with any other country.

The solid line in Figure 1 indicates the interbank exchange rate of Dutch guilders to U.S. dollars as you would see quoted in the press. Room is left for you to continue the graph if you like. Regular charting is not necessary, but a dot here and there as you observe currency moves may be useful to you if you acquire or plan to acquire Dutch securities.

In interpreting Figure 1, keep in mind that it shows only the rate of the guilder against the dollar and does not reflect the absolute value of the guilder. Movements of the U.S. dollar, higher or lower, with respect to other major currencies would smooth out or exaggerate the lines of such a graph.

The effective exchange rate (see p. 40), indicated by the broken line, shows the exchange rate against a basket of seventeen other currencies. This rate comes closer to the real value of a currency than, of course, the exchange rate with only a single currency such as the U.S. dollar. As you can see, the guilder has fallen against the dollar, particularly in 1981, but it has held its own against most other currencies.

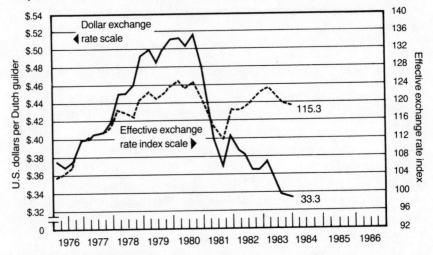

Figure 1. Exchange rate of the Dutch guilder with the U.S. dollar and the effective exchange rate with other major currencies.
Source: *Federal Reserve Bank of St. Louis*

SECURITIES TRADED ON THE AMSTERDAM STOCK EXCHANGE

There are no restrictions on the purchase or sale of securities on the Amsterdam exchange. Profits and revenues may be repatriated by U.S. citizens at will.

common stock: Most Dutch shares are in bearer form, although some, designated "CF" (Centrum Function), are registered. Dividends are semiannual and subject to a 15% withholding tax. Should you hold the certificates yourself, dividends are claimed by coupon; otherwise your broker or banker can take care of this for you. Shares of the large multinational corporations are traded widely; however, shares of smaller domestic companies sometimes do not enjoy the same degree of liquidity.

bonds: Both corporate and government bonds are exchange-listed. Interest on both is paid without withholding tax, usually once a year. Most bonds are available in bearer form and in denominations of DFl 1,000. Corporate bonds may be regular or convertible. Be careful to determine whether a bond you are considering amortizes the principal over the last five or ten years of its maturity.

options: As of 1978, options are available on the new European Options Exchange (see "Options").

investment companies: Shares of investment companies and funds are available on the Amsterdam exchange (see "Investment Companies").

A new market, called the "parallel market," has been introduced on the Amsterdam exchange to encourage smaller companies to seek equity or debt financing (i.e., to issue stocks or bonds). Although the shares are traded on the Amsterdam floor, the transactions do not make use of the *hoekman* system, but are traded on a "best effort" basis through two members called "specialists." As on the over-the-counter market in the United States, the listing requirements are less stringent than for securities on the regular market. These issues and the issues of smaller companies, in general, represent a relatively high degree of risk for the international investor. Usually, less information is available, and the relatively small amount of trading can make these shares susceptible to wide price swings on an increase in volume.

MAJOR STOCK INDEXES

The index you will see most often quoted in the press is the broadly based ANP/CBS General Index (Figure 2).[2] This is a general price index

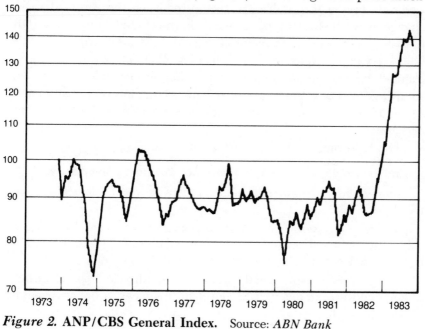

Figure 2. **ANP/CBS General Index.**   Source: *ABN Bank*

[2]ANP is the National Press Agency; CBS is the Central Bureau of Statistics.

made up of an average of seven separate industry indexes (international, industry, shipping and aviation, banks, insurance, trade, and local). Large international corporations constitute 48% of this index so that it is influenced by the state of the other world markets as well.

TRADING DUTCH SECURITIES IN THE UNITED STATES

All the stocks listed below are available in this country as ADRs, and their dividends, of course, are paid in U.S. dollars. In corporate reports you sometimes may see a reference to "New York shares." Those are ADRs.

KLM Royal Dutch Airlines—major air carrier

Royal Dutch Petroleum—diversified petroleum company

Unilever N.V.—foods and consumer goods

Among Dutch shares available over the counter are AKZO, Hoogovens, and Philips.

WHEN YOUR BROKER TRADES IN AMSTERDAM

The only reason to purchase a stock directly on the Amsterdam exchange would be that it is not available in the United States as an ADR. In that case, it could be convenient to have the bearer-form certificates held for you in an account in Holland so that the dividends can be claimed via coupon (both banks and brokerages provide this service). As always, it is best to use a broker with a large international section. As yet, there are no U.S. brokers with memberships on the Amsterdam exchange.

The following kinds of trades are possible:

at best price (bestens): A market order executed immediately.

limited order (gelimiteerde): No purchase above, or sale below, a specified price.

without force (sans forcer): A discretionary order giving the broker or banker the right to determine the method and time of the transaction. This type of order may not be available through a U.S. broker.

stop-loss order: Same as in the United States. An order to purchase only if the price has risen to a specified level, or to sell only if the price falls to a specified level.

yield order: To be executed at a price on which a given yield can be obtained.

standing order: The order is valid until canceled.

day order: The order is valid only for the day.

period order: The order is valid only for the first or second period of trading during the day.

Short selling is permitted but your U.S. broker may not allow it for a Dutch stock that is not available as an ADR.

It is common for holders of Dutch stocks to be offered a choice of dividends in cash or stock. The stock dividend is usually selected since its market value is almost invariably greater than the cash amount. The date and amount of dividends are always set at the annual meeting. Often you will not be notified of the dividend particulars until you actually receive it (unless you are required to select between shares or cash). There is a small .75% broker fee for claiming your dividends or interest payments. Shares usually trade ex-dividend the day after the annual meeting.

The hours of the Amsterdam exchange are 10:00 A.M. to 4:30 P.M. although the official hours are 11:30 to 12:15 and 12:45 to 1:15. Some stocks are traded continuously and others are traded at their assigned pitches only during the two official sessions.

As mentioned before, when investing in relatively small markets it is best to restict the majority of your purchases to the securities of major companies. The twenty largest companies in the Netherlands by market capitalization are listed in Table 1. The market value is given in Dutch guilders as of June 29, 1984.

COMMISSIONS, FEES, AND SETTLEMENT

Quotations you get through a U.S. broker from Amsterdam will usually include the Dutch brokerage commission, which varies from .7% to 1.5% depending on the size of the transaction (Table 2). There is also a stamp tax of .12% and a contract fee of DFl 7.50 per transaction.

As mentioned before, banks in The Netherlands provide safekeeping for securities. The fee is charged annually and calculated on the average value of your portfolio for four quarters. For an amount of up to DFl 5 million the fee is .8%.

The base fee for collection of dividends, when coupons must be submitted, is .75% for amounts up to DFl 5,000. For any amount above DFl 5,000 the fee is .375% for that amount in addition to the base fee.

Settlement for purchases on the Amsterdam exchange is usually the next day so your U.S. broker may therefore require one-day settlement of you. For new issues, however, you usually have up to thirty days to pay.

Table 1

THE TWENTY LARGEST STOCK ISSUES ON THE AMSTERDAM STOCK EXCHANGE

COMPANY	MARKET VALUE OF STOCKS IN MILLIONS OF DFL
1. Koninklijke Olie (Royal Dutch Petroleum)	40,232.4
2. Philips	8,433.6
3. Unilever	8,056.5
4. Robeco	6,554.1
5. Rorento	4,892.5
6. Nationale Nederlanden	4,641.9
7. Rolinco	3,663.9
8. Akzo	3,153.4
9. Algemene Bank Nederland (ABN)	2,655.1
10. Heineken	2,485.4
11. AMRO	1,982.8
12. AMEV	1,831.2
13. Aegon	1,752.8
14. Dordtsche Petroleum	1,533.8
15. Heineken Holding	1,087.3
16. Rodamco	1,058.1
17. KLM	921.3
18. NMB	851.9
19. Wereldhave	842.2
20. Gist Brocades	837.5

Source: Amsterdam Stock Exchange, *Facts & Figures,* first six months of 1984.

Table 2

AMSTERDAM COMMISSIONS

	STOCKS	BONDS
On the first DF1 5,000	1.5%	1.5 %
On the balance up to Dfl 20,000	1.0%	1.0 %
On the balance up to DF1 100,000	.7%	.7 %
On the balance up to DF1 500,000	.7%	.4 %
On the balance up to DF1 1,000,000	.7%	.25%
On the balance above DF1 1,000,000	.7%	.16%

INVESTMENT COMPANIES

Among the many firsts of the Amsterdam Stock Exchange is the first investment company, the *Eendragt maakt Magt* (Unity is Strength). Founded in 1774, it had the same purpose as investment companies and mutual funds of today: professional management and the safety of diversity. The largest investment company outside the United States is located in The Netherlands. Named the Robeco Group (for Rotterdamsch Beleggingsconsortium), it is similar to a closed-end investment company and its shares are traded on the Amsterdam exchange.[3] You can expect its price to be close to its net asset value due to the buying and selling of shares by the fund itself. Robeco also has four investment funds almost identical to the following AMRO funds, and they are, furthermore, available through AMRO Bank.

A variety of funds are available, managed by major banks such as the ABN Bank (Algemene Bank Nederland). The AMRO Bank (Amsterdam-Rotterdam Bank) manages the AMRO Investment Funds, which are made up of four funds of different proportions of shares to bonds:

AMRO Share Fund (AAF)—shares only

AMRO Share Combination (AAK)—shares and bonds with an emphasis on shares

AMRO Bond Combination (AOK)—shares and bonds with an emphasis on bonds

ARMRO Bond Fund (AOF)—bonds only

There is a transaction charge of .5% for both purchases and sales, and a 1% tax on purchases. Robeco funds, if purchased through AMRO, have a 1% transaction charge up to DFl 42,000, and .82% on any amount above that. Minimum purchase for both funds is only DFl 50. The above funds invest, as do most funds in The Netherlands, in securities from financial markets throughout the world.

ABOUT BONDS: GOVERNMENT AND CORPORATE

Interest from both corporate and government bonds is paid without withholding tax. Corporate bonds are issued by banks, financial institutions, and other companies. New issues can be subscribed through banks and brokers, and issues can be bought on the secondary market through the Amsterdam Stock Exchange.

Both state and corporate bonds are in bearer form. State bonds are issued in denominations of DFl 10,000. Some state bonds are issued with the option to convert to new bonds at the same coupon rate as a

---

[3] There are some technical differences between funds such as this and what we think of in this country as a closed-end investment company. In Holland, they describe them as "closed-end funds with open-end aspects."

means of stretching maturities. Local authority bonds have been widely issued and, while considered safe, are not usually guaranteed by the state. (Some are, however, such as those of the Dutch Water Council.)

Most corporate bonds are for a maximum maturity of only ten years. Bonds are not usually called (paid off) early, but it is usual for a company to begin amortizing the principal for the last five or ten years before maturity. Bonds are bought and sold with accrued interest, and they trade ex-coupon fifteen days before the payment date. Unfortunately, there is no bond rating service so you must rely on your bank or broker for recommendations.

BANKS

The Netherlands prides itself on being a country where you can "eat in any language." You can also bank in any language, and The Netherlands is one of the easiest continental countries in which to do so.

Two leading commercial banks are the Amsterdam-Rotterdam Bank (AMRO) and the Algemene Bank Nederland (ABN). Nonresidents can open checking accounts in any currency and use the account to pay for securities or to pay or receive currencies. Checking accounts may also be interest-bearing. Portfolio managment is available but you should check for the minimums required. A variety of savings accounts are available but they must be denominated in guilders. "Numbered" accounts are also available; there is no extra charge for them but they are expected to be of a substantial amount.

To open an account by mail you will need to have a bank or notary public certify your signature. Should you wish to give another person either full or limited power of attorney for the operation of your account, you should know that under Dutch law, power of attorney ends upon the death of the account holder. To get around this you may open a joint account and specify that the other account holder cannot operate the account so long as you are alive.

Safe-deposit boxes at Dutch banks are among the cheapest in Europe. A small box (about 400 cubic inches) will cost about $15 (U.S.) a year, and the contents are automatically insured free of charge for up to $25,000 (U.S.).

OPTIONS

A new exchange for options, the European Options Exchange (EOE), was created in 1978. It is the first options exchange in Europe and the only exchange where options are traded on stocks from different countries. It is completely independent of the Amsterdam exchange, and options trade on Dutch, American, and other European stocks. Both call and put options are available for expirations of up to nine months. Expirations are always the third Friday of the expirations month.

Gold, silver, and bond options are also available in puts and calls for expirations up to nine months. By special arrangement with exchanges in Montreal and Vancouver, the EOE offers sixteen-hour trading. If negotiations with Hong Kong are successful, the European Options Exchange may be able to offer twenty-four hour trading in gold options. Expiration months for gold and bond options are February, May, August, and November. Expiration months for silver options are March, June, September, and December.

COMPLAINTS

The Amsterdam exchange has a reputation for being scrupulous in all its operations. It even assumes the protection of shareholders. In this capacity it has recently initiated a new Complaints Commission. If you have a problem with a broker or banker in The Netherlands concerning security transactions, you should write to them in care of the exchange. They are empowered to make binding decisions if:

1. Your complaint is not also currently pending in court.
2. You have first registered your complaint with the bank or brokerage involved.
3. No more than one year has elapsed since you lodged your complaint with the brokerage or bank.

WITHHOLDING TAX

Citizens of the United States pay 15% withholding tax only on cash dividends, and U.S. tax credit may be obtained for these payments as described before. There is no capital gains tax, but capital gains are usually taxed in the country of the investor. Interest is not taxed, either from bonds or from interest-bearing accounts.

DUTCH INVESTMENT JARGON

commissionairs: Stockbrokers.

ex-claim (excl.): Ex-rights.

for all exchanges: An order indication specifying that the order can be executed on any stock exchange (Amsterdam or otherwise), or after official business hours.

CF: Stands for Centrum voor Fondsenadministratie (Securities Administration Center), a subsidiary of the stock exchange. It indicates that a share or bond has no coupons and therefore the certificate must remain in the custody of the CF.

hoekman: Similar to the jobber on the London stock exchange. The *hoekman* makes a market in specific securities and is the trader through whom other members of the exchange, brokers and bankers, must trade.

K: Stands for "classic," which indicates that the share or bond certificate is in bearer form with a separate sheet of coupons.

New York shares: ADRs.

parallel market: Analogous to the NASDAQ market in this country, in that its listing requirements are less rigorous than for securities regularly listed. Trades take place on the Amsterdam floor, although the time and place may be somewhat restricted. Mostly smaller companies. Founded in 1982.

SOURCES OF INFORMATION

Not later than September, all companies on the Amsterdam exchange, including those on the parallel market, must publish their annual report. This may constitute the bulk of information you get from some Dutch companies although others publish a semiannual report. Those listed on a U.S. exchange are required to send at least semiannual reports and to make available to the press quarterly earnings figures.

Investment newsletters in Holland are primarily in Dutch, and thus of limited use to most U.S. investors. However, English readers have the excellent coverage of the London *Financial Times.* Banks are probably the best source of investment information in English. A number of them publish general investment letters monthly and some include specific stock and bond recommendations as well as industry analyses. The Algemene Bank Nederland publishes *Companies Profiles* and the *Monthly Review.* The AMRO Bank publishes the *AMRO Stock Market News* monthly.

USEFUL ADDRESSES

THE AMSTERDAM STOCK EXCHANGE

Vereniging voor de Effectenhandel
Bostbus 19163
1000 GD Amsterdam

BANKS

The following two banks provide
brokerage service and mutual funds.

Algemene Bank Nederland (ABN)
Vijzelstraat 32
Postbox 669
Amsterdam

Amsterdam-Rotterdam Bank
(AMRO)
Rembrandtplein 47
1017 CT Amsterdam

CHAPTER 15:

THE MILAN STOCK EXCHANGE

Courtesy of the Milan Stock Exchange

BORSA VALORI DI MILANO

The Milan Stock Exchange was founded in 1808 by decree of Viceroy Eugene Napoleon. It has since become the major stock exchange of Italy and accounts for over 90% of the exchange volume in equities and 80% of the exchange volume in fixed-income securities. A significant portion of large bond transactions in Italy, however, is dealt off the exchange. The other Italian exchanges are in Rome, Turin, Genoa, Naples, Florence, Bologna, Venice, Trieste, and Palermo.

Although the Milan exchange is the principal exchange of Italy, it is small compared to the size of the country and its economic base. The total value of its listed bonds is about $100 billion (U.S.). The total value of its listed shares is only $20 billion (U.S.), and as if that weren't small enough, it is estimated that about half of all listed shares are closely held.

The securities of 149 Italian companies trade on the Milan exchange. There are 201 shares and 1,190 bonds. Of the bonds, about 65% are issues of the government or public agencies. Of the shares, only about thirty enjoy a healthy turnover. The ten most active account for 45% to 55% of the exchange volume each year, indicating a market of little breadth.

There are no foreign shares listed on the Milan exchange. Any demand for such shares has been effectively curtailed by punitive deposit requirements. Italian investors who buy foreign securities must place 50% of the purchase price of such shares on deposit with the Bank of Italy (through a bank agent) in a noninterest-bearing account. The only exceptions are bonds issued by European Economic Community (EEC) authorities. The deposit is refunded only on the sale of the securities. It is hoped that in the future this kind of protectionism will be abandoned in favor of regulations aimed at increasing the efficiency and competitiveness of Italian markets with other world markets.

Investment of foreign capital is needed in Italy, and generally encouraged by the government. Nonresidents may buy or sell all types of securities, including money market instruments, and repatriate profits and revenues freely. The foreign investor, however, should be aware that the Italian securities market is, at least for the present, a troubled

---

THE MILAN STOCK MARKET AT A GLANCE
(official list only)

Capitalization:
Market value of shares in U.S.$* .... $20.5 billion
Nominal value of bonds in U.S.$* .... $103 billion
Volume:
Average daily volume of shares .... 21.9 million†
Percent of total volume represented by ten most active shares......... 54%
Listings:
Domestic equities... 201
Domestic fixed-interest securities.................................. 1,190
Foreign securities.. 0
Dividend (average yield) 3.16%
PE ratio (average) 22
Rank in the world:
Capitalization 12th
Turnover/shares.. 11th

*Exchange rate as of Dec. 30, 1983: $1 = L.1674.
*Source: The Milan Stock Exchange, *Annual Report,* 1983.

one. The lira is weak, inflation is high, state borrowings are enormous, and frequent changes in the government have not helped establish sound or consistent financial policies.

The Italian securities market, in general, has been the focus of a great deal of criticism, both from within Italy and from abroad. In the United States, it has been portrayed as a market of excessive speculation, insider trading, and little regulation. While these reports may have been exaggerated, there has definitely been some cause for concern. Large off-the-floor deals, at prices significantly lower than those on the exchange, have been commonplace. New issues—which can be problematic under the best of circumstances—have not, in the past, even required the issuing of a prospectus, although now prospectuses are "strongly recommended."

Changes have begun, however, and it is possible that the Milan Stock Exchange and the Italian securities market in general will be profoundly altered within a few years. Many of the changes are the result of new legislation, and many are the result of a new regulatory body, the Commissione Nazionale per le Società e le Borse (CONSOB), the Italian equivalent of the SEC.

REFORMS: A MARKET IN TRANSITION

CONSOB, founded in 1974, oversees official listing of securities and required financial disclosures. It is also responsible for the general operations of all the stock exchanges. Its most important task, however, is to modernize the securities trading system, which has seen no major reform in the last sixty years.

This undertaking is not made easier by the fact that the commission is chronically understaffed (some of the employees are even on loan from other agencies), and the office of the presidency, a political appointment, has been allowed to remain vacant for months at a time.

Some feel that the government has purposely dragged its feet with respect to CONSOB. If a strong risk-capital market should emerge in Milan, it is possible that it might absorb investment capital to which the state might otherwise have access. (Government issues are large and frequent.) At any rate, among the efforts of CONSOB has been the weeding out of failing companies from the official list. That alone halved the average 1982 PE ratio from the previous year and brought the percentage of exchange-listed securities that pay dividends up to 75%. As supervisor of trading, CONSOB has improved the handling of unlisted securities considerably, and has also initiated investigations into the trading practices of a number of Italian brokers.

In addition to the efforts of CONSOB, there has recently been considerable legislative initiative. Among the major reforms:

1. Semiannual reports are required from listed companies. By 1984 all companies with capital of 10 billion lire to 50 billion lire must have their reports audited; by 1985, all other companies; and banks must follow suit in 1986.
2. Double taxation of corporate profits has been abated.
3. An Italian depositary, "Monte Titoli," has been established.
4. A stamp tax has been levied that is higher for off-floor transactions. This is a small tax, but clearly a step toward limiting the major volume of trading to the stock exchanges.
5. Reasonable reevaluation of assets is now permitted.
6. Italian-managed mutual funds have been permitted and are given tax incentives to invest in industrial securities (i.e., not government securities).
7. Holding companies have been given incentives to divest industrial subsidiaries and to list them independently on the exchange.

Many more reforms have been proposed, and bills seem perpetually to be before Parliament. If you are interested in Italian securities, you should keep abreast of the most recent regulatory and legislative developments. An excellent source of information is the annual report of the Milan exchange, which has an English summary. Also, you may write to CONSOB for its bulletin and annual report (see "Useful Addresses").

ITALIAN CURRENCY AND EXCHANGE RATE WITH THE U.S. DOLLAR

The currency is the Italian lira, which, when used to designate amounts, is usually used in its plural form, "lire," abbreviated "L." Sometimes you will see the less desirable "Lit." Italy participates in the EMS and so maintains an exchange rate within EMS guidelines.

Securities must be bought and sold through one of two different types of accounts, *conto speciale* and *conto capital,* depending on how settlement is made. The requirement for these two types of accounts dates back to the 1950s, when there were two different exchange rates. Since that is no longer the case, however, there is currently no difference between the accounts.

In Figure 1 you can see a steady decline of the lira against the average of the world currencies (represented by the effective exchange rate) although it held its own against the U.S. dollar from 1977 to 1979. Room is left for you to continue the graph if you would like to do so.

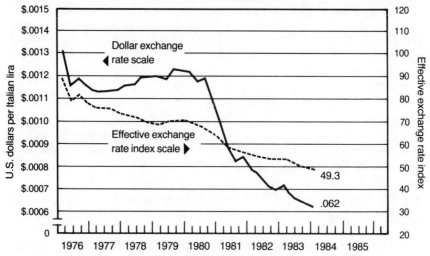

Figure 1. Exchange rate of the Italian lira with the U.S. dollar and the effective exchange rate with other major currencies.
Source: *Federal Reserve Bank of St. Louis*

SECURITIES TRADED ON THE MILAN STOCK EXCHANGE

stocks: Common and preferred. All are in registered form except for the new nonvoting savings shares (see below).

bonds: Straight, convertible, and indexed are available.

options: A small market in the stocks of major Italian companies. Options may either be exercised or allowed to expire. There is no secondary market.

rights: Most new shares are offered first through rights. They are usually good for five weeks.

A NEW TYPE OF STOCK

The nonvoting savings shares mentioned above, or *azioni di risparmio,* have a cumulative fixed dividend which is higher than that of common stock. These shares are a fast-growing new instrument in the Italian securities industry. Currently, there are over thirty issues. They may be issued by companies *in addition to* their common (voting) shares, and both may be listed on an exchange. Companies are given special tax incentives to issue such shares: distributed dividends are tax-deductible (i.e., for the company)! To the investor they are similar to preferred shares, although to the company they are structured quite differently.

These are particularly appropriate instruments for the Italian market because equities have been out of favor for a long time due to their low yield in a high-inflation economy. Their purpose is to attract investment back to industries that are badly in need of capital.

THREE SECURITIES MARKETS

Securities are traded in one of three markets:

listed securities: These make up the "official list." See the requirements below.

unlisted securities (mercato ristretto): These are traded on the exchange (as of 1977) and consist of shares only. This is an important market because it consists of the stock of many banks and financial institutions. Transactions are for cash.

over-the-counter market: This is an over-the-telephone market between brokers and banks. Almost any security can be traded in this fashion.

The principal requirements for listed securities are:

1. Minimum capital of 500 million lire.
2. Net assets of 1.5 billion lire.
3. Profit during the last two years.
4. A dividend in the previous year.
5. Shares with full rights (voting), freely transferable.
6. Minimum public distribution of 20% of shares.

Although CONSOB is considering more stringent requirements, it is currently allowing time for shares presently on the official list to come up to the above standards. Government securities are admitted to the official list automatically.

Italian shares purchased by a nonresident ordinarily remain in Italy in a bank depositary. However, bearer-share certificates (which are illegal for Italian nationals to own) may be brought out of the country if they are stamped "circotanti all 'estero." As such, they are negotiable outside Italy.

THE MAJOR STOCK INDEX

The major stock index is the Milan Indice Generale (MIB). It is a broadly based composite of fifteen industrial indexes. It is calculated on a base of 1,000 as of January 1, 1975, although it is often represented from a base of 100. The volatility of the index is apparent from its extremes. The high of 419 in 1981 is over six times the low of 65.5 that occurred only three years and four months earlier.

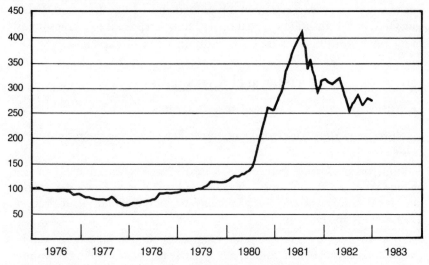

Figure 2. **Milan General Index (MIB), calculated from 100 in January of 1975.** Source: *The Milan Stock Exchange,* Annual Report, 1983.

Tables 1 and 2 list the the companies with the largest market capitalization, and the stocks having the largest turnover, respectively.

Table 1

THE TEN LARGEST STOCK ISSUES ON THE MILAN STOCK MARKET

	COMPANY	PER-SHARE PRICE IN LIRE*
1.	Assicurazioni Generali—insurance	33,550
2.	S.T.E.T.—holding company	1,749
3.	Banca Commerciale Italiana	26,600
4.	Credito Italiano—bank	3,223
5.	Banco di Roma	24,799
6.	S.I.P.—telephone	1,697
7.	S.I.P. risparmio (savings shares)	1,860
8.	Alleanza Assicurazioni—insurance	32,750
9.	Fiat—automobiles	3,360
10.	Banco Lariano	4,580

*Jan. 1, 1984.
Source: The Milan Stock Exchange, *Annual Report,* 1983.

MILAN TRADING FLOOR OPERATIONS

Only brokers may be members of an Italian stock exchange, and by law only Italian nationals may be brokers. The Milan exchange has 107 broker-members. Each must operate as an individual, that is, not as a brokerage firm, although each may have as many as three representatives assisting on the trading floor.

Table 2

THE TWENTY MOST ACTIVE STOCK ISSUES ON THE MILAN STOCK EXCHANGE

	COMPANY	% OF TOTAL MARKET TURNOVER
1.	Assicurazioni Generali—insurance	10.41
2.	Fiat—automobiles	9.16
3.	Olivetti—business machines	6.06
4.	Montedison—chemicals and synthetic fibers	6.06
5.	Riunione Adriatica de Sicurità—insurance	5.98
6.	Fiat (preferred)—automobiles	4.88
7.	Snia B.P.D.	3.75
8.	Farmitalia Carlo Erba	2.88
9.	La Rinascente ordinaria—retailer	2.64
10.	Italmobiliare	2.15
11.	I.F.I.—holding company	1.86
12.	Pirelli S.p.A.—tires	1.82
13.	Mediobanca—banking	1.80
14.	Dalmine—steel tubes	1.73
15.	La Centrale—holding company	1.67
16.	S.I.P.—telephone	1.53
17.	Italcementi—cement	1.40
18.	Alleanza Assicurazioni—insurance	1.25
19.	Bastogi I.R.B.S.—holding company	1.20
20.	Toro—insurance	1.05

Source: The Milan Stock Exchange, *Annual Report,* 1983.

Trading is by means of a roll-call system. Prices are fixed to accommodate the greatest number of buy and sell orders. The prices of actively traded securities may be fixed several times throughout the trading session. The types of orders possible are "at best" (at the market), "at discretion," "at limit," and "circa." Brokers may not take positions in the securities themselves.

The size of trading lots is specified for each issue. They vary from lots of 25 to 100, 500, or 1,000 shares. The smaller-sized lots are generally for actively traded shares. Odd lots are usually available through banks.

Trading hours for securities on the official list are from 10:00 A.M. to 1:45 P.M., Monday through Friday, although the closing time can vary, depending on volume. Trading in unlisted securities is only on Wednesdays beginning at 3:30 P.M. The official exchange rate of the lira is set at 1:45 P.M. daily in one of the trading rings.

MUTUAL FUNDS

Until recently, mutual funds were not permitted in Italy. Those funds that specialized in Italian securities (there were about ten) were based in Luxembourg. However, in 1984, mutual funds were legalized, and a state-owned credit institution, Istituto Mobiliare Italiano (IMI), immediately initiated two funds, Imigest and Imicapital. IMI already directed two highly successful Italian mutual funds based in Luxembourg, Fonditalia and Interfund. The second largest Italian insurance company, Riunione Adriatica de Sicurta, launched the Gestiras Fund.

It is expected that about twenty funds will be initiated within a year. If so, they may substantially increase turnover on the Milan Stock Exchange and improve the Italian risk capital market in general.

COMMISSION AND SETTLEMENT

Commission rates are .7% for stocks, .3% for bonds, and .15% for government securities. A stamp duty is also added which consists, successively, of lire 10, 20, 30, etc., for each hundred thousand lire of the total amount of the transaction.

Settlement for listed securities is "for the account." An account period, although it may vary from year to year, usually runs from mid-month to mid-month with the settlement day coming at the end of the month. Unlisted securities are traded for cash, meaning within three days.

Settlement for bonds is usually for cash. Exceptions are convertible bonds and some government bonds which may be traded "for the account." Carry-over transactions to postpone settlement dates are possible, but are not available to nonresidents.

WITHHOLDING TAX

Withholding tax on stock dividends is 15%. Government bonds, including provincial, municipal, public agencies, etc., are all exempt from withholding tax. Also exempt are straight bonds and convertible bonds issued before 1974. Other than those exceptions, withholding on corporate bonds is 20% (although for some bonds of credit institutions and some convertible bonds, the rate is 10%).

ITALIAN INVESTMENT JARGON

azioni: Shares.

azioni di risparmio: From the investor's point of view, these are the same as nonvoting cumulative preferred shares.

borse: Exchange.

borse valori: Stock exchange.

CONSOB: Commission equivalent to the SEC.

conto capital and *conto speciale:* Types of accounts within which non-residents must hold securities.

for the account: Settlement for securities on a day at the end of the month for the prior mid-month to mid-month.

mercato ristretto: Market constituting the unlisted shares of (mostly) banks.

obbligazioni: Fixed-interest securities.

reddito fisso: Fixed interest.

privilegiato: Preferred stock.

savings shares: See *azione di risparmio.*

titoli: Securities.

USEFUL ADDRESSES

THE MILAN STOCK EXCHANGE

Comitato Direttivo
degli Agenti di Cambio
Borsa Valori di Milano
Piazza degli Afferi, 6
20123 - Milan

THE ITALIAN SECURITIES
REGULATION AGENCY

CONSOB
Via Isonzo 19/dc
00198 Rome

BANKS
*The following two banks accept
securities accounts and publish limited
investment information in English.*

Banca Commerciale Italiana
Piazza della Scala 6
Milan

Banco di Roma
Via del Corso 307
Rome

PROFILES OF OTHER STOCK EXCHANGES

The Brussels Stock Exchange

THE EXCHANGE

Belgium recently provided another example of a moribund securities market brought to life by favorable tax legislation. Although obviously aided by the general recovery, incentives for both investors (deductions of up to Bf 40,000) and for corporations (deduction of some dividends) helped double volume on the Brussels exchange from 1981 to 1983. And as if the exchange could not accommodate the additional volume fast enough, a lively over-the-counter market developed as well.

There are stock exchanges in four Belgian cities: Brussels, Antwerp, Ghent, and Liège. The largest, Brussels, has 306 members and conducts three to four times the business of the other exchanges combined.

There are 342 stocks listed on the Brussels exchange, 138 of which are of foreign issue. Foreign investment is welcome in Belgium al-

---

THE BRUSSELS STOCK MARKET AT A GLANCE

Capitalization:
Market value of shares in Belgian francs* . . . . Bf 600 billion
Nominal value of bonds in Belgian francs . . . . Bf 1,924 billion

Volume:
Yearly volume of shares in Belgian francs . . . . Bf 137 billion
Yearly volume of bonds in Belgian francs . . . . Bf 133 billion
Average daily volume of shares in Belgian francs . . . . Bf 560 million

Listings:
Belgian shares 204
Foreign shares 138
Belgian corporate bonds 33
Foreign corporate bonds 7
Belgian government bonds 206
Foreign government bonds 1

*Exchange rate as of Dec. 31, 1982: $1 = BF 46.73.
Source: Brussels Stock Exchange, *Annual Report,* statistics for 1983.

though both interest and dividends are subject to 15% withholding for nonresidents; in some cases this can be reduced to 11%. However, interest from deposits of, or securities issued by, financial institutions is not subject to withholding tax.

International ownership and transfer of securities are efficiently managed through the CIK. (Interprofessional Organization of Deposits and Transfers). There are no foreign exchange controls.

Shares are issued in both registered and bearer forms. "Jouissand shares" (profit-sharing certificates) resemble common stock and are the

Courtesy of the Brussels Stock Exchange

most frequently traded type of share. Preferred shares are also available. Bonds may be either straight or convertible and are issued either in bearer or registered form.

Securities are traded in three distinct markets on the Brussels exchange:

parquet market: This is for securities traded infrequently; settlement is the next day.

corbeille market: This is for securities that trade more frequently than on the parquet market. Settlement is the next day.

Both the above markets trade by means of the roll-call system. The following market trades by continuous auction.

marché à terme (account settlement market): This is for the most actively traded major securities. Minimum transaction lots are set by the exchange (from 5 to 100 shares), and settlement is at the end of the two-week accounting period.

Brussels is a relatively small equity market when compared to other major markets, so investors are advised to stick with shares of the larger companies. In many cases, these are large multinationals, and, in some

Table 1

THE TWENTY MOST ACTIVE STOCKS ON THE BRUSSELS STOCK EXCHANGE

COMPANY	VOLUME IN BILLIONS OF BELGIAN FRANCS
1. Petrofina	13,138
2. Intercam	6,582
3. Réserve (Sté Générale)	6,320
4. Ebes	4,574
5. GBL	3,614
6. Philips	3,032
7. Solvay	2,872
8. Inco	2,717
9. Stilfontein	2,001
10. Unerg	1,958
11. Genstar	1,938
12. Sony	1,865
13. De Beers	1,740
14. Amax	1,673
15. Royal Dutch	1,658
16. Boeing	1,573
17. ITT	1,553
18. Eastman	1,540
19. President Brand	1,517
20. Electrobel	1,498

Source: Brussels Stock Exchange, *Annual Report,* statistics for 1983.

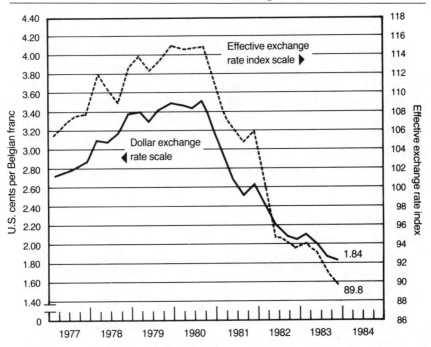

Figure 1. Exchange rate of the Belgian franc with the U.S. dollar and the effective exchange rate with other major currencies.
Source: *Federal Reserve Bank of St. Louis*

cases, foreign issues. The twenty most active shares traded in 1982 are shown in Table 1.

There are no restrictions on foreign investment. Brokerage fees, in comparison with other countries, are low. Both stock brokers *(agents de change)* and banks can accept security orders although only brokers can execute orders on the floor of the exchange.

The Federal Reserve Bank of St. Louis has plotted the exchange rate for the Belgian franc against the U.S. dollar and for the Belgian franc against seventeen other currencies in order to provide an effective exchange rate. Shown in Figure 1, this graph is similar to the ones in earlier chapters except that the U.S. rate is given in cents, not dollars.

The Hong Kong Stock Exchange

BACKGROUND

Financial markets in Hong Kong are overshadowed by uncertainty over China's intentions with respect to the future of the Colony. At issue is almost 90% of the land that presently constitutes Hong Kong, without which it is felt the Colony could not economically survive. The recent treaty, initialed by the ambassadors of both Great Britain and China, is likely to be ratified by the governments of both countries. In it, China publicly claims that it wants to keep Hong Kong a viable marketplace, but China's definition of a viable marketplace may be different from that of free-wheeling Hong Kong. Its markets are typified by a laissez-faire attitude of noninterference by the government, and there is also the problem of extensive trade with a number of countries with which China has no diplomatic relations.

Hong Kong is made up of a combination of territories that were acquired by the British in three separate stages. The island of Hong Kong, only thirty-two square miles (Manhattan, by comparison, is twenty-two square miles) was acquired in 1842. Theoretically, it belongs to the United Kingdom in perpetuity as does Britain's second acquisition in 1860, Stonecutter's Island and the Kowloon Peninsula (both, an additional thirteen square miles). The third and final acquisition is the one over which there are the most problems. Leased in 1887 for ninety-nine years, the New Territories make up the largest segment of Hong Kong, 365 square miles. It consists of a relatively large segment of the mainland bordering the Kowloon Peninsula and 235 small islands.

Private investment, needed to upgrade present industrial facilities, has slowed considerably, awaiting more tangible evidence of China's future course of action. If Hong Kong is to enjoy the economic activity for the next twelve years that it has up to now, China must signal the rest of the world that investments in Hong Kong will be safe. Probably the happiest (and most realistic) solution would be a substantial Chinese investment in Hong Kong that would create jobs and help repair the Colony's ailing industries. So far, there has been limited Chinese investment in some Hong Kong factories and a few banks, but nothing on the scale needed to reassure the world investment community of the future of the Colony.

THE STOCK EXCHANGES

There are presently four stock exchanges in Hong Kong. The oldest was founded in 1891 under the name "Association of Stockholders." Another exchange, founded in 1921, eventually merged with it after World War II to form the present Hong Kong Stock Exchange. Because of the refusal of the Hong Kong exchange to admit many businessmen, a rival exchange, the Far Eastern Stock Exchange, was founded in 1969. Two additional exchanges, the Kam Ngan Stock Exchange and the Kowloon Stock Exchange, were founded in 1971 and 1972 respectively. Other exchanges were in the planning stage but at this point the government stepped in to prevent formation of any more stock exchanges.

Today the four exchanges are loosely joined in the Hong Kong Federation of Stock Exchanges which, among other things, imposes the same listing requirements for all corporations. There has been a movement to further consolidate the exchanges but, so far, objections of various members have not been overcome. Older firms on the Hong Kong exchange enjoy a priority in bid selection that might be lost in a merger with the younger exchanges. The price of a seat on the exchanges differs widely, and those members who deal primarily for their own account (mostly individuals) fear that a merger would bring on increased capital requirements that would force them off the exchange.

Speculation on the exchanges seems to be the order of the day with shares selling sometimes at extreme multiples. Hong Kong Land has traded at 300 times its earnings. Volume, also, can vary enormously. The Hang Seng Index, which is the oldest of the indexes in Hong Kong, is probably the most volatile in the world. From 1973 to 1974 it tumbled from 1,774 to 150. The index is composed of over thirty-three stocks which usually account for about 70% of the total Hong Kong volume. It is based on a value of 100 as of July 31, 1964. Highly capitalized stocks carry a great deal of weight in the index, and a large percentage of stocks are issues of property companies or companies with property interests.

Membership, which may be individual or corporate, on the four exchanges totals over 1,000, and includes a few foreign firms. The majority of members trade for their own accounts and not for customers. In volume, the Far Eastern and Kam Ngan exchanges have surpassed the Hong Kong exchange, and the Kowloon exchange now has only a very modest turnover.

Trading is by auction in front of huge trading boards. Orders to buy or sell securities are written on the board, and the offer can be accepted by anyone in the room (with priority given to senior members). Other information such as dividends is included on the board. Columns beneath the company names list buyers and sellers. Odd lots are available but most trading is in board lots (round lots) which vary from 1,000 to 2,000 shares (although there are some lots set at either higher or lower amounts). Minimum increments have been set at which prices may move (Table 2).

The above increments are important in another way in that they are used to determine limits on price moves. Although price volatility on the Hong Kong exchanges is notorious, there are restraints imposed by the exchange: the price of a board lot may not move more than four times its increment from one transaction to the next. There are, however, no limits on opening prices.

There are two trading sessions daily on each exchange, 10:00 A.M. to 12:30 P.M. and 2:30 P.M. to 3:30 P.M. Settlement is the following day, although registration of transfer may take up to six weeks. Commissions, although negotiable, are often around 5%. The minimum is HK$25, and there is an additional charge of 1% possible. Sellers must pay a stamp tax of HK$5.

One of the advantages of the Hong Kong market is taxes. There is

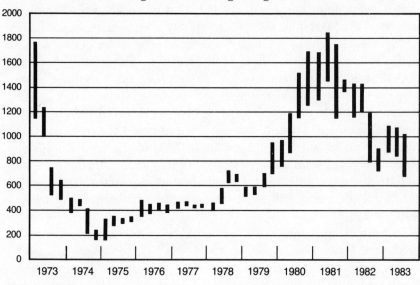

Figure 2. **Hang Seng Index.**

Table 2

MARKET PRICE	MINIMUM INCREMENT IN HONG KONG DOLLARS
Under 2.00	.02
2.00–4.99	.025
5.00–9.99	.05
10.00–29.99	.10
30.00–49.99	.25
50.00–99.99	.50
100.00–199.99	1.00
200.00 and above	2.00

no tax on capital gains or dividends. There are also no foreign exchange controls. Interest, however, is subject to 15% withholding.

There is no over-the-counter market so that bringing a company public means listing it on an exchange. Among the more important requirements for exchange listing are that a company must have HK$20 million in paid-in capital and the public offering must consist of at least HK$5 million.

There are almost 200 stocks listed on the Hong Kong Stock Exchange, and a few more than 200 on the Far Eastern Stock Exchange. Many issues are listed on all four exchanges. Market capitalization is concentrated in relatively few stocks so that the nonresident is best advised to stick to the larger companies.

Dividends are usually issued twice a year providing that an "interim" dividend is announced. Otherwise they are annual. Companies are required to publish their annual reports at least fourteen days prior to the annual meeting. Financial reporting for some of the smaller companies, in particular, is often lacking by U.S. standards.

The bond market is quite small and usually not of interest to nonresident investors because of the withholding tax. There are practically no government bonds, and the corporate bond market is almost dormant except for convertible bonds. These bonds, some with warrants, offer the possibility of sharing in the volatility of stock prices whenever the market price of the underlying stock exceeds that of the conversion price.

The following Hong Kong securities are available in the United States as ADRs. The depositary bank is Morgan Guaranty Trust. Five issues are also available through Citibank as marked. The ratio of shares to ADRs is given after each in parentheses.

Carrian Investments Ltd. (10:1)

Cheung Kong Holdings Ltd. (1:1)

China Light & Power Co., Ltd. (1:1)

Hongkong Electric Holdings Ltd. (1:1)

Hongkong & Kowloon Wharf & Godown Co. Ltd. (1:1)

Hongkong Land Co., Ltd. (2:1) (also Citibank)

Hongkong and Shanghai Banking Corp. (1:1) (also Citibank)

Hutchison Whampoa Ltd. (5:1)

Jardine, Matheson & Co., Ltd. (1:1)

Swire Pacific Ltd. (2:1) (also Citibank)

Swire Properties Ltd. (1:1)

Trafalgar Housing Ltd. (5:1)

Wheelock Marden and Co., Ltd. (5:1) (also Citibank)

Winsor Industrial Corp. Ltd. (5:1)

The Luxembourg Stock Exchange

BACKGROUND

The Grand Duchy of Luxembourg is an independent state that borders France, Germany, and Belgium. It is a constitutional monarchy with its own language, Luxembourgish, and a history that dates back to the tenth century (although it has been independent only since 1867).

The stock exchange, located in the capital city of Luxembourg, opened in 1929, five months before the New York Stock Exchange crash in October.

During World War II, the occupying authorities removed all foreign securities from the exchange, permitting only German or Luxembourgish securities to trade. At the end of the war, the exchange closed and did not reopen until October 10, 1945. It was not until the 1950s,

Courtesy of the Luxembourg Stock Exchange

THE LUXEMBOURG STOCK MARKET AT A GLANCE

Volume:
    Total volume of shares in Luxembourg francs .... Lf 1,600.7 million
    Total volume of bonds in Luxembourg francs .... Lf 11,288 million
Listings:
    Total listings 2,070
    Domestic equities.. 34
    Domestic fixed-interest securities..................................... 91
    Foreign shares.. 128
    Foreign fixed-interest securities 1,700
    Domestic investment funds... 73
    Foreign investment funds 44

Source: The Luxembourg Stock Exchange, *Facts and Figures,* data for 1983.

---

after foreign exchange restrictions were lifted, that Luxembourg began to emerge as an international securities trading center.

Today, the vast majority of security trading in Luxembourg is in Eurobonds. Most large transactions (over $100,000 [U.S.]) are conducted over the counter, that is, between banks, and only smaller transactions find their way to the stock exchange. Luxembourg, counting the over-the-counter market, handles the second largest volume of Eurobonds in the world (after London), and the stock exchange lists more Eurobond issues than the exchange of any other country.

THE STOCK EXCHANGE

There are forty-six members of the stock exchange: thirty-four banks and twelve brokerages. Two U.S. brokers have seats: E.F. Hutton & Co., and Merrill Lynch Europe S.A. The official hours of the exchange are 11:00 A.M. to 1:00 P.M., Monday through Friday. Each security is traded by auction when its name comes up in roll call. All transactions on the exchange are for cash.

Although prices for domestic securities are listed in Luxembourg francs, all foreign securities are quoted—and settlements made—in the currencies of their respective countries, thus allowing the investor to save foreign exchange fees. This is a special feature of the Luxembourg exchange. In fact, the first bond managed by an international banking syndicate and issued in a currency other than that of the country of issue was listed on the Luxembourg Stock Exchange in 1961.

Stocks account for only about 5% of the listings on the exchange.

Domestic bonds and investment funds account for even less. The rest are international bonds.

Brokerage fees range from .8% for stocks to .5% for local bonds. The accrued interest added to bond purchases is calculated from the last coupon date to the sixth calendar day *after* the transaction.

Investment funds (both closed-end and mutual funds) are popular in Luxembourg, where government regulations are particularly favorable. Over 100 are quoted on the exchange, including most of the leading funds of Europe. Many invest in equities of one special geographical zone, or only in equities issued by companies active in one sector, such as electronics or telecommunications. In 1983 the eight most actively traded funds were Capital Growth Bond Fund, Robeco, Pan Holding, Rolinco, Transpacific Fund, Japan Pacific Fund, Rorento, and Comète.

The trading of shares on the Luxembourg exchange is dominated by relatively few large foreign equities. Although the eight issues shown in Table 3 constitute a whopping 72% of the total share turnover in 1982, if one takes into account the enormous volume of bond trading (and the smaller amount of trading in investment funds) the percentage of the total exchange volume represented by the shares in Table 3 is only 8%.

The currency is the Luxembourg franc ("Lf" or "FLX"). The exchange rate is on par with the Belgian franc by virtue of the Belgian and Luxembourg Economic Union (BLEU). There are no foreign exchange restrictions although there are two different currency exchange systems (as in Belgium) depending on the transaction. The system used for the purchase of securities (the "free market") is usually at a rate 2%

Table 3

THE EIGHT MOST ACTIVE STOCKS ON THE
LUXEMBOURG STOCK EXCHANGE

COMPANY	VOLUME FOR YEAR IN MILLIONS OF LUXEMBOURG FRANCS
1. Arico-America Realestate Investment Co.	388.5
2. Royal Dutch	183.0
3. Belgo-Mineira	171.0
4. Philips	136.1
5. IFINT	84.5
6. Banque Internationale à Luxembourg	84.4
7. G.T. Western Land	63.6
8. ARBED	47.6

Source: The Luxembourg Stock Exchange, *Facts and Figures,* data for 1983.

or 3% lower than the rate for commercial transactions (the "official market").

In most cases, U.S. citizens are not charged withholding tax on interest from domestic bonds. Interest on Eurobonds and other foreign bonds is also tax-free. Dividends from domestic shares, however, are subject to a 7.5% withholding except for dividends from Luxembourg holding companies which are free of tax.

The Luxembourg Stock Exchange will supply you with additional information. Their *Annual Report* is available in English, from Bourse de Luxembourg, Boite postale 165, 2011 Luxembourg.

The Madrid Stock Exchange

BACKGROUND

The Madrid Stock Exchange is the largest of the four exchanges in Spain (the others are in Barcelona, Bilbao, and Valencia). It was founded in 1831 by decree of King Fernando VII.

The nineteenth century was a time of economic and political eclipse for Spain. The first half of the twentieth century was not much better, with two world wars disrupting the economies in most of the

Courtesy of the Madrid Stock Exchange

THE MADRID STOCK MARKET AT A GLANCE

Capitalization:

Market value of domestic shares in U.S.$*................. $11,177.0 million

Market value of corporate bonds in U.S.$* .... $6,813.9 million

Market value of government bonds in U.S.$*.............. $5,655.2 million

Volume:

Average daily volume of shares in U.S.$* .... $5.0 million

Average daily volume of bonds in U.S.$*...................... $1.7 million

Average daily volume of government bonds in U.S.$*........... $.5 million

Total listings 448

PE ratio (average) 6.87

Average price over book value.. 0.41

*Exchange rate as of Jan. 1, 1983: $1 = 125.5 pesetas.
Source: Madrid Stock Exchange, *Fact Sheet,* 1983.

---

countries of Europe. (Spain's questionable position in World War II did not help its isolationism.) The greatest devastation, however, was from the bloody revolution of 1936–1939.

The Spanish economy did not begin to improve until the mid-1960s, when an increase in tourism, foreign investment, and foreign loans brought capital to the country. The political climate improved markedly in 1976 with the orderly transition to a constitutional monarchy, but by then the worldwide recession had caused a reversal in growth of the real GNP and raised inflation to 14%.

In 1978, branches of foreign banks were permitted to open in Spain. Their growth, however, was cut short when the new socialist government came to power in 1982. A severe tightening of monetary policy and reserve requirements effectively undermined their ability to compete with domestic banks.

A certain amount of protectionism (such as for domestic banks) is understandable; however, it is not clear to what degree, if any, such protectionism will affect the securities markets in the future. Currently, there are no restrictions on the purchase or sale of Spanish securities by nonresidents except that a permit is needed if the transaction exceeds 50% of the total capital stock.

THE BOLSA

At the beginning of 1983 there were 448 companies listed on the Bolsa (the stock exchange), down fifty issues from the previous year. Volume, however, was healthy, with records broken successively for three years in a row, partly because of the recent introduction of new instruments such as treasury bills and commercial paper. For many years, volume in Madrid has been dominated by shares rather than bonds. In 1982, trading was 68.8% shares, 23% bank bonds, 7.1% government bonds, and 1.1% industrial bonds.

Unfortunately, there is not much depth to the Madrid market. The trading of the first six stocks in Table 4 frequently account for between 40% and 50% of the total exchange volume. Five of these companies are banks; one (Hidrola) is an electric company.

As a group, banks dominate the stock market, and are usually the securities of most interest to nonresident investors. Currently, their prices are still depressed because of the tightening of monetary policy and reserve requirements mentioned earlier. At the beginning of 1983 they were trading at an average of 66% of their book value and an average PE of 5.4.

Only brokers may trade on the exchange floor. They are appointed as individuals to the College of Stockbrokers after completion of a competitive state examination. Currently, there are seventy-six broker-members of the exchange. Trading is by open outcry in the trading rings.

The Madrid exchange is exclusively a spot, or cash market. Margin buying and short selling were introduced in 1981, but Bolsa officials are quick to point out that margin buying has not turned the exchange into a forward market. The difference is that in a forward market both the buyer and seller establish a price today, and agree on a future date when settlement will be made; the transaction only becomes effective

Table 4

**THE TEN MOST ACTIVE STOCKS ON
THE MADRID STOCK EXCHANGE**

COMPANY	TURNOVER IN MILLIONS OF PESETAS
1. Banco Central	13,739.7
2. Banco de Santander	11,838.7
3. Banco Hispano Americano	11,197.4
4. Banesto	9,190.3
5. Banco de Bilbao	7,577.6
6. Hidrola	6,316.5
7. Banco Popular Español	4,277.2
8. Fecsa p. A.	3,818.0
9. Telefónica	3,700.1
10. Iberduero	3,619.1

Source: Madrid Stock Exchange, *Statistical Summary,* data for 1982.

on the future date. In margin buying, the buyer and seller establish the price and make the transaction effective as of that day, and buyer and seller deliver a specific percentage of the total amount due. The rest is made up by (and owed to) the broker. The margin required is 25%, which is paid by *both* the buyer and seller. When the respective brokers are reimbursed, the buyer pays the 75% owed and the seller delivers the entire amount of securities. The point is that there is some collateral supporting the transaction.

Transactions effected during the first two weeks of the month will come due at the end of the month. Transactions effected during the final two weeks of the month will come due at the end of the following month. These initial periods may be prolonged twice for a possible extension of ninety days.

Spanish mutual funds may interest the nonresident investor with limited resources for diversity. Mutual funds are limited by the amount they may invest abroad with the result that most cover the Spanish securities market thoroughly.

Spanish banks will open accounts for nonresidents for the purchase of domestic securities. (There are no foreign securities listed on the exchange.) To open an account, it is easiest to go through a U.S. branch of a Spanish bank initially, although the account must reside in Spain for the purchase of securities.

The *Annual Report* of the Madrid Stock Exchange is published in an English version and furnishes an excellent source of information on stock market activity. You may also obtain a list of brokers in Madrid from the exchange. Write to Agencia General de Mercado de Valores, Bolsa de Madrid, Plaza de la Lealtad, 1, Madrid 14, España.

There is no withholding on dividends for nonresidents and no capital gains tax. Interest, however, is subject to 24% withholding. Although you can receive tax credit for this amount, Spanish bonds are, for this reason, of little interest to nonresident investors.

The Rio de Janeiro and São Paulo Stock Exchanges

VOLUME ON THE TWO EXCHANGES

There are nine stock exchanges in Brazil, but only two, Rio de Janeiro and São Paulo, are significant enough to attract international investment. Table 5 compares the two exchanges with respect to volume

Courtesy of the São Paulo Stock Exchange

(shown in U.S. dollars); the last column gives the average exchange rate of the cruzeiro with the U.S. dollar.

The exchange in Rio is generally regarded as the larger exchange,

Table 5

VOLUME ON BRAZIL'S TWO MAJOR STOCK EXCHANGES

	VOLUME IN U.S. $			EXCHANGE RATE (NUMBER OF CRUZEIROS PER U.S. $)
YEAR	SÃO PAULO	RIO DE JANEIRO	TOTAL	
1973	1,834	1,131	2,965	6.126
1974	1,058	954	2,012	6.790
1975	1,373	1,929	3,302	8.127
1976	1,049	1,594	2,643	10.673
1977	1,054	1,625	2,679	14.144
1978	1,331	1,623	2,954	18.078
1979	1,559	1,699	3,258	26.818
1980	1,743	3,629	5,372	52.811
1981	1,305	4,864	6,169	93.349
1982	2,217	3,741	5,958	178.886
1983*	1,947	989	2,936	513.528

*Until October.
Source: Comissão de Valores Mobiliários e Banco Central do Brasil.

and the market prices of its shares, rather than São Paulo's, are quoted in the U.S. press. However, for many years, São Paulo has conducted the greater volume in stock. Rio's volume comes primarily from futures contracts. In Table 6, you can see that because of the drastic drop in futures trading the total volume of the São Paulo exchange, as of October, 1983, is almost double that of Rio de Janeiro.

Table 6

SUMMARY OF STOCK EXCHANGE TRANSACTIONS*

	1981		1982		1983†	
MARKETS	SÃO PAULO	RIO DE JANEIRO	SÃO PAULO	RIO DE JANEIRO	SÃO PAULO	RIO DE JANEIRO
Cash	876	760	1,246	977	1,110	575
Forward	7	18	52	30	192	9
Call options	304	—	636	35	638	332
Futures	119	4,086	283	2,699	7	73
Total	1,305	4,864	2,217	3,741	1,947	989

*All figures in millions of U.S. dollars calculated at exchange rates shown in Table 4.
†Until October.
Source: Comissão de Valores Mobiliários e Banco do Brasil.

The drop in share futures trading (defined below) was the result of two highly restrictive regulations *(instrucão* #19 and #25) passed by the securities regulation body (the Comissão de Valores Mobiliários e Banco Central do Brasil) in 1981 and 1982 respectively. In general, they restrict speculation in share futures trading to specific percentages of investors' portfolios.

THE TWO MARKETS

The Bovespa (short for Bolsa de Valores de São Paulo) lists the securities of 594 companies. The Rio de Janeiro exchange lists just over 500. Both trade listed and unlisted securities in a continuous auction system. Both exchanges are made up of the following four markets:

cash market: Settlement is in five days.

forward market: Settlement may be in five, thirty, sixty, or ninety days. Margin is required, and minimum-sized trading lots are stipulated. Forward contracts may be closed before the settlement date.

options market: Established in 1979. Only calls are now available although there are plans to introduce puts soon. There is a limit of 500 contracts per investor. There has been some intervention in this market, such as the compulsory closing of some contracts in November 1981. The market has grown steadily and today almost 450 trades are executed daily in São Paulo. In Rio, options were introduced somewhat later, and volume is about half that of São Paulo.

futures market: Futures contracts are for round lots of securities. Maturity dates are set by the exchange. Margin is, of course, required, and the investor is exposed to possible margin calls. Due to the regulations mentioned earlier, trading was severely curtailed in 1983.

The currency is the cruzeiro (abbreviated "Cr"), which contains 100 centavos. At the beginning of 1984 the exchange rate was $1 = Cr 926.5.

The brokerage fees range from 1.5% to 2% with a minimum of Cr 800. There are also registration fees of .1% on futures contracts, .2% on options contracts, and .1% for each thirty days on forward contracts. There is a transfer fee on registered stock of Cr 447, and a transaction notice fee to cover the cost of mailing the transaction verification to the investor.

Nonresidents may purchase Brazilian stocks only on a Brazilian stock exchange through Brazilian brokers designated as "foreign investment companies." There is a requirement that investment funds be "applied toward the subscription or acquisition of a diversified portfolio of shares issued by open [public] companies." There is also a requirement that 50% of investment funds be "invested in the acquisition of shares issued by open companies controlled by private national capital."[1]

The Bovespa Index *(Indice Bovespa)* is a broadly based index that represents 80% of the total volume on the São Paulo Stock Exchange (Figure 3). It is calculated from a base of 100 on January 1, 1973. The increases in the index have been matched by increases in volume. However, one's enthusiasm for the price performance of any stocks in Brazil must be viewed in light of the staggering inflation in that country.

If you are interested in South American securities you may want to start with a mutual fund. The following is a list of funds and their management:

Brasilinter S.A., Brasilvest S.A., and Brazilian Assets S.A., managed by Unibanco Banco de Investimento do Brasil S.A., Rua da Quitanda, 157–4ọ andar, São Paulo, SP.

[1]"A Profile of the Bolsa de Valores de São Paulo," mimeograph copy available from the Bovespa.

Brazilian Selected Securities, managed by Banco Montreal de Investimento S.A., Montrealbank, Travessa do Ouvidor, 4–21ọ andar, Rio de Janeiro, RJ.

The Brazil Fund, managed by Banco de Investimento Lar Brasileiro S.A., Rua do Ouvidor, 97–8ọ andar, Rio de Janeiro, RJ.

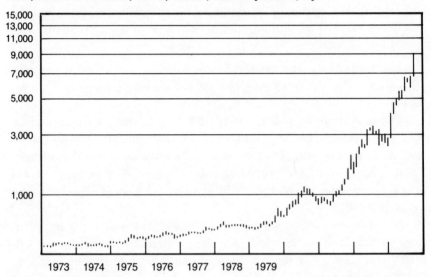

Figure 3. **The Bovespa Index.**　Source: *The São Paulo Stock Exchange*

Brazilian tax on dividends is 23%. Tax on interest depends on the maturity of the security: for maturities less than twenty-four months, 40%; for maturities from twenty-four to sixty months, 35%; and for maturities over sixty months, 30%.

Brazil is a large country with vast resources, but anyone investing in Brazilian securities should be aware of the huge financial problems the country is facing. From 1973 to 1983 inflation went from 15.5% to 127%. The foreign debt, rising by an even greater percentage, went from $12.6 billion to $90 billion (U.S.), making it the world's largest debtor. Twenty percent of the work force is unemployed, and the country is in a deep recession.

At present, default on foreign debts seems to have been avoided, but Brazil will not be back from the brink for many years to come. In the meantime, there is the risk of various "political" solutions to the nation's economic problems, which could decimate foreign investments or freeze them within the country indefinitely.

The Johannesburg Stock Exchange

BACKGROUND

The Johannesburg Stock Exchange was founded in 1887, one year after the discovery of the Witwatersrand goldfields. For fifty years it remained primarily an exchange for the shares of mining companies. Although gold now accounts for only 29% of all South African exports, and there are three times as many industrial companies listed on the stock exchange as there are mining companies, gold is still the primary reason for nonresidents to invest in South Africa. Over the years, yields from the dividends of gold-mining shares have averaged 7% to 8% and often have been higher. When the price of gold rises, the price of gold shares will often rise faster, creating opportunities for substantial capital gains in addition to the dividends.

Courtesy of the Johannesburg Stock Exchange

THE EXCHANGE

The Johannesburg Stock Exchange is the only stock exchange in South Africa. Its hours are from 9:30 A.M. to 4:00 P.M., Monday through Friday. Trading, by two-way auction, is only between brokers. There are no jobbers or specialists as in London or New York.

THE JOHANNESBURG STOCK MARKET AT A GLANCE

Capitalization:
Total market capitalization in rands . . . . R85 billion
Market value of gold shares in rands. . . . . R22.7 billion
Market value of mining financial shares in rands. . . . . R19.7 billion
Market value of industrial sector shares in rands. . . . . R34 billion
Market value of other shares in rands. . . . . R8.6 billion
Volume:
Total volume for the year in rands . . . . R3.8 billion
Nominal value of government bond trades in rands. . . . . R22 billion
Listings:
Equities. 905
Fixed-interest securities 729

Source: Johannesburg Stock Exchange, *Annual Report,* 1983.

Despite popular belief, there is no domestic commodities market in South Africa. Investors who want to purchase gold may obtain two types of coins on the stock exchange. The most well known is the krugerrand, containing 1 ounce of fine gold; the other is the 2 rand, containing 7.3 ounces of fine gold. There are other smaller coins also available but they are not traded as actively.

Securities available on the Johannesburg Stock Exchange include both stocks and bonds. Stocks, which may be either common (called "equities") or preferred, are in registered form. Dividends are paid semiannually. Corporate bonds, called "debentures," pay interest semiannually. They are usually in bearer form with maturities from five to twenty years. Some issues amortize their capital over the life of the bond. Mutual funds are not traded on the exchange but are available from stockbrokers and banks.

The most actively traded stocks for the calendar year 1982 were the following:

S.A. Selected Holdings Ltd.—industrial engineering

Retco Ltd.—financial properties

Egoli Consolidated Mines Ltd.—gold mines

De Beers Industrial Corporation—diamond mining and marketing

Trumcor Ltd.—financial holdings

The total of the above shares equaled almost 17% of the exchange volume in 1982.

For information on the Johannesburg exchange write to the Public Relations Department, Johannesburg Stock Exchange, P.O. Box 1174, Johannesburg 2000.

APARTHEID

Many investors resist purchasing South African securities because of that nation's policy of apartheid, which discriminates against blacks. (The term "black" in South Africa refers to Asians, 3% of the population; true blacks, 72% of the population; and any persons of mixed races, 9% of the population. Whites make up 16%.) Often people who urge investment boycotts mistakenly assume that purchases of South African gold shares send money to South Africa. As with any shares, unless you are buying them directly from the company (such as is the case in an initial offering or a rights subscription), the money with which shares are purchased goes to the former owner of the shares and not to a country or a company. Purchasers of South African mining shares on the secondary market, however, can be said to be indirectly supporting apartheid in that they constitute part of the ongoing market support for these securities. Current market price levels will, of course, affect the receipts from future issues of shares.

The relationship of financial and economic policies to apartheid is often not clear, and appropriate courses of action are not necessarily obvious. For instance, in 1983 four black African nations that were members of the IMF had what seemed a golden opportunity to censure South Africa when it applied for its first IMF loan. To the surprise of the other member nations, the black delegates did not vote against the loan; instead, they abstained. Although they gave no reason for their action, it is generally believed that the economies of other African nations are so intertwined with South Africa's that serious economic problems in that country would have a detrimental effect on the surrounding countries.

There are a number of signs that apartheid is gradually weakening. New employment opportunities have been opening to blacks, including some of a supervisory nature (although for the present such jobs seem to be confined to public relations). In another development, the chairmen of four major gold-mining companies have taken public stands urging that labor laws which discriminate against blacks be rescinded. (The mines involved are the Anglo American Corporation of South Africa, the President Brand Gold Mining Company, the Free State Geduld Mines Ltd., and the President Steyn Gold Mining Company.) Apparently, the biggest stumbling block is the white labor unions which have threatened to strike if their members have to share supervisory privileges with blacks. The government has requested that the mine operators and the unions settle the problem among themselves.

THE SULLIVAN PRINCIPLES

Leon H. Sullivan, a director of General Motors Company and also a Baptist minister, proposed a set of principles for U.S. companies that have operations in South Africa. Among those principles are equal pay for equal work, nonsegregation of work facilities, improved housing and schools, and training programs for blacks.

Sullivan initially called for the withdrawal of all American companies from South Africa as a way of pressuring South Africa to end apartheid. He later saw that more could be accomplished if U.S. companies stayed and set an example through the implementation of the principles he enunciated.

There are about 285 U.S. companies with operations in South Africa and 125 have adopted these principles and agreed to periodic inspection that would verify compliance. While some argue that this action has come at a time when change is already taking place, it is safe to say that the U.S. companies employing the Sullivan Principles have been in the forefront of change in South Africa.

The Stockholm Stock Exchange

BEST PERFORMER TWO YEARS IN A ROW

The spectacular performance of the Stockholm Stock Exchange over the past few years has stimulated considerable interest on the part of investors all over the world. According to Capital International, Swedish stocks outperformed the stocks of all other countries, both in 1981 and 1982. In 1983, Sweden again made a strong showing by ranking fifth in the world. The percentage of stock price increases for those years over each of the previous years is shown in Table 7.

Table 7

YEAR	PERCENT OF INCREASE OVER PREVIOUS YEAR-END LEVEL
1981	66.2
1982	57.2
1983	61.2

In its 1983 *Annual Report* the Stockholm Stock Exchange attributed this remarkable record to the following conditions:

1. A high degree of liquidity.
2. A continuation of government tax incentives for savings.
3. Anticipation of increased inflation (the expectation was that substantial capital gains would offset inflation).
4. Continued interest in Swedish securities on the part of foreign investors (this was partly stimulated by a devaluation).
5. The acquisition of companies' shares in large numbers by other companies.

Not only have prices performed well, but volume in Stockholm has also shown impressive gains. In the last ten years (1973 to 1983) volume has increased over six and one-half times. Recently, the government decided to profit from this burgeoning turnover and imposed a .5% tax on all exchange transactions (both the buyer and the seller have to pay). As a result, a substantial number of orders are being routed to the London exchange where there are currently about twenty-five Swedish stocks listed.

THE STOCK EXCHANGE

The Stockholm Stock Exchange has one of the quietest trading floors in the world. Although trading is by two-way auction, member traders make their bid and asked prices known by entering them in a computer instead of by open outcry as is required on most other exchanges. Traders may continue to modify their prices until bid and asked prices match, at which time a deal is struck; again, all by computer.

Only members of the exchange may trade securities on the exchange floor (or, more correctly, on the exchange computer). Under certain well-regulated conditions, a member may represent both the

THE STOCKHOLM STOCK MARKET AT A GLANCE

Capitalization:

Market value of shares in kronor* .... Kr 241,989 million

Nominal value of bonds in kronor* .... Kr 484,430 million

Volume:

Total yearly volume of shares in kronor................. Kr 75,796 million

Total yearly volume of bonds in kronor................. Kr 18,201 million

Listings:

Domestic equities... 214

Domestic bonds 1,623

Foreign shares.. 1

Foreign bonds.. 6

*The exchange rate as of Jan 1, 1984: $1 = Kr 8.005.

Source: Stockholm Stock Exchange, Annual Report, data for 1983.

buyer and the seller in the same transaction. Currently, there are twenty members of the exchange: twelve banks and eight brokerage firms.

At the beginning of 1984 there were 215 stocks listed on the Stockholm exchange, including one foreign issue. There were 1,623 bonds listed, which included six foreign issues. Among the bonds, straight and convertible are both available.

All exchange securities are divided into several sections called lists, according to the size and financial strength of their issuer. Stocks are divided into lists AI and AII. The AI list is made up of the largest companies and accounts for about 95% of the share volume on the exchange. Official trading hours are from 9:30 A.M. to 2:30 P.M., Monday through Friday. Different lists are traded at different times throughout the day and, in some circumstances, scheduled trading may be as infrequent as once a week. Members may also trade after hours or among themselves anytime, although such transactions must be reported to the exchange and will become part of the following day's transaction data.

A small over-the-counter market has recently been initiated for the trading of unlisted securities. Currently, over-the-counter trading accounts for only about 1% of total volume, but substantial tax advantages to the issuer may cause this sector of the market to grow substantially in the next few years.

Like most European stock exchanges, the Stockholm exchange can trace its roots back to outdoor trading in public squares. In the case of Stockholm, the square is the Stortorget, the site of the mass execution of bishops and nobles by Kristian II in 1520. In the mid-eighteenth century plans were drawn up for an exchange building on the square but it was 1776, the year of the American Revolution, before Stockholm got its stock exchange.

Today, protectionist measures have closed much of the Swedish securities market to nonresidents. Many companies with shares on the Stockholm exchange list two classes of shares—A shares and B shares. Only B shares may be purchased by nonresidents, and often, because of their limited supply, their price is at a substantial premium above the A shares available to Swedish residents. Only a handful of Swedish companies are known in the United States. These include Volvo (the automotive giant), Astra and Pharmacia (two pharmaceuticals), and Ericsson (telecommunication).

In the last few years there have been definite signs that the Swedish authorities are beginning to adopt a less insular perspective. In 1981, Pharmacia made the first public offering of shares in the United States by a Swedish company. A year later Pharmacia announced a pre-tax profit increase of 143%, and the stock has split several times. Current owners would now have ten shares for every three they originally purchased.

Another hopeful sign has been the sale of a Swedish company, Luxor, to a foreign conglomerate, Oy Nokia of Finland. This sale is significant, not only because Luxor was state-owned, but because the sale was to a non-Swedish concern. In the 1970s, the Swedish socialist government acquired many companies such as Luxor to rescue them from bankruptcy and save workers' jobs. Entire industries were eventually acquired, such as the steel industry and shipbuilding.

Since the sale of Luxor, plans have subsequently been made to sell other companies, such as the government's 40% stake in Sodra, a forestry group. The motivation behind these divestitures is the strong rise in equity prices coupled with the government's budget deficit which reached 10.9 billion (U.S.) in 1983. Although not exactly in line with socialist dogma, these sales will give the government the opportunity to recoup some of the more than 7.7 billion (U.S.) that it has poured into unprofitable state companies since 1975.

CURRENCY

The currency is the Swedish krona (plural: kronor, abbreviated Kr or SEK), which contains 100 ore. The Federal Reserve Bank of St. Louis has graphed the exchange of the krona to the dollar and calculated the effective exchange rate as was done for most of the major currencies in earlier chapters. As you can see from Figure 4, in 1983 the krona began performing better against the dollar than against the average of other major currencies.

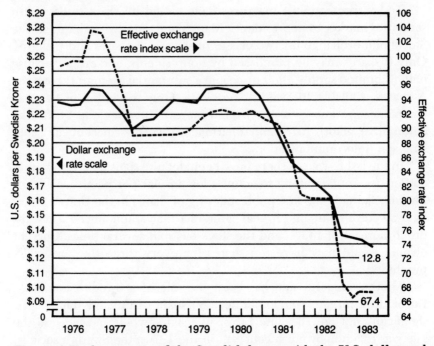

Figure 4. Exchange rate of the Swedish krona with the U.S. dollar and the effective exchange rate with the average of other major currencies. Source: *Federal Reserve Bank of St. Louis*

SWEDISH INVESTMENT TERMS

Unfortunately, there is almost no information in English available on Swedish securities, so the following brief glossary of standard investment terms is provided. Obviously, you will not be able to read an annual report in Swedish with only the following information, but sometimes you will find these terms used in reports or articles about Swedish securities.

aktie: Share.

aktiebolag: Corporation, also called a joint stock company.

bundna aktier: "Unfree shares," shares that can only be owned by Swedish citizens.

börspost: Round lot.

courtage: Broker's commission.

efterbörs: After-hours trading.

emission: New issue.

fondkommissionärer: Licensed (state approved) brokers.

fria aktier: "Free shares," shares that can be owned by non-Swedish citizens.

investmentbolag: Investment company.

konvertibla skuldebrev: Convertible bonds.

kurs: "Price," meaning the quotation ("buying price," "selling price").

nominellt värde: Par value.

obligaion: Bond.

preferensaktie: Preferred stock.

premieobligation: Bonds for which interest is drawn in a lottery twice a year.

stamaktie: Common stock.

You may obtain a copy of the annual report of the Stockholm exchange, which is printed with an English translation, from Stockholms Fondbörs, Källargränd 2, Postadress: Box 1256, S 111 82 Stockholm.

The Tel Aviv Stock Exchange

BACKGROUND

The thirty-year history of the Tel Aviv Stock Exchange is punctuated by three dates: 1953, 1963, and 1973. In 1953 the exchange was founded; in 1963 the exchange's clearinghouse was established, but in 1973 the Yom Kippur War erupted. Neither the Israeli economy (particularly as reflected in the inflation rate) nor the securities market has recovered from the war. For a while after 1973 inflation became so severe (200% a year!) that the most practical investment became bonds whose yields were linked to the cost of living. Subsequently, those bonds became such a burden to the government that new issues were indexed only to a percentage of the cost of living, and finally new issues dried up altogether.

While inflation is still a problem, some sectors of the securities market have shown healthy gains. Volume, for instance, has increased dramatically. From an average daily low in 1968 of only $100,000, the

Courtesy of the Tel Aviv Stock Exchange

average daily volume in 1983 reached over $25 million (U.S.). The number of issues listed has also been increasing. In 1982 alone there were seventy-six new shares listed and only four deletions.

THE EXCHANGE TODAY

The Tel Aviv exchange is the only stock market in Israel. There are thirty members, including eighteen banks which conduct most of the

---

THE TEL AVIV STOCK MARKET AT A GLANCE

Capitalization:
Market value of shares in U.S.$* .... $15.8 billion
Market value of bonds in U.S.$*............................. $4.5 billion
Volume:
Average daily volume of shares in U.S.$* .... $26.4 million
Average daily volume of bonds (including convertibles)
in U.S.$*... $10.2 million
Listings:
Shares 487
Bonds... 790

*Exchange rate as of Jan. 26, 1984: $1 = IS 122.
Source: The Tel Aviv Stock Exchange, *Fact Sheet,* 1983.

brokerage business in Israel, and twelve brokerages. (In the United States, however, Israeli securities must be purchased through a broker, not a bank.) Leumi Securities Corporation is the largest Israeli stockbroker in this country. It is a subsidiary of Israel's largest bank, Bank Leumi le-Israel, which is also the largest trader on the Tel Aviv exchange.

At the beginning of 1983 there were 790 bond issues and 487 share issues (including warrants) traded on the exchange. In all, 210 companies list their securities in Tel Aviv. Of those shares, more than half are issues of banks or bank subsidiaries.

Securities available are stocks, bonds (including convertibles), warrants, and shares in mutual funds. Securities are traded primarily on a roll-call market although there is some continuous trading, too. Studies are now under way to substantially enlarge the continuous trading part of the market. The exchange is open Sunday through Thursday, 9:00 A.M. to 3:30 P.M., and all transactions are for immediate settlements.

Commissions are charged according to the schedule shown in Table 8 (applicable in the U.S.).

Table 8

PURCHASE AMOUNT	COMMISSION
U.S. $500–2,499.99	3.0%
$2,500–4,999.99	2.5%
$5,000–9,999.99	2.0%
$10,000 and over	1.5%

Source: Leumi Securities Corporation.

The minimum commission is $15. There is also a 2% war tax on sales, and both sales and purchases are affected by a 1% surcharge on foreign currency transactions imposed in April 1983.

Limits on price fluctuations are imposed by the Tel Aviv exchange that are similar to restrictions imposed by other exchanges. Initially, flucuations are limited to 10% of the previous day's closing price. If there is still an imbalance of orders, all trades are postponed to the following session, where a 15% limit is imposed. If this does not accommodate all orders, trading is delayed to a third session, at which all restrictions are removed.

For bonds the limitation on price fluctuations is similar to that for stocks except the initial limit is 3%. New issues have no fluctuation limits on the first day of trading. New issues, incidentally, are never registered with the SEC. and are therefore not available to U.S. residents until 90 days after the inception of trading.

There is no capital gains tax in Israel. There is 25% withholding on dividends and on interest if the bond is issued for maturity of twelve years or longer. U.S. investors can claim credit or a deduction for that amount on their income tax returns.

ISRAELI SECURITIES

The following Israeli securities trade on the American Stock Exchange. None are ADRs; all trade in their original certificate form. (This is called trading "ordinary" shares.)

Alliance Tire and Rubber Company, Ltd. (class A shares)

American Israeli Paper Mills Ltd. (common stock)

ETZ Lavud Ltd. (common stock)

Laser Industries Ltd. (common stock)

Ampal Ltd. (class A shares)

In addition, American Israeli Paper Mills Ltd. has a bond (11¾% debenture) that trades on the American Stock Exchange.

Twenty-three Israeli securities trade over the counter in the United States. A few are ADRs but most trade "ordinary" shares; a few are also bonds.

Over 100 mutual funds trade on the Tel Aviv exchange. Most are load funds with a charge from 2% to 4%. The shares, called certificates, will be repurchased by the fund at the net asset value.

SOURCES OF INFORMATION

Leumi Securities Corporation publishes a periodic price list for stocks and bonds. It also contains the broadly based General Share Index, made up of nine industry subindexes. The monthly *Tel Aviv Stock Exchange Newsletter* is available through Leumi as are annual reports of many listed companies. Leumi also maintains a recorded quotation service with quotes directly from Tel Aviv on selected Israeli securities (212-759-1120). The stock exchange itself publishes a periodic *Guide to Shares.*

There is an investment letter, *Israel Securities Review,* which is published bimonthly in this country. It covers Israeli securities, both in the United States and in Israel. Subscription is a modest $20 per year.

USEFUL ADDRESSES

Leumi Securities Corporation
18 E. 48th St.
New York, NY 10017
(800) 221-4838

Public Relations Department
The Tel Aviv Stock Exchange
54, Ahad Haam St.
Tel-Aviv 65543 Israel

Israel Securities
American Israel Venture Corp.
461 Beach 124th St.
Bell Harbor, NY 11694

The Vienna Stock Exchange

BACKGROUND

The Vienna Stock Exchange, founded in 1771 during the reign of the Empress Maria Theresa, began as a state institution established primarily for the trading of Austrian government bonds (although other securities were traded as well). Unfortunately, adequate facilities were not

Courtesy of the Vienna Stock Exchange

provided so that for 100 years the exchange was periodically relocated in various buildings throughout the city. This lack of appropriate accommodations encouraged both the growth of unlicensed street trading and undercover stock markets, primarily in coffee houses.

A permanent building for the exchange was finally erected on the famous Schottenring and dedicated by the Emperor Franz Joseph in 1877. It contained one of the largest and most lavishly appointed trading floors of its day. In 1956, however, the interior of this magnificent building, except for one room, was completely destroyed by fire.

The Council of the Vienna Stock Exchange decided to leave the exterior and to rebuild only the interior. The great trading floor, having become too large for the amount of capital trading, was made into an interior courtyard ringed by modern offices. The room that survived the fire was refurbished and is now used mostly for ceremonial occasions. The rest of the building, greatly modernized, houses not only the stock exchange, but the currency exchange and the commodity exchange as well.

The Austrian shilling (written variously as "AS" or "As") is a relatively stable currency. Although Austria is not a member of the EMS, the exchange rate of the shilling is usually kept within EMS guidelines for the deutschemark because of the close link between the German and Austrian economies.

THE EXCHANGE

Perhaps the most surprising thing about the Vienna Stock Exchange is its small size. As the sole stock exchange of the country, it lists only 113

THE VIENNA STOCK EXCHANGE AT A GLANCE

Capitalization:
Market value of Austrian shares........................... AS 25.9 billion
Market value of Austrian bonds .... approx. AS 500 billion
Volume:
Market value of shares traded............................. AS 1.2 billion
Market value of bonds traded............................. AS 3.9 billion
Listings:
Domestic shares 76
Foreign shares... 37
Average yield from dividends.. 2.17%
Average yield from bonds 8.15%

Source: Vienna Stock Exchange, *Annual Facts Sheet,* for 1983.

stocks, seven of which are foreign. Of those domestic issues, the floats are often small and thus subject to erratic price movements. This situation has been brought about partly by nationalizations, which have removed a number of issues from the market or significantly reduced their float. Several important industry sectors are weakly represented on the exchange or are absent altogether, such as consumer goods, pharmaceuticals, department stores, utilities, and heavy industry.

In 1983 the downward trend in stock prices seemed to have reversed itself. The average share price rose by 10% and volume doubled. Biggest gains were shown by breweries, with a 50% average rise. Insurance and building materials closed 17% higher.

The bond market is considerably larger than the share market; 1,780 issues were listed in 1983, but only 10.7% of those represented industry or utilities. The rest were government issues (68%), banks (18.5%), and the sole foreign issuer, the World Bank, accounted for 2.6%. Maturities range from fifteen years for government bonds to twenty-five years for mortgage bonds. Denominations are sometimes as low as As 1,000.

There are sixty-seven members of the stock exchange (all banks) and seven official brokers *(Börse-Sensale)*. All trading by members is through the official brokers who set prices so as to balance the largest number of buy and sell orders. As on many other European exchanges, trading is by means of the call-over system. Types of orders accepted are only "at the market" and "limit."

All stock exchange transactions executed within one week are settled on the same clearing day, *Kassatag,* which is the second Monday following the transaction. Only the *balance* resulting from a week's dealing actually has to be delivered or accepted; thus money and securities handling is reduced to a minimum. Trading hours are from 11:30 A.M. to 1:00 P.M., Monday through Friday.

There is a semiofficial market but the volume and number of issues traded is quite small. Some securities, if not traded on the exchange officially or semiofficially, may be traded on the phone *(Telefonverkehr)* between banks or brokers.

Most domestic stocks are in bearer, rather than in registered form. An unusual feature of Austrian shares is that they are quoted in percent of par value, similar to bonds. Dividends are also declared at a percent of par.

In order to limit share-price volatility, which is characteristic of thin floats, the Vienna exchange has a "5% rule" whereby no domestic share or bond may vary in price from its previous quote by more than 5%.

This may not seem like much control to persons accustomed to continuous trading, but it represents a reasonably effective restraint for shares traded by the roll-call system.

Commissions, subject to an As 30 minimum, are 1.25% for shares and rights, and .75% for bonds. Custody fees, charged by banks for safekeeping, range from 1.5% to 5%, depending on whether the shares are stored collectively (i.e., as undifferentiated segments of large blocks), in individual deposits, or in separate securities accounts.

Banks in Austria offer all financial services including underwriting, safe custody, portfolio guidance, and mutual funds, and even float their own issues. They also control much of the industry since loans are preferred to equity or bond issues as a means of raising capital. Many of the larger banks, including the largest, Creditanstalt-Bankverein, are majority-owned by the government.

It is possible to open anonymous savings accounts with many of the major Austrian banks. A code word is used on the bankbook itself, and the bank will know the account only by that name. In that not even bank officials have a record of the identity of the beneficial holder, these accounts are even more "secret" than their Swiss counterparts. In order to open an account one must have resided in the country for several months, but that requirement is difficult to enforce. As with most Austrian accounts, one may also use them to purchase securities and gold. (Careful on gold, however, since your profits will be subject to an 18% value added tax when it is sold.)

There are no restrictions for nonresidents regarding the purchase or sale of Austrian securities. Dividends, interest, and proceeds from sales may be freely repatriated. There is withholding tax on interest from convertible bonds. Interest from bonds issued after Jan. 1, 1984, is subject to a 7.5% interest earnings tax (ZESt).

Investment funds are usually managed through bank subsidiaries. The two banks listed below, in addition to providing all investment services, manage a number of investment funds, shares of which can be purchased directly from the bank.

USEFUL ADDRESSES

THE VIENNA STOCK EXCHANGE

Wiener Börsekammer
Wipplingerstrasse 84
1011 Wien 1
Austria

BANKS

Creditanstalt-Bankverein
Schottengasse 6–8
1010 Wien (Vienna)
Austria

Girozentrale und Bank der
Österreichischen Sparkassen
Aktiengesellschaft
Schubertring 5
1010 Wien
Austria

Appendix 1

TIME ZONES OF THE MAJOR STOCK EXCHANGES

The times shown are the zonal times at noon in New York (Eastern Standard Time). Some countries use a daylight savings time in the summer which differs from one to one-half hour from normal time.

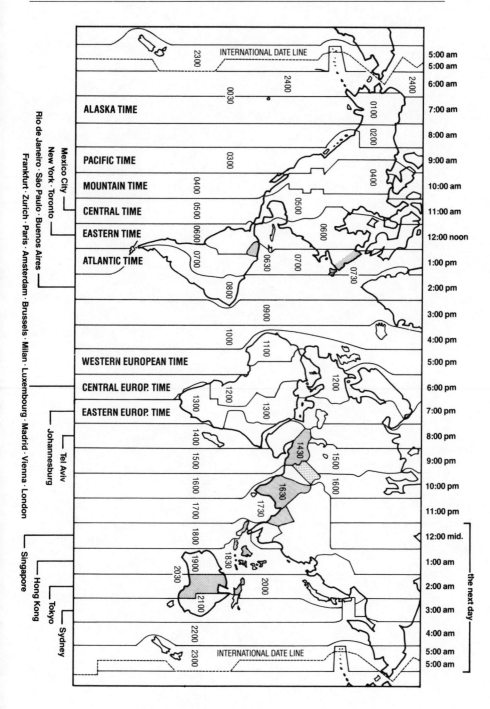

INTERNATIONAL DATE LINE

5:00 am
5:00 am

2300

2400

6:00 am

0030

2400

0100

ALASKA TIME

7:00 am

0200

8:00 am

PACIFIC TIME

0300

0400

9:00 am

MOUNTAIN TIME

0400

10:00 am

CENTRAL TIME

0500

0500

11:00 am

EASTERN TIME

0600

0600

12:00 noon

ATLANTIC TIME

0700

0630

0700

0730

1:00 pm

0800

2:00 pm

0900

3:00 pm

1000

4:00 pm

WESTERN EUROPEAN TIME

1100

1200

5:00 pm

CENTRAL EUROP. TIME

1200

1300

6:00 pm

EASTERN EUROP. TIME

1300

7:00 pm

1400

8:00 pm

1500

1430

1500

9:00 pm

1600

1600

10:00 pm

1700

1630

1730

11:00 pm

1800

12:00 mid.

1900

1830

1:00 am

2030

2000

2:00 am

2100

3:00 am

4:00 am

2200

2300

INTERNATIONAL DATE LINE

5:00 am
5:00 am

Mexico City
New York · Toronto
Rio de Janeiro · São Paulo · Buenos Aires
Frankfurt · Zurich · Paris · Amsterdam · Brussels · Milan · Luxembourg · Madrid · Vienna · London

Tel Aviv
Johannesburg

Singapore

Hong Kong

Tokyo

Sydney

the next day

Appendix 2

WORLD CURRENCIES

COUNTRY	CURRENCY	FRACTIONAL CONTENT OF ONE UNIT
Afghanistan	Afghani	100 puls
Albania	Lek	100 quintar
Algeria	Dinar	100 centimes
Angola	Kwanza	100 cents
Antigua	East Caribbean dollar	100 cents
Antilles, French	French franc	100 centimes
Antilles, Netherlands	Guilder	100 cents
Argentina	Argentine peso	100 centavos
Australia	Dollar	100 cents
Austria	Schilling	100 groschen
Azores	Portuguese escudo	100 centavos
Bahamas	Dollar	100 cents
Barbados	Barbados dollar	100 cents
Belgium	Franc	100 centimes
Belize	Belize dollar	100 cents
Bermuda	Bermuda dollar	100 cents
Bolivia	Peso Boliviano	100 centavos
Botswana	Pula	100 thebe
Brazil	Cruzeiro	100 centavos
Bulgaria	Lew	100 stotinki
Burma	Kyat	100 pyas
Cambodia	Riel	100 sen
Cameroon	Equatorial C.F.A. franc	100 centimes
Canada	Dollar	100 cents
Canary Islands	Spanish peseta	100 centimos
Cayman Islands	Cayman dollar	100 cents
Central African Republic	Equatorial C.F.A. franc	100 centimes
Chad	Equatorial C.F.A. franc	100 centimes
Chile	Peso	100 centavos
China (People's Republic)	Renminbi (Yuan)	10 chiao, 100 fen
Colombia	Peso	100 centavos
Congo	Equatorial C.F.A. franc	100 centimes
Costa Rica	Colón	100 centimos
Cuba	Peso	100 centavos
Cyprus	Pound	1,000 mils
Czechoslovakia	Crown (Kc.)	100 halers
Denmark	Kroner	100 oere
Dominican Republic	Peso	100 centavos
Ecuador	Sucre	100 centavos
Egypt	Pound	100 piastres; 1,000 millièmes
El Salvador	Colón	100 centavos
Ethiopia	Birr	100 cents
Falkland Islands	Pound	100 new pence
Faroe Isles	Danish kroner	100 oere
Fiji Islands	Dollar	100 cents
Finland	Markka	100 penni
France	Franc	100 centimes
Gambia	Dalasi	100 bututs
Germany, Democratic Republic (East)	Mark of the DDR	100 pfennig

COUNTRY	CURRENCY	FRACTIONAL CONTENT OF ONE UNIT
Germany, Federal Republic (West)	Deutschemark	100 pfennig
Ghana	Cedi	100 pesewas
Gibraltar	Pound	100 new pence
Grenada	East Caribbean dollar	100 cents
Great Britain	Pound sterling	100 new pence
Greece	Drachma	100 lepta
Greenland	Danish kroner	100 oere
Guatemala	Quetzal	100 centavos
Guiana, French	Franc	100 centimes
Guinea	Syli	100 cory
Guyana	Guyana dollar	100 cents
Haiti	Gourde	100 centimes
Honduras	Lempira	100 centavos
Hong Kong	Hong Kong dollar	100 cents
Hungary	Forint	100 filler
Iceland	New króna	100 aurar
India	Rupee	100 paise
Indonesia	Rupiah	100 sen
Iran	Rial	100 dinars
Iraq	Dinar	1,000 fils
Ireland	Pound	100 new pence
Israel	Shekel	100 agorot
Italy	Lira	100 centesimi
Ivory Coast	West C.F.A. franc	100 centimes
Jamaica	Jamaica dollar	100 cents
Japan	Yen	100 sen
Jordan	Dinar	1,000 fils
Kenya	Shilling	100 cents
Korea, North	Won	100 chon
Korea, South	Won	100 chon
Kuwait	Dinar	1,000 fils
Laos	New kip	100 at
Lebanon	Pound	100 piastres
Liberia	Dollar	100 cents
Libya	Dinar	1,000 durhams
Liechtenstein	Swiss franc	100 centimes
Luxembourg	Franc	100 centimes
Macao	Pataca	100 avos
Madeira	Portuguese escudo	100 centavos
Malaysia	Ringgit	100 sen
Malta	Pound	100 cents; 1,000 mils
Mexico	Peso	100 centavos
Monaco	French franc	100 centimes
Mongolia	Tughrik	100 mongo
Morocco	Dirham	100 centimes
Mozambique	Metical	100 centavos
Namibia	South African rand	100 cents
Nepal	Rupee	100 paisas
Netherlands	Guilder	100 cents

COUNTRY	CURRENCY	FRACTIONAL CONTENT OF ONE UNIT
New Caledonia	C.F.P. franc	100 centimes
New Zealand	Dollar	100 cents
Nicaragua	Cordoba	100 centavos
Niger	West C.F.A. franc	100 centimes
Nigeria	Naira	100 kobo
Northern Ireland	Pound sterling	100 new pence
Norway	Krone	100 oere
Oman	Riyal-Omani	1,000 baiza
Pakistan	Rupee	100 paisas
Panama	Balboa	100 centesimos
Papua-New Guinea	Kina	100 toea
Paraguay	Guarani	100 centimos
Peru	Sol	100 centavos
Philippines	Peso	100 centavos
Poland	Zloty	100 groszy
Polynesia, French	C.F.P. franc	100 centimes
Portugal	Escudo	100 centavos
Romania	Leu	100 bani
Samoa, Western	Tala	100 sene
San Marino	Italian lira	100 centesimi
Saudi Arabia	Riyal	20 qursh; 100 halalah
Senegal	West C.F.A. franc	100 centimes
Sierra Leone	Leone	100 cents
Singapore	Singapore dollar	100 cents
South Africa, Republic of	Rand	100 cents
Spain	Peseta	100 centimos
Sri Lanka	Rupee	100 cents
Sudan	Pound	100 piastres; 1,000 millièmes
Surinam	Surinam guilder	100 cents
Swaziland	Lilangeni	100 cents
Sweden	Krona	100 oere
Switzerland	Franc	100 centimes
Syria	Pound	100 piastres
Taiwan	New Taiwan dollar	100 cents
Tanzania	Shilling	100 cents
Togo	West C.F.A. franc	100 centimes
Trinidad and Tobago	Dollar	100 cents
Tunisia	Dinar	1,000 millimes
Turkey	Pound	100 kurus
Uganda	Shilling	100 cents
Union of Soviet Socialist Republics	Rouble	100 kopecks
United Arab Emirates	Dirham	100 fils
United Kingdom	Pound sterling	100 new pence
Upper Volta	West C.F.A. franc	100 centimes
Uruguay	New peso	100 centesimos
Venezuela	Bolivar	100 centimos
Vietnam, Socialist Republic	Dong	10 hao, 100 xu
Yemen (Arab Republic)	Riyal	100 fils

COUNTRY	CURRENCY	FRACTIONAL CONTENT OF ONE UNIT
Yemen (Democratic People's Republic)	South Yemen dinar	1,000 fils
Yugoslavia	Dinar	100 para
Zaire	Zaire	100 makuta; 10,000 sengi
Zimbabwe (Rhodesia)	Dollar	100 cents

INDEX